Analyzing qualitative data

The last decade has witnessed considerable growth in the development of qualitative research. Most methodological development has been concerned with data collection. As a consequence, texts, readers and monographs remain relatively silent on the conduct of data analysis, yet this is an area on which most researchers require some guidance.

This collection brings together a range of distinguished contributors who have worked with qualitative data. Among the examples provided are accounts of ethnographers, case study workers, lone researchers, team-based investigators and those who use specialist approaches including discourse analysis.

Together they demonstrate that a range of approaches are involved in qualitative data analysis, and suggest different ways in which qualitative data can be handled to overcome problems with these data.

The book will be essential reading for undergraduates and postgraduates following research courses and conducting empirical studies, as well as for those coming to qualitative research for the first time.

Alan Bryman is Professor of Social Research, Loughborough University, and **Robert G. Burgess** is Professor of Sociology, University of Warwick.

Analyzing qualitative data

Edited by Alan Bryman
and Robert G. Burgess

London and New York

First published 1994
by Routledge
11 New Fetter Lane, London EC4P 4EE

Simultaneously published in the USA and Canada
by Routledge
29 West 35th Street, New York, NY 10001

Reprinted 1995, 1996, 1999, 2000

Routledge is an imprint of the Taylor & Francis Group

Typeset in Times by
Mews Photosetting, Beckenham, Kent
Printed and bound in Great Britain by
TJ International Ltd, Padstow, Cornwall

British Library Cataloguing in Publication Data
A catalogue record for this book is available from the British Library

Library of Congress Cataloguing in Publication Data
A catalogue record for this book is available from the Library of Congress

ISBN 0-415-06062-1 (hbk)   ISBN 0-415-06063-X (pbk)

Contents

Illustrations

FIGURES

TABLES

Contributors

Alan Bryman is Professor of Social Research in the Department of Social Sciences, Loughborough University. His main research interests lie in the fields of organization studies and research methodology. He has a special interest in leadership in organizations, an area in which he has co-directed a number of funded research projects. He is author or co-author of the following books: *Leadership and Organizations* (1986), *Quantity and Quality in Social Research* (1988), *Research Methods and Organization Studies* (1989), *Quantitative Data Analysis for Social Scientists* (1990), and *Charisma and Leadership in Organizations* (1992). He is also editor of *Doing Research in Organizations* (1988).

Robert G. Burgess is Director of CEDAR (Centre for Educational Development, Appraisal and Research) and Professor of Sociology at the University of Warwick. His main teaching and research interests are in social research methodology, including qualitative methods and the sociology of education, especially the study of schools, classrooms and curricula. He has written ethnographic studies of secondary schools and is currently working on case studies of schools and higher education. His main publications include: *Experiencing Comprehensive Education* (1983), *In the Field: an Introduction to Field Research* (1984), *Education, Schools and Schooling* (1985), *Sociology, Education and Schools* (1986), *Schools at Work* (with Rosemary Deem, 1988) and *Implementing In-Service Education* (with John Connor, Sheila Galloway, Marlene Morrison and Malcolm Newton, 1993), together with fourteen edited volumes on qualitative methods and education. He has been President of the British Sociological Association for the last two years and is currently President of the Association for the Teaching of the Social Sciences. He is a member of the Economic and Social Research Council (ESRC) Training Board and the ESRC Research Resources Board.

Nan Paulsen Chico, Ph.D. is Assistant Professor of Sociology at California State University, Hayward. She has published on sterilization and reproductive issues. She is currently doing a qualitative analysis of alumni of several California State University campuses on their undergraduate experiences and is beginning a quantitative study of students at Hayward who have taken a 'death and dying' course to assess death anxiety, experience of loss, etc.

Nellie Droes, D.N.Sc. is currently Assistant Professor of Nursing at the Orvis School of Nursing, University of Nevada, Reno. Her research interests include health in correctional institutions and health among the under-served. She has published on nursing in correctional settings and on the image of nursing. She and Diane Hatton are currently involved in a study of self-care among homeless women and children.

Keith Evans is the Technical and Vocational Education Initiative (TVEI) Coordinator for Central Warwickshire. Prior to this he was a Schoolteacher Fellow at CEDAR where he worked on the Records of Achievement projects. He has held senior and middle management positions in schools, where his subject specialism has been history. His whole-school interests include assessment, staff development and school-based evaluation. Among his research interests are leadership and management in comprehensive schools, together with the work on records of achievement.

Diane Hatton, D.N.Sc. is currently Assistant Professor of Nursing at the Philip Y. Hahn School of Nursing, University of San Diego. Her research interests include health and illness among vulnerable populations. She has published on the work of translators in bilingual health-care settings and on the image of nursing. She and Nellie Droes are involved in a study of self-care among homeless women and children.

Christina Hughes is a lecturer in Continuing Education at the University of Warwick; she was previously a research fellow in the Centre for Educational Development, Appraisal and Research at the University of Warwick. Her publications include *Stepparents: Wicked or Wonderful?* (1991) and *Educating the Under Fives in Salford* (with Robert Burgess and Susan Moxon, 1989). She is currently writing *Stepmums, Stepkids, Step by Step*. Her research interests continue to focus on the family and education and the development of research methodologies.

Jennifer Mason is a lecturer in the Department of Applied Social Science at Lancaster University. She has had a long-standing interest in the use of qualitative research methods to explore family, kin and gender relations. During the past six years she has been researching with colleagues on ESRC-funded research projects designed to exploit the potential of integrating 'qualitative' and 'quantitative' methods: first in a study entitled 'Family obligations', and currently in one entitled 'Inheritance, property and family relationships'. She is co-author, with Janet Finch, of *Negotiating Family Responsibilities* (1993), a book based on the 'Family obligations' research.

Judith Okely is Reader in the Department of Social Anthropology, University of Edinburgh. She was a lecturer in the Department of Sociology, University of Essex (1981–90) and a lecturer in the Department of Anthropology, University of Durham (1976–80). Her main publications are *The Travellers: Gypsies* (1983), *Simone de Beauvoir: a Re-Reading* (1986), and she was joint editor of *Anthropology and Autobiography* (1992). Her main research interests include Gypsies, feminism and gender, and anthropological methodology. She has done field research among Gypsies in Britain and elsewhere in Europe. Recent fieldwork in Normandy and East Anglia examines rural representations, landscape, ageing and agricultural change.

Virginia Olesen, Ph.D. is Professor of Sociology and Co-Director of the Women, Health and Healing Program, Department of Social and Behvioural Sciences, School of Nursing, University of California, San Francisco. She has published on qualitative research contexts and is currently writing on feminist models of qualitative inquiry with particular attention to tensions between classic and postmodern approaches. She is also conducting (with Professor Anne Davies) a study of professional socialization among university student nurses in the People's Republic of China and is writing on the confluence of emotions and organizational structure in contemporary health-care systems.

Christopher J. Pole holds a joint post with CEDAR and the Sociology Department, University of Warwick, where he teaches Field Studies in Social Research and Sociology of Education. In CEDAR he is currently engaged in an ESRC funded research project which examines the socialization and supervision of first year Ph.D. students in the Natural Sciences. His publications include: *The Management of TVEI* (with S. Stoney and D. Sims, 1986), the *TVEI Experience* (with S. Stoney and D. Sims, 1987) and *Assessing and Recording Achievement: Implementing a New Approach in School* (1993).

Marilyn Porter took degrees in History, at Trinity College, Dublin, and Education, at Oxford University, before 'converting' to Sociology at Bristol University. Since then she has taught at Bristol and Manchester Universities before moving to Newfoundland in 1980 where she is currently Associate Professor of Sociology at Memorial University. An initial interest in women and class consciousness (see *Home, Work and Class Consciousness* (1983)) developed into a focus on women in rural communities and women's economic lives in Newfoundland, in *Women, Work and Family in Off-shore Oil Fields* (edited) and *Peripheral Workers: Towards an Understanding of Women's Lives in Newfoundland* (forthcoming). Most recently she has expanded those interests to examining women's 'development' issues in other parts of the world, notably Indonesia.

Jonathan Potter is Reader in Discourse Analysis at Loughborough University. His research interests are focused on the construction and use of factual discourse in a number of social realms: science, current affairs television, riots and uprisings, political reporting and racism. He has published numerous articles and is the author (with M. Wetherell) of *Discourse and Social Psychology* (1987) and (with D. Edwards) of *Discursive Psychology* (1992). He is a co-editor of the journal *Theory and Psychology*.

Christine Priestley is currently deputy head of a comprehensive school in York. She entered the teaching profession from industry as a mature graduate. She joined CEDAR as a schoolteacher fellow on secondment from a management post in a Warwickshire secondary school. Her work in CEDAR focused on research and evaluation of records of achievement and assessment schemes. Her research interests include the post-16 transition from school to work and management perspectives within education, in particular the application of strategic management processes in schools and colleges and organizational health. The main elements of her developmental activities centre on equal opportunities and staff development.

Lyn Richards is Associate Professor in Sociology at La Trobe University, Melbourne. She is author or co-author of three books on Australian families: *Nobody's Home: Dreams and Realities in a New Suburb* (1990), *Having Families* (revised 1985) and *Mothers and Working Mothers* (revised 1986). Her current research projects include qualitative longitudinal studies of women's experiences of using day-care and of the social construction of the menopause. Her work with Tom Richards in qualitative computing led to the development of software now used across the world for Non-Numerical Unstructured Data Indexing, Searching and Theorizing (NUDIST). She lectures and trains researchers in these qualitative computing techniques.

Tom Richards is a Reader in Computer Science at La Trobe University, Melbourne. With a background in analytical philosophy and mathematical logic, he has a Masters degree from Victoria University of Wellington and a D.Phil. from Oxford University. He has had a long-standing interest in scientific methodology, philosophy of language and philosophical logic. These predilections led naturally to a study of software science and artificial intelligence. He teaches software engineering and AI, researches issues of knowledge acquisition and representation, and applies this in the design of the NUDIST system for qualitative data analysis.

Jane Ritchie is Director of the Qualitative Research Unit at Social and Community Planning Research (SCPR), London. She is a social psychologist who has spent her career in applied policy research, and has a specialist interest in the fields of social security, income support and social care. She is concerned with the development of qualitative methodology and teaches qualitative methods both on an occasional basis and on courses run by SCPR.

Leonard Schatzman, Ph.D. is currently Emeritus Professor of Sociology, Department of Social and Behavioural Sciences, School of Nursing, University of California, San Francisco. He is the author (with Anselm Strauss) of the text, *Field Research: Strategies for a Natural Sociology* (1973). Reflecting his continuing and principal interest in qualitative research, his most recent published article described 'dimensional analysis' as a variant form of grounded theory. This new approach to the grounding of theory looks at qualitative analysis largely in terms of its structural components, as well as process. A separate volume on this method is now in the writing stage.

Liz Spencer is a Research Director in the Qualitative Research Unit at Social and Community Planning Research, London. A sociologist with a background in both academic and applied social policy research, she has explored fields as diverse as organizational values and behaviour, Church and state, women in management, employment training, and the public understanding of science. She is concerned with the development of qualitative methodology and teaches qualitative methods both on an occasional basis and on courses run by SCPR.

Barry A. Turner graduated in Sociology from Birmingham University in 1966, and gained his doctorate at Exeter University in 1976. He has carried out industrial research, usually with a qualitative emphasis, at Imperial College, at the Universities of Loughborough and Exeter and now at Middlesex Business School where he is Research Professor of European Business. He is chairman of an international cultural research network and his most recent book on corporate culture is *Organisation Symbolism* (1990). He also pursues research in hazard management and system failure and he is currently revising his book *Manmade Disasters*.

Margaret Wetherell lectures in the Social Sciences Faculty at the Open University. She is the author of *Social Texts and Context* (with J. Potter and P. Stringer, 1984), of *Discourse and Social Psychology* (with J. Potter, 1987) and of *Mapping the Language of Racism* (with J. Potter, 1992). She is a member of the editorial group of the journal *Feminism and Psychology*. She has published numerous articles on discourse analysis, particularly applied to the study of racism and gender issues. Her current research is on feminist psychology and the interface between discourse, social practice and subjectivity.

Preface

There are now numerous texts and sets of readings attempting to give guidance to researchers about the styles and strategies that can be used in qualitative research. While much has been written about the collection of data, the books are often silent about the processes and procedures associated with data analysis.

Indeed, much mystery surrounds the way in which researchers engage in data analysis. Accordingly, we invited a range of social scientists who have engaged in qualitative projects to discuss the approaches that they used. The idea was to contribute insight and understanding to the process of qualitative data analysis rather than to produce a guidebook for the intending researcher. Such a task involves a process of demystification, of making implicit procedures more explicit. While this may sound straightforward, we have found this far from simple. In these circumstances we have given our contributors the opportunity to present their work in a range of styles which include autobiographical accounts and more impersonal forms.

This book has been a long time in the making and we are most appreciative of the support and forbearance we have received from our authors and from Chris Rojek at Routledge. In the end, we hope that this volume will be a contribution to a developing literature on qualitative data analysis which will be of interest to undergraduate and postgraduate students as well as researchers who engage in qualitative research. If these essays help to demystify qualitative data analysis and encourage research novices to explore a range of analytic approaches, they will have achieved a major aim of producing this book.

Finally, we wish to thank Su Powell and Sylvia Moore who have made numerous contributions to the preparation of this manuscript, for which we are very grateful. As always, any errors or omissions are our own.

Alan Bryman
Robert G. Burgess

Developments in qualitative data analysis: an introduction

Alan Bryman and Robert G. Burgess

The last decade has witnessed several shifts in emphasis among teachers and researchers when dealing with research methodology. First, method has given way to a discussion of methodology. Second, the pre-eminence and predominance of quantitative methodology has been replaced by an emphasis upon qualitative methodology in British sociology. Third, stages of social investigation have been replaced with the idea of research as a social process which requires careful scrutiny. Each of these developments has had an impact upon the other and in turn holds implications for the way in which the analysis of qualitative data is conducted and discussed. On this basis, it is important to examine each of these trends before turning to a detailed examination of a range of approaches to qualitative data analysis that is presented in the essays in this volume.

Despite discussions of the difficulties associated with conducting social research and the importance of adapting the principles of social investigation in the conduct of particular studies, it is apparent that the teaching of research methodology has until the recent past placed little emphasis either upon research practice or upon methodology as such. The course outlines (Peel 1968, Wakeford 1979) that have been collected from those engaged in teaching such courses to undergraduates in sociology demonstrate that there has been a strong emphasis upon the teaching of techniques. Indeed, this is also demonstrated in the most popular texts used by teachers (Marsh 1979). According to these outlines the three most widely cited methods texts that were used on undergraduate methods courses were Aaron Cicourel's *Method and Measurement in Sociology* (1964), Moser and Kalton's *Survey Methods in Social Investigation* (1971), and Oppenheim's *Questionnaire Design and Attitude Measurement* (1966). As Bulmer and Burgess (1981) remarked, Cicourel may provide a critical edge to methods teaching, but may also lead students away from empirical investigation. Meanwhile, the volumes by Moser and Kalton and Oppenheim give a focus to 'methods' which emphasize techniques: sampling, questionnaire design, interviewing and so on. Yet, the volume by Moser and Kalton gives little status to the diverse range of approaches covered by the term 'qualitative methods', which are briefly summarized in one chapter.

This approach to 'methods' was the subject of considerable revision in the 1980s, which witnessed the publication of a range of volumes focusing upon qualitative research. These included general texts (Burgess 1984a, Hammersley and Atkinson 1983) as well as more specialist volumes that took up aspects of qualitative research such as policy (Finch 1986), writing (Atkinson 1990), ethics (Burgess 1989), and reading and evaluating texts (Hammersley 1991). While many of these books focused upon major elements of research, there was little emphasis given to data analysis and only Miles and Huberman (1984) devoted a whole volume to this topic; in it principles of data analysis were discussed, although not in relation to research studies that had been conducted recently. However, one important aspect of research that was revealed in these texts was a shift from 'methods' and 'stages' of social research to a discussion of methodology in terms of a research process.

These trends in research and writing were also reflected in texts recommended on undergraduate courses concerned with social research. In the academic year 1990–1, Jon Gubbay conducted a project on the teaching of undergraduate sociology which included a special study of research methods teaching. By examining lists of recommended texts on sixty-eight 'research methods' courses, he found that the 'top seven' volumes included three books concerned with qualitative research: Burgess's *In the Field* (1984a), Hammersley and Atkinson's *Ethnography: Principles in Practice* (1983) and Burgess's *Field Research: a Sourcebook and Field Manual* (1982). However, it is interesting to note that the most frequently used volume was De Vaus's book on survey research (1991), alongside a wide range of volumes on quantitative and qualitative methodology.[1] Such a range of volumes indicated an emphasis on the practice of social research and a welcome attempt to teach quantitative *and* qualitative research.

Many of the volumes on qualitative research emphasized the research process and demonstrated that qualitative research cannot be reduced to particular techniques nor to set stages, but rather that a dynamic process is involved which links together problems, theories and methods. Here, the focus is upon the links between research design, research strategy and research techniques as well as the relationship between aspects of research design, data collection and data analysis. The importance of this approach to social research had been well summarized by Bechhofer when he stated:

> The research process, then, is not a clear cut sequence of procedures following a neat pattern, but a messy interaction between the conceptual and empirical world, deduction and induction occurring at the same time.
> (1974: 73)

Here, the difficulties involved in doing research and writing about it are vividly portrayed through the use of the word 'messy'. Indeed, research seldom involves the use of a straightforward set of procedures. Instead, the researcher has to move backwards and forwards between different sequences in the research process. For example, in designing a project, consideration needs to be given to the end-point and the concepts and theories that will be used in data analysis. Similarly, in terms of data collection, reference has to be made to the comparisons and contrasts that may be uncovered during a project. On this basis, there is not a sharp divide between different aspects of the research process in practice. Accordingly, while the contributors to this volume seek to examine critically the way in which qualitative data analysis is handled in practice, it is evident that they need to move between other aspects of the research process and qualitative data analysis, while keeping the latter as the central theme. However, before turning to some accounts of this process we need to look at some of the procedures that are advocated by those methodologists who have chosen to write about this aspect of doing research.

QUALITATIVE TEXTS

General texts on research methods have ignored qualitative data analysis despite allocating space to data collection (Frankfort-Nachmias and Nachmias 1992, Kidder and Judd 1986). Sometimes the analysis of qualitative data is only briefly covered (Babbie 1979) through 'coding' and the generation of theory from data.

It is not surprising that in texts concerned primarily with qualitative research, data analysis has been allocated fairly detailed treatments. As with the general texts, there is a tendency for gaining access, data collection strategies and fieldwork relationships to make up the bulk of the discussion before the move on to analysis (Bogdan and Biklen 1982, Bogdan and Taylor 1975, Burgess 1984a, Hammersley and Atkinson 1983, Goetz and LeCompte 1984, Lofland 1974 and Whyte 1984). Typically, these treatments discuss the major strategies for analyzing qualitative data, frequently using examples from the writers' own or others' research. In recent years, some books which focus more or less exclusively on qualitative data analysis have emerged. One of the best known is Miles and Huberman (1984), which offers a distinctive approach. Strauss (1987) and Strauss and Corbin (1990) provide detailed elaborations of grounded theory, while Tesch (1990) and Fielding and Lee (1991) pay a great deal of attention to analysis in the context of the development of computer software, which is increasingly being used by researchers. Two main approaches to qualitative data analysis can be found in texts: first, a discussion of the main general frameworks; second, provision of the main emphases of qualitative data analysis. These two approaches can be described as 'general strategies' and 'general processes', to which we now turn.

GENERAL STRATEGIES

The general strategies approach can be found in such texts as Bryman (1988), Burgess (1984a) and Hammersley (1989, 1992), as well as Bulmer's (1979) examination of concept generation during the analysis of qualitative data. The usual approach involves an articulation of two of the best known general strategies: analytic induction and grounded theory.

Analytic induction is closely associated with studies of social problems, though it has more general applicability. Its main elements have been outlined by Robinson (1951) and comprise a sequence of steps. The researcher begins with a rough definition of a problem or issue (e.g. drug addiction). Appropriate cases are examined and a possible explanation of the problem is formulated and the investigator then examines further appropriate cases to establish how well the data collected fit the hypothetical explanation. If there is a lack of fit, the hypothesis is likely to need reformulation and further research is conducted. There then follows an iterative interplay between data collection and revision of the hypothesis as research reveals cases that do not fit with each reformulated hypothesis. Indeed, the original problem itself may be redefined in the process. The sequence continues until cases that are inconsistent with what ends up as the last reformulated hypothesis do not appear. Analytic induction is extremely demanding in that the appearance of a single case that is inconsistent with a hypothesis (or a reformulated one) necessitates further revision of the hypothesis and a return to the field. However, there are very few instances of the use of analytic induction and it is striking that writers such as Bryman (1988) and Hammersley (1989) employ old studies – Lindesmith (1947) and Cressey (1950) respectively – as illustrations. It may be that the extremely stringent requirements implied by analytic induction have been responsible for its relatively infrequent use.

Grounded theory bears certain similarities to analytic induction in respect of the meshing of theorizing and data collection. Detailed presentations of the approach can be found in Glaser and Strauss (1967), Strauss (1987) and Strauss and Corbin (1990), but Turner 1981 (see also Martin and Turner 1986) has provided an especially helpful account of its main steps, which collectively are concerned with 'the discovery of theory from data' (Glaser and Strauss 1967: 1). After some data collection and reflection in relation to a general issue of concern, the researcher generates 'categories' which fit the data. Further research is undertaken until the categories are 'saturated', that is, the researcher feels assured about their meaning and importance. The researcher then attempts to formulate more general (and possibly more abstract) expressions of these categories, which will then be capable of embracing a wider range of objects. This stage may spur the researcher to further theoretical reflection and in particular he or she should by now be concerned with the interconnections among the categories involved and their generality. Hypotheses about links between categories will need to be formulated and tested in the field. Links with other theoretical schemes are then explored and as further revisions of hypotheses are carried out, as a result of both data collection and theoretical reflection, the emerging theory is tested once again in the field.

Coding represents a key step in the process. It has been described by Charmaz (1983) as 'simply the process of *categorizing* and *sorting* data' (p. 111), while 'codes' are described as serving to 'summarize, synthesize, and sort many observations made out of the data' (p. 112). As such, coding provides the link between data and the conceptualization. At first, the coding will be 'open coding' (Strauss 1987), or 'initial coding' as it was referred to in earlier writings on grounded theory (Charmaz 1983, Glaser 1978): 'the process of breaking down, examining, comparing, conceptualizing, and categorizing data' (Strauss and Corbin 1990: 61); coding here represents the gradual building up of categories out of the data. Later, 'axial coding' will be employed. This involves 'a set of procedures whereby data are put back together in new ways after open coding, by making connections between categories' (1990: 96). It should be noted that, as Richards and Richards (1991) observe, the term 'coding' is widely used in qualitative analysis but is applied in more than one way: to the task of fitting data and concepts together in such a way that conceptualization is under constant revision (as in grounded theory); to a process that is more or less identical to the coding of open-ended questions in survey research, where the aim is to quantify different categories of a variable.[2] Another key element in grounded theory is 'memo writing', whereby the analyst is constantly writing memos, perhaps relating to codes or to connections between emerging concepts, which elaborate the data and which represent the first step in the emergence of theory.

Grounded theory has been widely cited and writers of computer software for qualitative analysis often claim that it influenced their construction of the programs or that the programs were designed with doing grounded theory in mind (see Seidel and Clark 1984: 112, and Richards and Richards, this volume). The part played by grounded theory can be discerned very clearly in the following account by Sutton of how he analyzed his data on 'dying' organizations to produce a 'process model of organisational death':

> The method of data analysis used here draws on recommendations by Glaser and Strauss (1967) and Miles and Huberman (1984). The method entailed continuous comparison of data and model throughout the research project. I began the research by developing a rough working framework based on the existing literature, conversations with colleagues, and pilot interviews. I travelled back and forth between the emerging model and evidence throughout the data gathering and writing. In doing so, some elements suggested by the literature and prior intuitions could be grounded in evidence, while others could not. Other elements proposed at the outset or suggested by a subset of cases were retained but were modified considerably to conform to the evidence.
>
> (1987: 547)

However, in general there are relatively few genuine cases of grounded theory using the approach that is specified above. Very often, the term is employed in research publications to denote an approach to data analysis in which theory has emerged from the data. Rarely is there a genuine interweaving of data collection and theorizing of the kind advocated by Glaser and Strauss. Even the example of Sutton's description of his analytical procedures seems to imply that a model emerged at a much earlier stage (in terms of the amount of data collected prior to its specification) than the grounded theory approach would seem to suggest. As a result, grounded theory is probably given lip-service to a greater degree than is appreciated (Bryman 1988: 54–5). Richards and Richards make a similar point when they observe that grounded theory 'is widely adopted as an approving bumper sticker in qualitative studies' (1991: 43). Moreover, the precise process whereby a grounded theory analysis was undertaken is often imprecise.

A further strategy that has been identified by Williams (1976) and Hammersley (1989) is the *pattern model*, which does not separate explanation from description. According to this model,

> the activity of describing the relation between one action and others in a context is equivalent to interpreting or explaining the meaning of that action. Describing its place and its relation to other parts is therefore to explain it.
>
> (Williams 1976: 128)

However, this model operates at a higher level of generality than analytic induction and grounded theory and provides relatively few guide-lines when confronted with data.

Tesch (1991) has also identified different approaches to analysis. First are approaches based on language: discourse analysis, symbolic interactionism and ethnomethodology, in which the focus is on how language is employed. Second, there is a 'descriptive or interpretive approach', which seeks to establish a coherent and inclusive account of a culture from the point of view of those being researched. Classic ethnography and life history studies fall into this type. Finally, there are 'theory-building' approaches, as in grounded theory and in Miles and Huberman (1984), in which the generation of theory is a primary goal. The chief problem with this delineation is that it does not address the process of analysis. Also, the distinctions are not without difficulties. Tesch notes that symbolic interactionists, while being included primarily in the first category, are also concerned to build theory. It is also questionable whether the first two categories are quite as unconcerned with theory-building as the distinction implies.

GENERAL PROCESSES

The *generation of concepts* is one of the most frequently mentioned aspects of qualitative data analysis in the texts that have been reviewed. Hammersley and Atkinson (1983) recommended immersing oneself in the data and then searching out patterns, identifying possibly surprising phenomena, and

being sensitive to inconsistencies, such as divergent views (
different groups of individuals. They recognize that sometimes the r
will end up generating new concepts, but on other occasions will be
his or her observations to pre-existing notions (see Lofland 1971). Ir
the concepts may not be clearly defined and will require elaboratic
clues to the generation of new concepts, Woods (1986: 133–4) recommends
being sensitive to repetitions of incidents or words, irregularities, unusual
occurrences and how people say things (for example, if accompanied by
droll laughter, embarrassment, anger). He shows how his notion of teachers'
survival strategies was built up from such evidence as a series of well-prepared
eighty-minute science classes to which the pupils were paying next to no
attention or from utterly chaotic lessons which teachers regarded as having
gone down well. Miles and Huberman (1984: 60) observe that there will be
a close connection between coding and the generation of concepts, regardless
of whether the latter are pre-specified (and later revised) or emergent. However,
for most practitioners codes are the building blocks for emergent rather than
pre-specified concepts.

Hammersley and Atkinson (1983), Spradley (1979, 1980), Woods (1986)
and others mention the *building of typologies and taxonomies* as an important
component of analysis. Here the researcher aims to delineate subgroups within
a general category. Such devices can become helpful in the identification of
differences in the data and can help with the elucidation of relationships among
concepts. Even the simplest of classifications, like Whyte's (1955) 'street
corner' and 'college' boys, or Jenkins's (1983) 'lads', 'citizens' and 'ordinary
kids', can help to organize amorphous material and to identify patterns in
the data. Differences between the components of such classifications in terms
of behaviour patterns are important in generating the kinds of linkages that
will form the basis for the development of theory.

A particularly helpful discussion of analysis is provided by Bogdan and
Biklen (1982), who distinguish between analysis in the field and analysis after
data collection. Their approach owes much to grounded theory. In analysis in
the field, the authors suggest that the researcher needs to be constantly engaging
in preliminary analytic strategies during data collection. Such strategies include:
forcing oneself to narrow down the focus of the study; continually reviewing
field notes in order to determine whether new questions could fruitfully be
asked; writing memos about what you have found out in relation to various
issues (this is a grounded theory tactic); and trying out emergent ideas. Analysis
after the field is essentially concerned with the development of a coding system.
They present 'families of codes' which are fairly generic and can apply to
a variety of different contexts. These include: setting/context codes; informants' perspectives; how informants think about people and objects; process
codes; activity codes; strategy codes; and personal relationship codes.

A further classification of codes and coding has been provided by Miles
and Huberman (1984), who distinguish between descriptive, interpretive,

explanatory and astringent codes, these last being ones which 'pull a lot of material together' (p. 57). Lofland (1971) has provided a classification of 'social phenomena' which can usefully be employed as the basis for a coding scheme:

> Ranging from the microscopic to the macroscopic, these [social phenomena] are as follows:
> 1 *Acts*. Action in a situation that is temporally brief, consuming only a few seconds, minutes, or hours.
> 2 *Activities*. Action in a setting of more major duration – days, weeks, months – consuming significant elements of persons' involvements.
> 3 *Meanings*. The verbal production of participants that define and direct action.
> 4 *Participation*. Persons' holistic involvement in, or adaptation to, a situation or setting under study.
> 5 *Relationships*. Interrelationships among several persons considered simultaneously.
> 6 *Settings*. The entire setting under study conceived as the unit of analysis.
>
> (1971: 14–15)

While there is a range of strategies and processes described in the texts, the question that arises is: How (if at all) are these used in practice? Some clues are provided in autobiographical writing, to which we now turn.

AUTOBIOGRAPHICAL ACCOUNTS

Among the most popular volumes devoted to research methodology in the last decade have been those which provide first person or autobiographical accounts where researchers have been invited to discuss the ways in which they *actually* conducted their research, in contrast to the ways they might be supposed to conduct it. Yet, even in these cases it is important to remember that it is *post hoc* reflections that are provided, with the result that projects are tidied up by their authors before being presented to a wider public. One of the first set of accounts to be provided in this genre was from the USA, where Hammond (1964) published *Sociologists at Work*. One of the great strengths of this volume was the way in which the various authors made links between theory and research. Indeed, in a subsequent evaluation of the essays in this volume, Baldamus (1972) highlights the importance of formal and informal theorizing, which has a bearing upon our theme of analysis. Within these early autobiographical essays authors describe the way in which they search for 'integrating principles', 'theoretical amalgams' and 'conceptual frameworks'. But we might ask: How does this link with data analysis?

Regrettably, there are few clues in the accounts which have been produced. In an editorial preface to a special issue of the journal *Urban Life and*

Culture (now the *Journal of Contemporary Ethnography*), Lofland (1974) commented on the failings of autobiographical accounts. He considered that they provided little technical detail on the procedures associated with data collection and analysis. Instead, he argued that many accounts were little more than reviews of 'my adventures and nausea among the natives' (Lofland 1974: 307). In order to develop the level of discussion Lofland invited some successful fieldworkers (Cavan 1974, Davis 1974, Roth 1974, Wiseman 1974) to discuss data collection and analysis in one of their studies. To assist them in constructing their accounts, which would focus on procedures of data collection and analysis rather than on the social relations of fieldwork, he invited the researchers to address a set of questions. These included:

1 In what manner did you keep field and/or interview notes? Typed? Carbons? Dittoed? What was the rate of data accumulation, or waves of accumulation?
2 What workplace isolation or other place and physical devices did you employ to facilitate work on getting down material and working at its analysis?
3 How did you file, code or otherwise encode or sort the raw materials you accumulated? Marginal codes? Filing? Other?
4 How did the leading ideas that organized your present analysis evolve? A sudden flash? Slowly? Other?
5 What kinds of models or images are you aware of employing to organize the material? What were their sources?
6 To what degree did you organize your analysis before writing it out in text, versus writing it and then seeing what you had? Did you write a little every day, around the clock in bursts, or some other way?
7 In general, what were the most important difficulties *and* facilitants experienced in evolving the analysis and writing it up?
8 How would you, or have you, modified your practices since doing the particular work described here?

(Lofland 1974: 308)

While these questions focus on technical aspects of investigation, they should not be divorced from the social relations of fieldwork. The conduct of fieldwork is such that the social processes in which the fieldworker is engaged can have a direct influence on the modification of technical procedures and it is important for us to understand the dynamics of this relationship together with its implications for fieldwork.

Meanwhile, in Britain, Bell and Newby encouraged authors to contribute to the development of descriptive methodology through a series of accounts published under the title *Doing Sociological Research* (Bell and Newby 1977), in which authors were encouraged to write themselves into their accounts and to address such questions as:

Why did you do this or that piece of research, when you did it in the way you did? How did you actually go about your research – what were the false starts, brilliant ideas and so on? What were the reactions, if any, to publication? What have been the personal consequences for you of the research?

(1977: 12)

Although the editors indicated that their list of questions was not exhaustive, it is evident that no explicit mention is made of analysis apart from a general reference to the way in which individuals went about research.

Authors such as Bell and Newby, and Bell and Encel (1978), moved us away from textbook procedures, and in doing so they tended to focus more upon research narrative rather than any of the technical aspects of social investigation. Indeed, it was the 1980s that witnessed increasing systematization from the authors of these accounts. However, the contributors to Roberts (1981) tended to focus more upon the way in which feminist research involved particular aspects of data collection that called for serious amendment. Interview approaches came under detailed scrutiny (Oakley 1981). Some of these themes were subsequently taken up in a volume edited by Bell and Roberts (1984), which pursued similar issues to those that both editors had been associated with in the recent past. Their earliest volumes were predominantly associated with data collection: participant observation and interviewing alongside several others.

Yet the editors of subsequent collections demonstrated some unease with this approach. For example, Burgess (1984b) devised a set of questions that his contributors might address in writing about their research practice. His questions demonstrate that issues concerning data analysis cannot be relegated to one simple section on the implications of various procedures for data analysis. Instead questions concerning analysis were raised throughout the research process. For example, when addressing matters of research access authors were invited to consider: 'How did these relationships [between sponsors and gatekeepers] influence data collection and analysis?' (p. 8). Similarly, analysis also figured in questions of language when he asked, 'What language skills were required in data collection and data analysis?' (pp. 8–9). Such questions prefaced enquiries about data analysis which were summarized as follows:

What was the relationship between data collection and data analysis? What were the informal processes involved in data analysis? What technical procedures were used for analyzing field data? What form did the writing up take?   (Burgess 1984b: 9)

In addition, he invited authors to make links between theory and analysis when he asked, 'What was the relationship between theory, data collection and data analysis?' (p. 9).

Such questions point to the overlap between different aspects of the research process, with research access, data collection and data recording having implications for analysis, while analysis also links to the process of theorizing and writing. In the accounts that followed, authors demonstrated how analysis was not an activity to be relegated to the end of a research project, but was rather a central part of the continuous process of doing research. Several investigators demonstrated how the notes that were taken during a project were an important element in understanding the social structures under study (King 1984). The process of note taking was therefore highlighted not only as a means of data collection, but also as an important location for formal and informal analysis through commentary and coding.

Some authors demonstrated very clearly how analysis relates to formal and informal procedures, where themes emerge from data and from interview transcriptions (Porter 1984, Stenhouse 1984). Other strategies that are discussed involve looking for incidents (Delamont 1984) and the generation of theory from data using the model devised by Glaser and Strauss (1967). Yet sociologists have also been involved in devising new concepts in the course of conducting research so that data analysis gives rise to exploration and theory development.

Some of these procedures have been elaborated upon in other volumes (Burgess 1990, 1992), but many autobiographical essays remain silent on analysis in an explicit way. For example, Bryman (1988) encouraged his contributors to write about the formal and informal aspects of doing research in organizations, but he did not include analysis in his guide to topics on which his authors might write. Yet his volume contains an important essay by Turner (1988), who demonstrates the ways in which some of the principles associated with the work of Glaser and Strauss can be developed in practice.

Among the latest accounts in this genre is a collection of autobiographical accounts edited by Walford (1991), whose contributors focus on studies in education. While the volume continues to add to our knowledge of research practice, the focus is upon the practical and social aspects of conducting research. Accordingly, the editor tells us, 'all the chapters aim to share some of the challenges and embarrassments, the pains and triumphs, the ambiguities and satisfactions of trying to discover what is unknown' (1991: 5). As a consequence, there is a tendency to return to the story-telling mode of such essays, where a segment of the research process is scrutinized. Nevertheless, three qualitative essays do feature aspects of data analysis in an implicit or explicit way. For example, Measor and Woods (1991) tell us a little about analysis, since the main sections of their essay are devoted to research planning and design, access, and collaborative research. However, it is only in the subsection on writing that we get a glimpse of analysis through comments that Measor makes on an early draft of material written by Woods, where she talks of examples that are 'proof' of their analysis. Meanwhile, essays by Mercer (1991) and Ball (1991) give insights into the explicit processes associated with analysis in educational studies. In both instances they demonstrate that analysis is not a mere segment of the research process but is integral to other aspects of the conduct of investigation.

THE ORGANIZATION OF THIS VOLUME

The contributors to this volume were all invited to provide an exposition of the way in which they went about the analysis of qualitative data by providing a chapter in which there would be a balance between technical procedures and research examples. Our strategy was to issue invitations to those who had been involved in different kinds of qualitative investigations: studies based on the classic lone researcher approach, joint investigations, and research teams involved in multi-site studies, as well as studies that highlight the use of computers, policy issues and theorizing. Each of the contributors to this collection focuses on qualitative data analysis, but does so in his or her own way. Indeed, two essays that follow illustrate that there is no standard approach to the analysis of qualitative data; secondly, that data analysis relates not only to technical procedures but also to the social relations aspects of fieldwork; finally, that much of the work in which investigators engage in this phase of the research process is as much implicit as explicit.

Our collection opens with an essay from Judith Okely, an anthropologist who works within the classic tradition of ethnographic inquiry, but unlike the classical anthropologists such as Malinowski she focuses on the study of an aspect of her own society. Yet in this instance, the situation she was studying was simultaneously familiar (her own society) yet strange (the world of Gypsies) – an aspect of her work which had an important influence on her understanding and subsequent writing. The approach that was used by anthropologists has subsequently been taken up and developed by sociologists who have conducted ethnographic studies in schools, hospitals, factories and other social institutions. Yet it is relatively rare for the sociologist to move from public settings into the private domain of the family. But this is what Christina Hughes did in conducting a study of stepparents. Her chapter provides another example of the lone researcher developing insights from her fieldwork experience.

Alongside those studies conducted in anthropology and sociology that follow a classical approach, there is also a range of studies in a variety of social science disciplines utilizing more specialist approaches to qualitative data collection and analysis. Among the approaches used have been ethnomethodology, conversation analysis and discourse analysis. It is the last approach that is represented by Jonathan Potter and Margaret Wetherell so that comparisons can be made with the more conventional approaches. Indeed, a further major development in the social sciences has been the impact of feminism on data analysis. Accordingly, the chapter from Marilyn Porter discusses the role of team leader and illustrates the ways in which issues in feminist studies had an impact upon her analysis. Furthermore, although her chapter is single-authored, the study on which she is writing was produced by a team of social scientists.

It is this use of research teams that is explored through a series of chapters. First, by Jennifer Mason who was part of a two-member team. Here, she highlights the way in which she worked with her co-researcher to develop, collect, analyze and report data. In a further team-based chapter, Virginia Olesen and her co-investigators demonstrate much of the rich texture on the process of memo writing and exchange which assists in the development of analytic insights. Finally, a chapter from Robert Burgess and his team illustrates the way in which multi-site work can be developed through a systematic division of labour between team members, but where a discussion of key issues, insights and themes becomes essential for common conceptual development.

Certainly, conceptual development is a critical issue in the conduct of data analysis. In the final contributions to this volume, further themes are explored in this direction. First, the chapter from Lyn and Tom Richards discusses the development of conceptual themes on the basis of computer analysis. Second, there is a chapter from researchers in a qualitative research unit (Jane Ritchie and Liz Spencer) where interview-based studies are to the fore and topics and categories are extracted from transcripts for policy purposes as well as the development of social science. In a further contribution we turn to an essay by Barry Turner, who highlights the way in which thinking and theorizing are conducted in order to develop conceptual categories that will contribute to the social sciences as well as to our understanding of substantive fields. Finally, we provide some reflections on qualitative data analysis.

The essays that follow are therefore accounts of different approaches to data analysis in action. Together they illustrate that there is no standard approach but that a rich variety of approaches is characteristic of conducting qualitative research.

NOTES

1 From the study by Jon Gubbay (University of East Anglia), personal communication.

Most frequently cited methods texts in undergraduate research methods courses in Britain 1990–1

Rank order	Citations
1 D. De Vaus, *Surveys in Social Research*	10
2 R.G. Burgess, *In the Field*	4
2 M. Hammersley and P. Atkinson, *Ethnography: Principles in Practice*	4

Rank order	*Citations*
4 M. Bulmer (ed.), *Sociological Research Methods*	3
4 R.G. Burgess (ed.), *Field Research: a Sourcebook and Field Manual*	3
4 G. Rose, *Deciphering Sociological Research*	3
7 C. Bell and H. Roberts, *Social Researching*	2
7 A. Bryman, *Quantity and Quality in Social Research*	2
7 Frances Clegg, *Simple Statistics*	2
7 C. Marsh, *The Survey Method*	2
7 C. Marsh, *Exploring Data*	2
7 K. Plummer, *Documents of Life*	2
7 J. Scott, *A Matter of Record*	2
7 *Social Trends*	2

Notes:

(a) These data are based on a study of 68 courses.
(b) These texts were on lists which indicated students must read them in order to cope with the course.

2 It is not easy to specify how far coding in grounded theory and qualitative data analysis generally differs from that which takes place in quantitative data analysis. In part, this difficulty derives from an occasional tendency to caricature quantitative coding. Thus, Charmaz has written,

> Qualitative coding is not the same as quantitative coding .... Quantitative coding requires preconceived, logically deduced codes into which the data are placed. Qualitative coding ... means *creating* categories from interpretation of the data.
>
> (1983: 111, emphasis in original)

However, this statement applies more to pre-coded questions in quantitative research or the coding of answers to open-ended questions to which an explicit coding frame can be applied in advance (which can be quite rare in social science research). Very often when conducting 'quantitative coding' of open-ended questions, a researcher has to create a coding frame out of an initial reading of the answers provided to the questions, so that at least the initial categorization has an emergent quality. The difference between this coding and that which occurs in grounded theory lies in the tendency for coding in qualitative data analysis to be more provisional (since conceptualization is under constant revision) and for codes to represent different levels of elaboration (some will be highly speculative; others, at a later stage of elaboration, will be more developed in terms of theoretical abstraction). In quantitative data analysis, codes become 'fixed' more rapidly and tend to be similar in terms of their level of theoretical development.

REFERENCES

Atkinson, P. (1990) *The Ethnographic Imagination*, London: Routledge.
Babbie, E.R. (1979) *The Practice of Social Research*, 2nd edn, Belmont, Calif.: Wadsworth.

Baldamus, W. (1972) 'The role of discoveries in social science', in T. Shanin (ed.) *The Rules of the Game*, London: Tavistock.

Ball, S.J. (1991) 'Power, conflict, micropolitics and all that!' in G. Walford (ed.) *Doing Educational Research*, London: Routledge.

Bechhofer, F. (1974) 'Current approaches to empirical research: some central ideas', in J. Rex (ed.) *Approaches to Sociology: an Introduction to Major Trends in British Sociology*, London: Routledge & Kegan Paul.

Bell, C. and Encel, S. (eds) (1978) *Inside the Whale*, Oxford: Pergamon.

Bell, C. and Newby, H. (eds) (1977) *Doing Sociological Research*, London: Allen & Unwin.

Bell, C. and Roberts, H. (eds) (1984) *Social Researching*, London: Routledge.

Bogdan, R.C. and Biklen, S.K. (1982) *Qualitative Research for Education*, Boston, Mass.: Allyn & Bacon.

Bogdan, R. and Taylor, S.J. (1975) *Introduction to Qualitative Research Methods*, New York: Wiley.

Bryman, A. (1988) *Quantity and Quality in Social Research*, London: Unwin Hyman.

Bulmer, M. (1979) 'Concepts in the analysis of qualitative data', *Sociological Review* 27: 651–77.

Bulmer, M. and Burgess, R.G. (eds) (1981) 'The teaching of research methodology', *Sociology* 15 (4) (special issue).

Burgess, R.G. (ed.) (1982) *Field Research: a Sourcebook and Field Manual*, London: Unwin Hyman.

—— (1984a) *In the Field: an Introduction to Field Research*, London: Allen & Unwin.

—— (ed.) (1984b) *The Research Process in Educational Settings: Ten Case Studies*, Lewes: Falmer Press.

—— (ed.) (1989) *The Ethics of Educational Research*, Lewes, Falmer Press.

—— (ed.) (1990) *Reflections on Field Experience*, London: JAI Press.

—— (ed.) (1992) *Learning about Fieldwork*, London: JAI Press.

Cavan, S. (1974) 'Seeing social structure in a rural setting', *Urban Life and Culture* 3(3): 329–46.

Charmaz, K. (1983) 'The grounded theory method: an explication and interpretation', in R.M. Emerson (ed.) *Contemporary Field Research*, Boston, Mass.: Little, Brown.

Cicourel, A. (1964) *Method and Measurement in Sociology*, New York: Free Press.

Cressey, D. (1950) 'The criminal violation of personal trust', *American Sociological Review* 15: 738–43.

Davis, F. (1974) 'Stories and sociology', *Urban Life and Culture* 3(3): 310–16.

Delamont, S. (1984) 'The old girl network: recollections on the fieldwork at St Luke's', in R.G. Burgess (ed.) *The Research Process in Educational Settings: Ten Case Studies*, Lewes: Falmer Press.

De Vaus, D. (1991) *Surveys in Social Research*, 2nd edn, London: UCL Press.

Fielding, N.G. and Lee, R.M. (eds) (1991) *Using Computers in Qualitative Research*, London: Sage.

Finch, J. (1986) *Research and Policy*, Lewes: Falmer Press.

Frankfort-Nachmias, C. and Nachmias, D. (1982) *Research Methods in the Social Sciences*, London: Edward Arnold.

Glaser, B.G. (1978) *Theoretical Sensitivity*, Mill Valley, Calif.: Sociology Press.

Glaser, B.G. and Strauss, A.L. (1967) *The Discovery of Grounded Theory: Strategies for Qualitative Research*, Chicago: Aldine.

Goetz, J.P. and Le Compte, M.D. (1984) *Ethnography and Qualitative Design in Educational Research*, Orlando, Fla.: Academic Press.

Hammersley, M. (1989) *The Dilemma of Qualitative Method: Herbert Blumer and the Chicago Tradition*, London: Routledge.

—— (1991) *Reading Ethnography*, London: Longman.

—— (1992) *What's Wrong with Ethnography?*, London: Routledge.

Hammersley, M. and Atkinson, P. (1983) *Ethnography: Principles in Practice*, London: Tavistock.

Hammond, P. (ed.) (1964) *Sociologists at Work*, New York: Basic Books.

Jenkins, R. (1983) *Lads, Citizens, and Ordinary Kids: Working-Class Youth Styles in Belfast*, London: Routledge & Kegan Paul.

Kidder, L.H. and Judd, C.M. (1986) *Research Methods in Social Relations*, 5th edn, New York: Holt, Rinehart & Winston.

King, R. (1984) 'The man in the wendy house: researching infants schools', in R.G. Burgess (ed.) *The Research Process in Educational Settings: Ten Case Studies*, Lewes: Falmer Press.

Lindesmith, A.R. (1947) *Opiate Addiction*, Bloomington, Ind.: Principle Press (published in 1968 as *Addiction and Opiates*, Chicago: Aldine).

Lofland, J. (1971) *Analyzing Social Settings: a Guide to Qualitative Observation and Analysis*, Belmont, Calif.: Wadsworth.

—— (1974) 'Analyzing qualitative data: first person accounts', *Urban Life and Culture* 3(3): 307–9.

Marsh, C. (1979) 'Social sciences methods bibliography: British universities 1978', Cambridge: Social and Political Sciences Committee, University of Cambridge (mimeo).

Martin, P.Y. and Turner, B.A. (1986) 'Grounded theory and organizational research', *Journal of Applied Behavioural Science* 22: 141–58.

Measor, L. and Woods, P. (1991) 'Breakthroughs and blockages in ethnographic research: contrasting experiences during the changing schools project', in G. Walford (ed.) *Doing Educational Research*, London: Routledge.

Mercer, N. (1991) 'Researching common knowledge: studying the content and context of educational discourse', in G. Walford (ed.) *Doing Educational Research*, London: Routledge.

Miles, M.B. and Huberman, M. (1984) *Qualitative Data Analysis*, Beverley Hills, Calif.: Sage.

Moser, C.A. and Kalton, G. (1971) *Survey Methods in Social Investigation*, London: Heinemann.

Oakley, A. (1981) 'Interviewing women: a contradiction in terms', in H. Roberts (ed.) *Doing Feminist Research*, London: Routledge.

Oppenheim, A.N. (1966) *Questionnaire Design and Attitude Measurement*, London: Heinemann.

Peel, J. (1968) *Courses Mainly Concerned with Sociological Theory and Methods in 29 Universities*, 15th Conference of Sociology Teachers Section of the BSA, London: British Sociological Association.

Porter, M.A. (1984) 'The modification of method in researching postgraduate education', in R.G. Burgess (ed.) *The Research Process in Educational Settings: Ten Case Studies*, Lewes: Falmer Press.

Richards, L. and Richards, T. (1991) 'The transformation of qualitative method: computational paradigms and research processes', in N.G. Fielding and R.M. Lee (eds) *Using Computers in Qualitative Research*, London: Sage.

Roberts, H. (ed.) (1981) *Doing Feminist Research*, London: Routledge.

Robinson, W.S. (1951) 'The logical structure of analytic induction', *American Sociological Review* 16: 812–18.

Roth, J. (1974) 'Turning adversity to account', *Urban Life and Culture* 3(3): 347–59.

Seidel, J.V. and Clark, J.A. (1984) 'The Ethnograph: a computer program for the analysis of qualitative data', *Qualitative Sociology* 7: 110–25.

Spradley, J.P. (1979) *The Ethnographic Interview*, New York: Holt, Rinehart & Winston.

—— (1980) *Participant Observation*, New York: Holt, Rinehart & Winston.

Stenhouse, L. (1984) 'Library use and user education in academic sixth forms: an autobiographical account', in R.G. Burgess (ed.) *The Research Process in Educational Settings: Ten Case Studies*, Lewes: Falmer Press.

Strauss, A.L. (1987) *Qualitative Analysis for Social Scientists*, Cambridge and New York: Cambridge University Press.

Strauss, A.L. and Corbin, J. (1990) *Basics of Qualitative Research*, Newbury Park, Calif.: Sage.

Sutton, R.I. (1987) 'The process of organizational death: disbanding and reconnecting', *Administrative Science Quarterly* 32: 570–89.

Tesch, R. (1990) *Qualitative Research: Analytic Types and Software Tools*, Lewes: Falmer Press.

—— (1991) 'Software for qualitative researchers: analysis needs and program capabilities', in N.G. Fielding and R.M. Lee (eds) *Using Computers in Qualitative Research*, London: Sage.

Turner, B.A. (1981) 'Some practical aspects of qualitative data analysis: one way of organising the cognitive processes associated with the generation of grounded theory', *Quality and Quantity* 15: 225–47.

—— (1988) 'Connoisseurship in the study of organizational cultures', in A. Bryman (ed.) *Doing Research in Organizations*, London: Routledge.

Wakeford, J. (1979) 'Research Methods Syllabuses in Sociology Departments in the United Kingdom', Lancaster: Department of Sociology, University of Lancaster (mimeo).

Walford, G. (ed.) (1991) *Doing Educational Research*, London: Routledge.

Whyte, W.F. (1955) *Street Corner Society*, 2nd edn, Chicago: University of Chicago Press.

—— (1984) *Lessons from the Field: a Guide from Experience*, Beverley Hills, Calif.: Sage.

Williams, R. (1976) 'Symbolic interactionism: fusion of theory and research', in D.C. Thorns (ed.) *New Directions in Sociology*, London: David & Charles.

Wiseman, J. (1974) 'The research web', *Urban Life and Culture* 3 (3): 317–28.

Woods, P. (1986) *Inside Schools: Ethnography in Educational Research*, London: Routledge.

Chapter 1

Thinking through fieldwork

Judith Okely

In this chapter, I describe the way in which I interpreted and wrote up my material from an intensive fieldwork study of Gypsies and aspects of government policy. The approach and methods which informed this work were those of social anthropology. I give details of how I recorded my material and, more relevant for this collection, how I made use of it along with the totality of my field experience for the ensuing publications. Since the term 'qualitative' has been applied to a range of different methodologies within the social sciences, it is important to outline the distinctive characteristics of social anthropological research. 'Qualitative' can refer to research using only a small sample of interviews, whether structured or unstructured. In either case the qualitative material is bounded by the cultural conventions of the interview. Paradoxically, the interview format is associated first and foremost with quantitative surveys whose positivistic conventions have set the agenda (cf. Oakley 1981). 'Qualitative' has also come to be used to describe the research which this chapter addresses, namely that which emerges from participant observation.

There are significant contrasts between anthropological and sociological empirical research, with implications for analysis. The two disciplines came from different contexts. Social anthropology was formerly associated with the study of non-western societies, mainly by westerners. Sociology's empirical work was concerned mainly with western societies of which the sociologist was a member. Unlike the sociologist, the anthropologist could not take much as given, he or she could not isolate one theme extracted from a wider context, since the society as a whole was largely unknown to the researcher, and undocumented. Rigidly formulated questionnaires were inappropriate. These and the interview mode are culture bound. The sociologist could be more presumptuous in knowledge of the wider social context. Whereas Durkheim (1897) could claim to identify and sub-classify suicide in France, Malinowski (1926) had first to discover and then redefine such a practice among the Trobrianders. He had no statistics to play with.

The way in which the anthropologist carries out fieldwork affects the sort of material produced, then analyzed and presented in the final texts. The anthropologist rarely commences research with an hypothesis to test. There are few pre-set, neatly honed questions, although there are multiple questions in the fieldworker's head. There are theories, themes, ideas and ethnographic details to discover, examine or dismiss. The anthropologist, despite months of literature reviews, possibly years of theoretical and comparative reading, will have to eject hypotheses like so much ballast. The people may not live as recorded, there could be famine, strife or civil war. Rituals may be missionized, nomads dispersed, leaders imprisoned, documentation a distortion or deflection from the outsider's gaze. The ethnographer must, like a surrealist, be *disponible* (cf. Breton 1937), and open to *objets trouvés*, after arriving in the field. This approach inevitably affects the subsequent interpretation and analysis.

Although early field anthropologists made claims for the scientific status of their work, they have been less vulnerable than empirical sociologists to demands for positivist legitimacy in methods. Formerly, it was considered sufficiently impressive that anthropologists actually uprooted themselves and went to live elsewhere for extended periods. Social scientists who stayed at home were not in a position to challenge the techniques of pioneers in the unknown fields of exotica. There has been greater freedom in the analysis of fieldwork research. A great deal is taken on trust about the way material is written up. There can be no easily replicable formulae. The notion of techniques to be applied uniformly across the globe is inappropriate. Granted, social anthropologists of the earlier school have been too cavalier in both preparing students for the field and in conveying advice about how to write up. The lacunae are best filled by detailed autobiographical accounts of fieldwork and the ways in which interpretations are arrived at. These are relatively rare and split off from what are seen as the core concerns of the discipline (Okely 1992). The increasing bureaucratic and pedagogic demand for explicit methods 'training' has sometimes meant that social anthropologists have half-heartedly and inappropriately fallen back on textbooks devised for sociologists and others.

The historically divisive association of sociology with western societies and anthropology with non-western societies is no longer appropriate. Each discipline has strayed into the other's territory. While retaining its traditional methods, social anthropology can be used in the study of *any* group or society. I have, for example, applied it in the study of transport, the elderly and planning in East Anglia (Okely 1991), in addition to the study of Gypsies and government policy in England. Others have adopted an anthropological approach in Britain for scrutinizing the police (Young 1991) and views of death (Hockey 1990). These studies show that the kind of qualitative material which anthropology's methods and theories generate is different from other disciplines within the social sciences.

Each discipline retains its different historical approaches to methodology. Within sociology there appears to be a widespread association of participant observation with the theoretical perspective of symbolic interactionism (Hammersley and Atkinson 1983, Silverman 1985).[1] By contrast, the research material gathered by anthropologists can be placed in as many of the theoretical perspectives as there exist in both the social sciences and, if relevant, the humanities.

It is the custom for the anthropologist to be both fieldworker and analyst-author. Division of research labour into discrete tasks, or between individuals, is at a minimum. The anthropologist fieldworker records, interprets and writes up his or her own material. For the anthropologist, the stages of knowledge as the research progresses are not sectioned between persons. So there is no need to formulate mechanical procedures and managerial-type instructions to ensure uniformity of perspective along some chain of command. The anthropologist does not have to check and double-check whether numerous assistants and interviewers have understood or even faked the collection of data. He or she has instead to look to his or her specific relationship with the people who are the subject of study. The anthropologist becomes the collector and a walking archive, with ever unfolding resources for interpretation. By contrast, a social scientist in a prestigious research centre asserted that in order to follow the correct social science procedure and to attain 'objectivity', ideally someone other than I, the fieldworker, should write up the final report with the aid of my field notes. The fact that I completed the task myself was seen uneasily as a form of intellectual cheating rather than a scientific necessity and standard anthropological practice. Such a division between collection and analysis might be possible in a research tradition where the researcher delegates the former to a reserve army of interviewers with pre-ordained questionnaire and clone-like application.[2] The pre-selected choice of answers gives material which can be mechanically classified as part of the analysis.

Agar, the anthropologist, has offered an alternative descriptive term for research and fieldwork which is not hypothesis bound. A somewhat mechanistic metaphor, which doubtless allays the worries of those wanting proof of 'tools' of research, is what he names the 'funnel approach' (1980: 13). From the outset of fieldwork, the anthropologist adopts an open-ended approach to the full range of information and to all manner of people. This is the essence of the holistic approach. The material and ethnographic concerns are not cut to size at the start. The people who are the subject of study are themselves free to volunteer their concerns in their own voice and context. All this has implications for the kind of material and field notes which the anthropologist is faced with when it comes to writing up.

Both during the fieldwork and after, themes gradually emerge. Patterns and priorities impose themselves upon the ethnographer. Voices and ideas are neither muffled nor dismissed. To the professional positivist this seems like chaos. The voices and material lead the researcher in unpredictable, uncontrollable directions. This is indeed not a controlled experiment. The fieldworker cannot separate the act of gathering material from that of its continuing interpretation. Ideas and hunches emerge during the encounter and are explored or eventually discarded as fieldwork progresses. Writing up involves a similar experience. The ensuing analysis is creative, demanding and all consuming. It cannot be fully comprehended at the early writing-up stages by someone other than the fieldworker.

Long-term participant experience helps to make sense of even the most detached survey data. Leach, in a critique (1967) of an extensive survey of landownership in Ceylon (Sarkar and Tambiah 1957), was able to draw on his fieldwork in just one village to counter some interpretations of the statistics for 57 villages. The survey had concluded that 335 households were landless. However, from his detailed first-hand observation of inheritance practice in the region, Leach was able to point out that over time, a considerable number of the younger informants would inherit land. The same applied to many sharecroppers who were in fact heirs of the owners. He also suggested that some of the interpretation of the apparently unproblematic survey data was convincing only because the main researchers, already familiar with the region, arrived inadvertently 'at their conclusions by intuitive methods . . . . The numerical apparatus in which these conclusions are embedded seems to me to be very largely a complicated piece of self deception' (1967: 76).

After fieldwork, the material found in notebooks, in transcripts and even in contemporary written sources is only a guide and trigger. The anthropologist-writer draws also on the totality of the experience, parts of which may not, cannot, be cerebrally written down at the time. It is recorded in memory, body and all the senses. Ideas and themes have worked through the whole being throughout the experience of fieldwork. They have gestated in dreams and the subconscious in both sleep and in waking hours, away from the field, at the anthropologist's desk, in libraries and in dialogue with the people on return visits. Photographs point to details hitherto unnoticed by the fieldworker in the midst of the action. They may also revive hidden memories. The anthropologist may notice ethnographic detail which photographers do not perceive. The photograph on the cover of my 1983 book shows the interior of a Gypsy trailer-caravan. The professional who provided it failed to notice both before and after the event that the kitchen area had no sink. This is a crucial clue to Gypsies' pollution taboos. Other sources have also to be carefully scrutinized. Snatches of music may conjure up images and for-gotten or half-submerged insights. The act of interpretation and writing from past fieldwork may be as evocative and sensory as Proust's description of the tasting of the madeleine cake in *A la recherche du temps perdu* (1954).

The understanding and ways of making sense of the material and of writing cannot be routinized and streamlined as instructions for methodology text-books. Nor can it be fully assessed at this stage by a non-participant. Instead, to admit to the vastness, unpredictability and creative turbulence in which the ethnographic writer is immersed can be a reassurance that positivism is no guide. The methods in which many social scientists have been instructed have been an intellectual carapace. The puzzled novice researcher may be contaminated by positivistic notions of 'contamination', 'detachment', 'prediction', 'operationalization' or 'typicality'. Since ethnographic openness or *disponibilité* have defied hypotheses, the material cannot be subjected to strict formulae. The problem is how to convince researchers from other traditions or those who are schooled in positivistic formulae.

Years after my intensive fieldwork on Gypsies, and after follow-up research, there are still reverberations, there are still things to write about or to reinterpret, especially in the light of shifts in the theoretical and substantive concerns of social anthropology. It is only now that I feel free to detail the way in which the material was written up for books published in 1975 and 1983. The reasons are both political and intellectual. The first book, *Gypsies and Government Policy in England* (Adams *et al.* 1975) was policy-oriented. It was believed by the research centre that overseered it that policy-makers would respond most effectively to quantitative data (Okely 1987). On the other hand, they had chosen to employ an anthropologist because this discipline was traditionally associated with the study of the exotic and non-literate 'other'. Thus there was a built-in contradiction which the centre had not properly confronted, if extensive quantitative data was to be the ideal. The details of the struggle for qualitative methods could not be easily published (Okely 1987). Although an anthropological methodology was eventually accepted, its description in any public sphere risked political controversy. A detailed account of participant observation among both local officials and a vulnerable ethnic minority, and the seemingly clinical way in which field notes were dissected, risked being misread and misrepresented. Simultaneously, an exploration of how cumulative field experience leads to imaginative and intuitive interpretation would have been unsettling or irrelevant to the bureaucrats and politicians whom the research was intended to influence. Their received notions of research were and are still drenched in scientistic clichés.

There are also intellectual reasons for the absence of earlier research descriptions. Few anthropologists by the late 1970s had devoted much space to a detailed description of fieldwork practice. Resisting pressure to put a description in an appendix, I included a chapter on my fieldwork (Okely 1983). This deliberately excluded references to note taking. An autobiographical account was not as free as I had wished. Subsequently, social anthropology has shown new interest in examining the construction of ethnographic texts. Key monographs have been scrutinized for the literary devices used in the presentation of non-fictional material (Clifford and Marcus 1986, Geertz 1988).

It is standard practice for an anthropologist to live alongside a group of people for at least a year. I lived in a trailer-caravan on Gypsy encampments and went out to work with them: calling for scrap metal and joining a potato-picking gang. Research entailed periods amounting to about two years, including return visits, as well as participant observation among government officials and others in regular contact with Gypsies. Nothing approximating to an interview was used in the research for which I was responsible. Accordingly, the material which informs my writing is very different from that gleaned from one-to-one interviews with individuals divorced from daily practice and context. When I conducted research among government officials and non-Gypsies or 'Gorgios', as Gypsies call them, in the area, free-flowing conversations and dialogue occurred as I accompanied them about their business and at their leisure. All together, the number of people, whether Gypsy or Gorgio, whom I encountered and from whom I gained information amounted to several hundred, but my approach still places me behind what is considered to be the qualitative divide. The number of 'informants' is not an adequate guide to the distinction between very different research approaches.

Some of the themes and subsequent chapters in my early publication on Gypsies were explicitly affected by the demands and brief of the policy-oriented centre. The aim was to examine the Gypsies' position and preferences in the light of recent legislation which presumed long-term sedentarization and assimilation of this ethnic group. The needs of this travelling people and their conflict with the dominant society were unavoidably a key focus in the sort of questions addressed by the ethnographer at all stages of the research. Thus the political context and funding proposal influenced the way fieldwork was conducted, the themes selected in analysis and the projected readership (Adams et al. 1975). Even without the policy subtext, however, it still would have been impossible to write of a 'self-contained community' (Okely 1983). The non-Gypsy or Gorgio made an appearance every day on the Gypsy camps in body or spirit. Thus the Gorgio appeared in field notes and published text.

With minimal success, I had combed the anthropological monographs and other literature for guidance and for reassurance in the face of increasing scepticism among my employers about non-questionnaire research. Then a chance meeting with the Africanist anthropologist, Malcolm Mcleod, afforded me the best and only detailed methodological advice I was to find at the outset of fieldwork. From his experience, he suggested, 'write down everything you hear, smell and see; even the colour of the carpets . . . . Ideally you should fill an exercise book for each day.' So I jettisoned my earlier, increasingly unsatisfactory attempts at writing notes under prescribed headings. I had been prematurely deciding what was relevant and in the process omitting other details, possibly for ever. My notes took the form of a chronological journal. The only marker was the date on each page. Events were written up as soon as possible. The record for some days did indeed, when time allowed, stretch to exercise-book length. Ideas, tentative interpretations and dominant themes were also written into the text, as the field experience developed. However crude or speculative the ideas at that early stage, it did not matter. As both fieldworker and future author, I was free to allow the ideas to germinate in their own time and through my own thinking, not by proxy.

Subsequent participant observation and extended contemplation would sift out the wheat from the chaff.

Given the Gypsies' resistance to direct questioning, especially by outsiders, the material was acquired through daily, informal communication, which I recorded in detail. Thus the seemingly trivial descriptions of domestic objects, trailer interiors, and stray remarks volunteered in conversation, all meticulously noted, assumed massive significance when scrutinized and sifted, months and sometimes years later. Often the description, if properly open-ended, can seem innocent of deeper meaning when it is first recorded. Later, it is up to the anthropologist to read for the meaning.

At the end of fieldwork, I was faced with thousands of words: the experience written in chronological form. How to analyze? How to write up? First, the notes were typed up with wide margins, but single spaced, each page with the date on top. The final amount filled over eight box files of foolscap paper. Already, themes had emerged and I made a provisional list of topics, with subheadings. The broad headings were consistent with the holistic traditions of classical anthropology. The fieldworker aims for the total context, which includes kinship, the economy, politics and religion. Nothing can be taken for granted nor rigidly prearranged. So the classification is made after, not before, fieldwork. Major examples include:

(1) *Gypsy–Gorgio relations* with (i) council officials, (ii) customers, (iii) the police;
(2) *Work* (i) occupations, e.g. scrap metal, tarmac, antiques, (ii) ideology of self-employment, (iii) links with geographical mobility;
(3) *Gypsy identity* (i) Gorgio categories, (ii) self-ascription;
(4) *Kinship and the family* (i) choice of spouse, (ii) weddings, (iii) child care, (iv) shared residence, (v) alliances;
(5) *Education and socialization*;
(6) *Finance* (i) earnings, (ii) visible assets, (iii) budgeting;
(7) *Gorgio law* (i) courts, (ii) evictions, (iii) violence;
(8) *Gypsy law and community* (i) exchange and reciprocity, (ii) disputes, (iii) alliances;
(9) *Travelling* (i) ideology, (ii) case-studies, (iii) housing;
(10) *Sites* (i) official, (ii) official and temporary, (iii) illegal, (iv) rented, (v) Gypsy owned;
(11) *Religious beliefs*.

As I re-read through the notes, I added to the subheadings and categories. Paragraph by paragraph was bracketed. In many instances there was overlap. For example, a passage on kinship alliances could also be relevant to work partnerships. A case-study of a move from a camp could overlap with the topic of a police eviction. Details of a group discussion would involve individuals from several family or domestic units. The entire piece would be relevant to each unit. This overlap was no technical problem, since twelve photocopies were made of each page and the paragraphs were cut up according to each heading, stapled chronologically, and placed into the relevant named file. Each extract was marked with its original date in order to locate and cross-reference it in the chronology. Today, all this can be done by computer, without the labour-intensive cutting and pasting. Nevertheless, no computer can stand in for the ethnographer's discovery of emergent themes as fieldwork progresses, nor the final thinking and analysis. No computer can think through the fieldwork.

Without a fixed ideal number, I had always grabbed the opportunity to meet new individuals or families. It was a matter of balancing this with the benefits of increasing rapport with core clusters of families in the camps where I lived and in the locality as a whole. I was not under pressure as is a pollster interviewer to find select individuals and then hurry on after each interview. In working through my notes, I found that I had been able to obtain detailed, quantifiable information on seventy-five Gypsy families or domestic units, covering, for example, occupations, shelter, motor vehicles, visible assets, relative wealth or poverty, offspring, past and current marriages, kinship connections, literacy, housing experience and travelling patterns. All this was obtained without clip-board, and its accuracy was assured by the multiple contexts in which it emerged. This information was collated in anonymized family folders and quantified, along with the information on fifty families collected by my three colleagues. Numerical tables were presented in the first publication (Adams *et al*. 1975). The material was satisfactorily interpreted with the aid of knowledge which comes from long-term participant observation. The representative of the computer company which prepared the numerical print-out was intrigued by the fact that this relatively poor group showed, in the 1970s, such an 'atypically' high percentage of motor vehicle ownership. He advised us to make something of this extraordinary fact. Of course this qualitative aspect was unsurprising for a semi-nomadic Traveller-Gypsy group. But such detail was unlikely to have become apparent in a mass survey with quantitative priorities.

The numerical material may have given apparent credibility for policy-makers, but it was only a clue to systematic patterns. Since anthropology has delighted in the specific counter-example to ethnocentric universalisms, the presentation of its research does not rest on numerical majorities. It may require only one remark, one individual's example to unravel the elusive intelligibility of the group or context. People's beliefs, values and actions are not necessarily revealed by head counting. Instead, these crucial revelations are much more likely to emerge from chance incidents, extended comments, and both informal and ceremonial gatherings. All this is the stuff found in field notes or the fieldworker's selective memory. It is worked and thought through from event to text.

Having identified themes with many sub-classifications, and having stapled them sequentially in category folders, I would read and re-read the minutiae of this material. The detail and specificity were material to think with, a starting-point for an elaborated interpretation. The resultant chapters were in no way a collage of these bits and pieces. The folders provided confirmation of hunches, or unravelled false leads. The germs of ideas jotted down in the field offered organizing principles which had continued to simmer away since they first surfaced in crude and tentative form. The newly classified notes contained extended examples. There were first-hand statements whose words had often been forgotten long after the event, now preserved in aspic on paper. These voices were appropriately reproduced in the final text.

Preliminary outlines and drafts of chapters drew also on a wealth of other material. For dominant themes and proposed chapters I made card indexes with references and quotations from wider anthropological reading, from historical and folklore writing on Gypsies and from detailed notes on available contemporary records. Contrary to a still popular stereotyped view of participant observation and the discipline as a whole, anthropology does not ignore other sources. Archival, historical and current written records such as official reports, newspapers and the visual media are all grist to the writer's mill. Before ever encountering Gypsies and local agencies, I was steeped in non-Gypsy writing about this non-literate group who had few of their own records. Outsiders' typologies of 'real' and 'counterfeit' Gypsies offered an important perspective for understanding how the dominant majority rationalizes its repression of an ethnic minority. The racist and sometimes sentimental typology pointed to the constraints or opportunities available to the group in its relations with outsiders. Later, I looked at the use of stereotypes by Gypsies in economic relations with non-Gypsies (Okely 1979). I suggested that the ethnicity of the Gypsy could be exoticized ($+$), or concealed (0), or degraded ($-$), or neutralized ($+ -$). I was not concerned with how many times and how many Gypsies adopted the different strategies. My analysis was intended to demonstrate the underlying principles, rather than any quantitative information.

Given social anthropology's fundamental concern with a people's self-perceptions and view of the world, I was inevitably concerned with how the group defined its own members. Here, first-hand quotes and both ambiguous and unambiguous examples of individuals accepted as authentic members indicated the Gypsies' priorities and significant criteria. A key chapter in the 1975 publication (Okely 1975a) and a more theoretically exploratory chapter in the subsequent monograph (Okely 1983: 66–76) were devoted to questions of Gypsy identity and outsiders' interlocking or contrasting classifications. The theoretical perspective of Barth (1969), who posited the notion of self-ascription for ethnic groups, was an illuminating organizing principle.

Not only is the question of the construction of identity a continuing intellectual concern of anthropology, it is also used as a political weapon by non-Gypsies. The rejection of visible local Gypsies as 'counterfeit' in contrast to a mythically 'real Romany' legitimates a policy of harrassment and oppression. So the selection of this theme in writing up was grounded in the historical and political context of the minority. The larger society has itself generated the question about real or counterfeit Gypsies, and invented, beyond the academy, answers to which the academic has to respond. Received views on the 'other' become even more sensitive when the anthropologist is writing about people who inhabit both his or her own geographical territory, and that of the reader. Readers both within and outside the academy have ready-made stereotypes about the 'real' Gypsy. I was never allowed to escape the matter in everyday encounters outside the field. Once my research interests were identified, outsiders invariably offered pronouncements on the popular typology, before seeking my comments.

Written documentation provided the major source for chapters on the history of local policy (Okely 1975c) and an extended overview (Okely 1983: 105–24) of local and national planning. However, its reading and interpretation depended heavily on participant observation both among non-Gypsy officials and voluntary groups. Intensive fieldwork in only a limited locality helped to make sense of wider patterns, just as Leach had once found (1967, see above). I had, like Agar (1980), approached the material with an open mind. The local authority where I completed the bulk of fieldwork had been represented as one of the most liberal. Temporary sites had been established in the teeth of ferocious opposition. I was, until a subsequent incident outlined below, allowed completely free access to all the county council records and the photocopying machine. I filled two box files with copies of what I deemed to be essential documents: committee minutes and reports, correspondence, ministry directives, an informal census, residents' complaining letters and the odd petition. In the midst of the numerous and bulging filing cabinets was just one intervention from a Gypsy; a non-literate man on one of the camps where I had lived. He must have asked a literate acquaintance to write the letter, in its neat old-fashioned style. It requested the installation of a tap on his temporary council site, something which temporary army camps always regarded as a minimum requirement. The request remained unheeded throughout the three years of the site run by the authority which collected a weekly 'service charge' for the Elsans and rubbish skip. Officially, Gypsies had no political voice except for that one request in the council files. The interpretation and writing must therefore also confront the absences in the material.

Other absences may occur in the published text, not for want of material and analysis but because of powerful controls on information. The investigation of elites and those with power, which Nader has called 'studying up' (1974), is more precarious. As unexpected as the Gypsy's letter was the discovery of correspondence which revealed secret, illegal plans by senior county officials to set up an emergency committee and action group to chase specified Gypsies out of the county. The plan explicitly invited the police to collaborate with council officials. Their proposed task was to identify 'non-local' Gypsies (a contradiction in terms when considering travelling groups, who can rarely be fixed within a single county), and arrange for their deportation. The documentation belied the council's public protestations that the police acted as an independent and impartial body and that only legal methods were used to evict Gypsies from public or private land. The police chief's written response in fact rejected the emergency proposal. He argued that his force had already devised perfectly adequate screening methods. This correspondence could not be published. When my interest in these newly found documents was realized, my access to files was curtailed. The quality and amount of data to be scrutinized and interpreted was thereby diminished. Although I could not publish the evidence, it none the less informed my overall analysis (Okely 1975c), and especially that in my subsequent single-authored publication (Okely 1983: ch. 7).

In some instances, there were no comparable studies and traditions within anthropology to inform the analysis. This is another feature of such research, whose material can produce new theoretical paradigms and insights. The open-ended approach allows space for the previously unimagined. I had the opportunity to challenge classical concepts and typologies in both economics and kinship. For example, the classical typology of nomads in economic anthropology includes only hunter-gatherers and pastoralists. There was nothing on the specific nomadic formation found among Gypsies, and which, taking off from the articles of Cotten (1954, 1955), I helped to formulate (Okely 1975b and 1983). Gypsies, I suggested, are a unique type of nomad whose economy is directly dependent on a wider, usually sedentary economy. They can never claim to have or approximate to self-sufficiency, as has been said of other nomads. Hitherto, writers about Gypsies had tended to identify their economic activity by a description of the content of their occupations; e.g. horse dealer, tinsmith, knife-grinder, fortune-teller, scrap-dealer, hop-picker. No one except Cotten had attempted to look for a common form or structure. My notes gave me the huge variety of Gypsy occupations. They could be fitted into a common schema which I identified as the 'occasional supply of goods, services and labour where demand and supply are irregular in time and place' (1975b: 114 and expanded 1983: 50–1). My fieldwork confirmed again and again the Gypsies' conscious rejection of wage labour, which they spoke of with contempt. Thus, the popular argument that Gypsies were excluded from wage labour employment solely because of prejudice was untenable. It also explained the failure of well-meaning attempts to 'train' them for 'ordinary' employment.

Similarly, there seemed to be no available categories for the kind of marriage exchanges found in my field material (1983: 175–80). Some anthropologists inaccurately labelled them sister exchange. Segalen, Zonabend (and others) have, I discovered much later, offered the term 'chaining or renewal of alliance' (1987: 114–5) for marriage patterns in the French peasantry and which are to some extent similar to those found among British Gypsies. My analysis was here again intimately bound up with the manner in which the material was acquired. Contrary to standard advice in anthropology, dating back at least to Malinowski, the collection of genealogical information was not a way into the group and a means of establishing rapport. Bits and pieces were conveyed in the most unexpected circumstances. Any information on relationships, even names, was considered explosive. My genealogy file was composed of scribbles on cigarette packets, paper hankies and food packaging. I could not ask Gypsies about rules and choices of marriage partners, as I was not supposed to know about, let alone systematize any such matters. My completed diagrams (all anonymized), and perhaps banal to other anthropologists, represented a triumph over all adversity (1983: 175–80). Only other Gypsiologists would understand this.

The opening chapter to *The Traveller-Gypsies* (1983) includes some avowed speculation on the history of Gypsies. The circumstances of contemporary Gypsies derived from my intensive fieldwork, and placed alongside scattered historical data, is used to question the popular diffusionist theories which postulate that the Gypsies' presence in Europe from about the fifteenth century is to be explained only by migration from India. My alternative and still controversial suggestion is that, after the collapse of feudalism, groups of travelling people were formed from landless serfs and indigenous people, as well as from individuals from along the oriental trade routes. Fieldwork had shown how over time Gypsies used consanguines and affinal relations for internal solidarity. Simultaneously, they could incorporate isolated individuals through marriage. They banded together to exploit occupations which required flexibility in space and time and which were outside the fixed wage labour system. More detailed investigation is required by historians.

Meanwhile, the use of the present to analyze the past should be permitted to anthropologists as much as it is to others. Historians such as Thomas (1971) and Ladurie (1981) have made creative use of anthropological insights from living societies to explain rituals, witchcraft and animal symbolism in cultures which flourished centuries ago. Others may do it less explicitly. Mayall (1988) for example, uses the anthropologists' conceptual description of the Gypsy economy, formulated from accumulative participant observation and economic anthropology, of the kind outlined above (Okely 1975b, 1983), to make sense of his nineteenth-century data on Gypsies. Whereas an historian is expected to footnote the written source of every *fact*, he may project *concepts* backwards, without always fully acknowledging their source in recent anthropological analysis and fieldwork (Mayall 1988: 46–54). The use of qualitative anthropological research by historians should discredit a still popular belief in sociology that findings from participant observation are only applicable to the fieldworker's single locality in both time and space.[3]

Chapter priorities emerge through the experiencing, thinking and rethinking. For example, at the outset I had no preconceived notion, let alone hypothesis, that pollution beliefs and animal classification among the Gypsies would turn out to be as significant as I realized they were at the time of the later publication (Okely 1983: chs. 6 and 12). Nor indeed did my policy-oriented research employers, who saw these aspects of Gypsy life as mere 'superstitions', that could only be of interest to denigrated folkloreists. Beliefs were not seen then as relevant to the prioritized and pre-defined issues of sedentarization and settlement. The Gypsies' use of pollution beliefs to construct ethnic boundaries became clearer to me through the repeated evidence in field notes of distinct practices; for example, the rejection of sinks in caravans, the use of multiple bowls, and explicit statements or just casual asides by Gypsies about the apparently dirty habits of non-Gypsies.

While unburdened by hypotheses, the anthropologist is of necessity steeped in the broader theoretical and ethnographic concerns of his or her time. A theoretical sensitivity to the subject of pollution or animal symbolism had also been formed from reading Douglas (1966), Leach (1972), Lévi-Strauss (1966) and Tambiah (1973). Once the groundwork has been done, chance plays its part with the open mind.

It was while I was browsing again through *The Journal of the Gypsy Lore Society* that signals I had been alerted to in the field and in anthropological studies were consolidated. A stray example in an article by Thompson, a 'gentleman scholar', gave a clue to the system of the Gypsies' animal classification, evidence of which I could see scattered throughout the field notes. Until then I had not found a pattern in the Gypsies' random comments in identifying one animal as clean and another as polluting. Thompson (1922: 23, cited in Okely 1983: 92) recorded a direct quote, without further investigation, from a Gypsy who denigrated cats and dogs as polluted because they licked themselves, whereas horses were considered clean because they did not have the same habit. Eureka! I saw the demarcation between the inside and outside of the body reflected in the Gypsies' selective focus on animal behaviour, and as consistent with their own view of the body. Ingestion of the 'outer body' broke the rules which governed the Gypsies' washing and eating practices. The bits and pieces, recorded in field notes and in the folklore literature, on dogs, cats, ponies and hedgehogs suddenly fell into a classification grid. In contrast to the work of Lévi-Strauss (1966) and Tambiah (1973), this classification also depended on a relationship with the perceived or actual classification of another, that of non-Gypsies. The analysis, while drawing on structuralists' codes, yet grounded the beliefs in the historical and materialist context of the Gypsies' relations with outsiders. Pollution beliefs among Gypsies elsewhere were to be found in studies carried out by anthropologists working contemporaneously (Kaminski 1980, Miller 1975 and Sutherland 1975). None of these studies had, however, cracked the animal code. As is sometimes the case, the material may be there, but not necessarily interpreted. Jane Dick Zatta (1989) has followed up my analysis of British Gypsy animal classification in a comparison with Italian Gypsies and with intriguing innovation. Qualitative research of this kind has implications beyond territorial boundaries.

Interpretations are attained not only through a combination of anthropological knowledge and textual scrutiny, but also through the memory of field experience, unwritten yet inscribed in the fieldworker's being. The ethnographer, as former participant observer, judges the authenticity of his or her conclusions and interpretations in terms of that total experience. Others cannot so easily do it for her. Anthropologists have not begun to articulate the way in which ideas and interpretations are arrived at. The self and its autobiographical experience are used to relive and rework the material, although many anthropologists are coy about explicitly discussing that self and its history (Okely 1992). The interpretation is intuitive (cf. Leach 1967 above), yet the intuition is a newly acquired one which has been formed from months of living in the different culture.

Ideas may emerge from only the most intangible link with recorded notes. They arise in part as a response to other theories and ideas, long after fieldwork. For example, when the first book had been sent to press, and I was no longer employed by the policy-oriented research centre but instead registered for a doctorate and in the very different atmosphere of a university anthropology department, new ways of thinking about my fieldwork and the Gypsies took shape. Again, the political as well as academic context had implications for the ensuing texts. An all-women seminar of anthropologists took place weekly. Banished by the professor from departmental buildings because men were discouraged, if not excluded,[4] it pursued its creative and co-operative course away from the usual academic cockfights. Suddenly I could see how my political feminism could link up with academic anthropological work and the rethinking of my field material. I had not previously placed women in a separate category when classifying and chopping up field notes. Gender was not consciously highlighted, except to analyze the division of labour. Although I was without a relevant file to think through, I nevertheless found ideas tumbling out. Perhaps the very absence of a file permitted lateral thinking. All the exotic and erotic images of the Gypsy woman in literature, opera and art assailed me. The ideas crystallized after a chance viewing of an old Hollywood movie on Gypsy Rose Lee, the stripper, who had no ethnic connections with the minority group. Key images pointed to the contradictions between the projected fantasy among Gorgios of the Gypsy woman which contrasted with the behaviour I had learned was required of the Gypsies I had encountered.

As a woman researcher, I learned also through personal experience about non-Gypsy projections. To outsiders learning of my research, I was sometimes seen as a 'Gypsy woman', with all the fantastic stereotypes. Vivid and contrasting examples of actual Gypsy women from my fieldwork were recalled. I pursued the contrast in a paper for the women's seminar. Thoughts came at unexpected times; on a walk, in the night, not necessarily when seated with pen and paper at a desk. After the broad schema of ideas was set down, I could look back for some exact details, incidents and statements in the chronological field notes. That is, the ideas and theories, having fermented in the subconscious, emerged by free association from unspecified experience. Only then was empirical evidence instrumentally sought as confirmation or elucidation. This form of analysis was the opposite to how I had worked on some of the other chapters; I now responded entirely to intuition and elusive memory before grounding myself in the recorded notes. There was a moment of relief and freedom when, after a discussion with Shirley Ardener, I felt it was right to trust my new intuitions, while being unable in any empiricist way to point to exact 'proof' in field notes that the ideas were sound. Since I had not and could not have predicted the paradoxes in Gypsy women's position either before or during fieldwork, it was logical that this would not be traceable in the notes. It was a matter of piecing together passing clues and seemingly neutral descriptions, while allowing an imagination, grounded in experience, its proper freedom. My approach rested absolutely on the initial fieldwork which itself helped to form the theories, in a mysterious and uncontrolled way.

In my text (Okely 1975d) I presented stereotypes from literature and opera as icons or as an epiphany to demonstrate the full range of possibilities in stereotypes, not as some numerically calculated evidence. This was misunderstood by some empiricists who complained that my 'proof' rested on just one opera (*Carmen*) and two or three quotes from novels or poems. Since these were labelled as 'only fiction', or 'numerically insignificant', they were not counted (literally) as sufficient evidence. These readers were inappropriately demanding a media content-analysis which entails mechanically counting the number of times a stereotype appears, for example, in newspapers.

To conclude, the interpretation of anthropological material is, like fieldwork, a continuing and creative experience. The research has combined action and contemplation. Scrutiny of the notes offers both empirical certainty and intuitive reminders. Insights emerge also from the subconscious and from bodily memories, never penned on paper. There are serendipitous connections to be made, if the writer is open to them. Writing and analysis comprise a movement between the tangible and intangible, between the cerebral and sensual, between the visible and invisible. Interpretation moves from evidence to ideas and theory, then back again. There can be no set formulae, only broad guidelines, sensitive to specific cases. The researcher is freed from a division of labour which splits fieldwork from analysis. The author is not alienated from the experience of participant observation, but draws upon it both precisely and amorphously for the resolution of the completed text.[5]

NOTES

1   After eight years in a department of sociology, where I taught the core courses in 'qualitative methodology', I was astonished to be told by a theoretical Marxist colleague, unfamiliar with my publications, that I was a symbolic interactionist. His apparent proof was that I had done intensive fieldwork, including participant observation.

2   This tradition is often marked by a gender division of labour, with a named male researcher-author and unnamed female assistants.

3   Sociology undergraduates are routinely asked to write essays on the 'limitations' of participant observation. Textbooks inform them that its results may be 'valid', but 'unreliable' anywhere beyond the locality. In this positivistic exercise, quantitative criteria for generalizations predominate.

4   He did not see the inconsistency in being a member of All Souls, one of the richest Oxford colleges, which then excluded women.

5   The construction of anthropological texts has recently been scrutinized. My insertion of some reflexivity (see also Okely 1992), multiple quotations as voices and cultural references as ideology anticipated this. Simultaneously, my intention was to demonstrate that aspects of the classic monograph could be transposed to a western context.

REFERENCES

Adams, B., Okely, J., Morgan, D. and Smith, D. (1975) *Gypsies and Government Policy in England*, London: Heinemann Educational.

Agar, M. (1980) *The Professional Stranger*, London: Academic Press.

Barth, F. (1969) 'Introduction', in F. Barth (ed.) *Ethnic Groups and Boundaries*, London: Allen & Unwin.

Breton, A. (1937) *L'Amour fou*, Paris: Gallimard.

Clifford, J. and Marcus, G. (1986) (eds) *Writing Culture*, Berkeley, Calif.: University of California Press.

Cotten, R.M. (1954) 'An anthropologist looks at gypsiology', *Journal of the Gypsy Lore Society* 3rd series 33(3–4): 107–20.

—— (1955) 'An anthropologist looks at gypsiology', *Journal of the Gypsy Lore Society* 3rd series, 34 (1–2): 20–37.

Dick Zatta, J. (1989) '"The has tre mule!", tabous alimentaires et frontières ethniques', in P. Williams (ed.) *Tsiganes: Identité, évolution*, Paris: Syros Alternatives.

Douglas, M. (1966) *Purity and Danger*, London: Routledge & Kegan Paul.

Durkheim, E. (1897) *Le Suicide*, Paris: Alcan.

Geertz, C. (1988) *Works and Lives*, Oxford: Polity Press.

Hammersley, M. and Atkinson, P. (1983) *Ethnography: Principles in Practice*, London: Tavistock.

Hockey, J. (1990) *Experiencing Death: an Anthropological Account*, Edinburgh: Edinburgh University Press.

Kaminski, I.M. (1980) *The State of Ambiguity: Studies of Gypsy Refugees*, Gothenberg: Anthropological Research.

Ladurie, E. le Roy (1981) *Carnival in Romans*, Harmondsworth: Penguin Books.

Leach, E.R. (1967) 'An anthropologist's reflections on a social survey' in D. Jongmans and P. Gutkind (eds) *Anthropologists in the Field*, Assen: Van Gorcum.

—— (1972) 'Anthropological aspects of language: animal categories and verbal abuse', in P. Maranda (ed.), *Mythology*, Harmondsworth: Penguin Books.

Lévi-Strauss, C. (1966) *The Savage Mind*, trans. anon., London: Weidenfeld & Nicolson.

Malinowski, B. (1926) *Crime and Custom in Primitive Society*, London: Routlege & Kegan Paul.

Mayall, D. (1988) *The Gypsy-Travellers in Nineteenth Century Society*, Cambridge: Cambridge University Press.

Miller, C. (1975) 'American Rom and the ideology of defilement', in F. Rehfisch (ed.) *Gypsies, Tinkers and other Travellers*, London: Academic Press.

Nader, L. (1974) 'Up the anthropologists: perspectives gained from studying up', in

D. Hymes (ed.) *Reinventing Anthropology*, New York: Vintage.

Oakley, A. (1981) 'Interviewing women: a contradiction in terms', in H. Roberts (ed.) *Doing Feminist Research*, London: Routledge.

Okely, J. (1975a) 'Gypsy identity', in B. Adams, J. Okely, D. Morgan and D. Smith *Gypsies and Government Policy in England*, London: Heinemann Educational.

—— (1975b) 'Work and travel', in B. Adams, J. Okely, D. Morgan and D. Smith *Gypsies and Government Policy in England*, London: Heinemann Educational.

—— (1975c) 'Conflict and accommodation', in B. Adams, J. Okely, D. Morgan and D. Smith *Gypsies and Government Policy in England*, London: Heinemann.

—— (1975d) 'Gypsy women: models in conflict', in S. Ardener (ed.) *Perceiving Women*, London: Malaby/Dent (part reproduced in Okely 1983).

—— (1979) 'Trading stereotypes', in S. Wallman (ed.) *Ethnicity at Work*, London: Macmillan.

—— (1983) *The Traveller-Gypsies*, Cambridge: Cambridge University Press.

—— (1987) 'Fieldwork up the M1: policy and political aspects', in A. Jackson (ed.) *Anthropology at Home*, London: Routledge.

—— (1991) 'The ethnographic method applied to rural transport, the elderly and planing', report to the Economic and Social Research Council.

—— (1992) 'Anthropology and autobiography: participant experience and embodied knowledge', in J. Okely and H. Callaway (eds) *Anthropology and Autobiography*, London: Routledge.

Proust, M. (1954) *A la recherche du temps perdu*, Paris: Gallimard.

Sarkar, N.K. and Tambiah, S.J. (1957) *The Disintegrating Village*, Colombo.

Segalen, M. and Zonabend, F. (1987) 'Social anthropology and the ethnology of France: the field of kinship and the family', in A. Jackson (ed.) *Anthropology at Home*, London: Routledge.

Silverman, D. (1985) *Qualitative Methodology and Sociology*, Aldershot: Gower.

Tambiah, S.J. (1973) 'Classification of animals in Thailand', in M. Douglas (ed.) *Rules and Meanings*, Harmondsworth: Penguin Books.

Thomas, K. (1971) *Religion and the Decline of Magic*, London: Weidenfeld & Nicolson.

Thompson, T.W. (1922) 'The uncleanness of women among English Gypsies', *Journal of Gypsy Lore Society* 3rd series, 2(3): 113–39.

Young, M. (1991) *An Inside Job*, Oxford: Oxford University Press.

Chapter 2

From field notes to dissertation: analyzing the stepfamily

Christina Hughes

Why do myths predominate about wicked stepmothers and not wicked step-fathers? Why do stepparents sometimes perceive their stepchildren as 'wicked'? Why does an 'ex-wife' similarly provoke anger and resentment in stepmothers? How do these notions arise, how are they maintained and what is their effect on stepfamily life?

(Hughes 1991a: 1)

These questions suggest starting-points for an analysis of the stepfamily. Indeed, they appear on the first page of my published work on stepparenting for that very reason (see Hughes 1991a). However, these questions did not form starting-points to my research as central issues to be explored. Rather they were raised only at the end of the fieldwork period when I began to grapple, in a formal way, with making sense of my data. Their life in print therefore portrays something of a misrepresentation of the process of analyzing field data.

I am concerned in this chapter to detail that process of analysis in respect of the research on the stepfamily I undertook for my Ph.D. The process I shall describe contains references to the work of Glaser and Strauss (1967) and Strauss (1987). Indeed, the notion of 'grounded theory' appears to have captured the sociological imagination, judging by its almost standard inclusion in key methodology texts (see Burgess 1984a, Hammersley 1992, Hammersley and Atkinson 1983).

Notwithstanding, I make no claims here to be offering a guide to the methodological techniques of 'grounded theory' in the sense that Strauss describes it: as a 'style of doing qualitative analysis that includes a number of distinct features, such as theoretical sampling, and certain methodological guidelines, such as the making of constant comparisons and the use of a coding paradigm, to ensure conceptual development and density' (1987: 5). However, there are elements in the process I followed which were informed by the thrust of work by Glaser and Strauss in terms of the need to keep an ongoing analytic record throughout the data collection, to look for supporting and non-supporting data when developing analytic categories and to develop an analytic framework in relation to other substantive areas of work.

Nevertheless, I would be concerned if this were to appear as a mechanical process devoid of the impact on the task of analysis of fieldwork relationships and the researcher's own professional development. Indeed, as the text will indicate, I take the position wholeheartedly that the analytic process must also take account of researchers as 'fully aware of themselves as instruments for developing that grounded theory' (Strauss 1987: 6).

With this in mind, I am concerned to detail the social as much as the technical processes of analyzing field data. The chapter is therefore concerned with the problems arising from familiarity with the field under study and with the interrelationship between developing analyses from data collected from the field and that gleaned from other substantive fields. Overall, I seek to contribute to the very necessary demystification of the process of analyzing field data through the use of a 'confessional account' (Burgess 1984b: 67).

THE STUDY

This chapter is based on a participant observation study I undertook of five stepfamilies for a twelve-month period from 1985 to 1986 (for a full account of the methodological approaches see Hughes 1991b). The analytic framework for the research is the developing of theories of the role of myth in stepfamily life in terms of management, strategies, decision-making and gender. The research therefore details the way that myths of wickedness form an overarching consideration in the lives of stepmothers but not stepfathers, and the process through which myths are developed about stepchildren and ex-partners.

However, it would be a mistake to consider that the analytic process centres only on one concept – in this case that of mythology. The research also seeks to link mythology to the concepts of motherhood and caring and to the notion of reciprocity in (step)family relationships. Thus I argue that myths of wickedness form the very opposite images to those created by notions of good motherhood and that reciprocity also has very contrary expectations to the giving nature of love which is embedded within the ideology of being a parent, and specifically a mother. My task now is to detail the process by which I arrived at these end-points.

DEVELOPING ANALYSES IN THE FIELD

The quality, or even adequacy, of a research project is not only the result of the questions asked or concepts used, it is also the result of keeping rigorous field notes. As Hammersley and Atkinson argue, recording field data 'constitute[s] a central research activity, and it should be carried out with as much care and self-conscious organisation as possible' (1983: 146). The form in which participant observation data are recorded can therefore form an essential medium through which the researcher can develop analytical ideas.

My own approach is broadly to follow the principles elaborated by Schatzman and Strauss, who argue that data should be recorded in 'distinct packages' of material according to whether they constitute 'Observational Notes' (ON), 'Theoretical Notes' (TN) or 'Methodological Notes' (MN) (1973: 99). In this way there will be a separate set of notes for each observation, each of which should serve a different purpose.

In particular, emphasis is given to developing theoretical insight into field material whilst collecting data through the form and content of recording. Here, the Schatzman and Strauss category, Theoretical Notes, constitutes an elementary stage of the analytic process through drawing theoretical inferences from the data in an ongoing way.

My own system of recording reflected the principles of keeping separate records of the same incident. As these extracts from my field notes indicate, one set of notes was directly related to the Schatzman and Strauss category, Observational Notes (ON), where I recorded 'events experienced principally through watching and listening. They contain as little interpretation as possible and are as reliable as the observer can construct them' (1973: 110). Thus my ON from part of a visit to a stepmother whose stepdaughter was getting married state:

> The wedding cake had arrived and Meg [stepmother] was none too pleased with it. An aunt of Sandy's [Meg's stepdaughter] had made it and consequently Meg felt she could not say anything to her about it as she would have if it had 'been bought in a shop'. She commented very specifically on what she felt was wrong with it. 'It's got no decoration on it. No bells or rings or birds. All it's got is a cheap looking champagne glass with Christmas ribbon hanging out of it.' She then added, 'What will people think? They'll think I don't care.'

I also kept another set of notes which corresponded to the category of Theoretical Notes (TN), which are 'self-conscious, controlled attempts to derive meaning from any one of several observation notes' (Schatzman and Strauss 1973: 101). Attempts to develop analytic concepts or to make sense of the data therefore took place here by considering more abstract meanings in the data. Moreover, as I will illustrate, each incident could be considered either as a discrete entity or could be linked to previous ones both within cases and across cases.

The corresponding Theoretical Note to the Observational Note above therefore, in an elementary way, attempts to draw inferences from the data of this one event (Meg's feeling about the cake) but also seeks to link this inference to a previous issue in Meg's career as a stepmother, in this case her stepdaughter Sandy's premarital pregnancy. Thus, the TN indicates that I was drawing an inference from the incident of the cake, in relation to developing the concept of the need for public shows of caring and the possible consequences if such displays are not evident. The TN read,

> I think Meg's feelings about the cake signify that she thinks she will be seen as failing Sandy. This can be linked to her feelings about Sandy's pregnancy. This could also be seen as a sign of Meg's failure as a step-mother. As an outward sign of lack of care. Perhaps why they wish for Sandy to get married. At least then there would be less stigma.

It would appear, therefore, that at the very least I had embedded within my field notes an elementary form of analysis. In this particular case, the concept of 'care' appears to be one way in which, as I shall indicate later, I can begin to develop the data in a more rigorous way. However, whilst I would always attempt to keep an ongoing analysis in this way, there were some incidents from which I could not, at the time, derive meaning. Importantly, this was not because such incidents had no analytic merit. Rather it was because they simply continued to leave me puzzled when asking questions of them. It is to this issue that I now turn.

SIGNIFICANT EVENTS, BUT WHY?

During the fieldwork I witnessed, and duly recorded, events in stepfamily life where a stepparent would become extremely concerned over seemingly innocuous and everyday events. Specifically, it was not the event in itself which concerned me but rather the amount of agitation or distress which it caused the stepparent. For example, my field notes record the following data about a visit to a stepfamily. There had been a telephone call to a stepdaughter from her natural mother's friend asking about the whereabouts of her mother. As the ON records this created consternation for the stepmother, who wanted to know the 'real' reason for the telephone call. The ON read,

> Jane [a stepmother] reported that Polly [her stepdaughter] had received a telephone call from her mother's friend Gill. Gill had been trying to get hold of Polly's mother but without success and had telephoned Polly to ask her if her mother had gone away. Jane said that she had asked Polly why Gill wanted her mother so urgently and Polly had replied that she did not know. Nevertheless, Jane commented that the fact that Gill had telephoned Polly was sufficient to suggest that 'something was afoot' which involved Polly and that consequently some sort of conspiracy was going on. When Simon [Polly's father] returned home Jane recounted the above incident and suggested that he should telephone Gill and see what it was she wanted. Jane said she thought 'something is going on with Polly'. [Polly meanwhile is trying to telephone her mother but is unable to reach her. She finally returns to say she does not know why Gill wants her mother. Simon has suggested that it was to arrange a squash game as Gill and his

first wife often played together.] 'It could be as innocent as that,' Simon commented. Jane accepted that this could be a possibility.

The Theoretical Note corresponding to this incident indicates something of my perplexity in trying to make sense of the data. It is clear from this TN that I considered it was telling me something about the insecurity evidenced in stepparent–stepchild relationships. However, I was particularly concerned at the amount of disruption the telephone call had caused to the family's evening. At least forty-five minutes were spent in post-mortem by Jane discussing the incident with me and repeating the events to her husband. Thus, as my TN indicates, I was unclear about the theoretical relevance of the events yet considered this very lack of clarity worthy of recording. The TN reads,

> Why should Jane make such a big thing about the phone call? She spent a lot of time talking about it and was getting very upset. I think her comments 'something was afoot' and 'something is going on with Polly' show her basic insecurity about her relationship with Polly and Polly's relationship with her mother, but why should a seemingly innocent phone call cause so much concern?

As I witnessed similar behaviour in the other stepfamilies, where lengthy periods of time were spent by stepparents questioning motives around seem- ingly innocent events, I became more exasperated by the fact that I could not make more sense of this type of behaviour. The degree to which such events interposed in the more everyday events of stepfamily life suggested that they were significant. Yet during the fieldwork I could only signal this as problematic.

It would appear, therefore, that whilst in the field I was able to make tentative analytical statements through the form of keeping field notes. Yet this was not in itself a total solution to developing a coherent analytical framework which would link my data together. As I shall now consider, the develop- ment of this stage of the process was hampered in part by my very familiarity with the fieldwork couples.

LOST IN THE DATA

Taking orderly field notes is useful in separating types of data and putting the search for analytic categories at the forefront of the research process, but it is just the beginning of a lengthy process of developing wider categories in understanding the stepfamily. The recognition that this is so can be seen by the emphasis given to the role of 'analytic memos' in the literature (see for example Schatzman and Strauss 1973, Strauss 1987). Such memos enable the researcher to 'elaborate upon the inference, or to tie up several inferences in a more abstract statement' (Schatzman and Strauss 1973: 104).

I have to confess that my own system of developing analyses from field notes was rather less a self-conscious attempt to analyze and rather more an attempt just to write something coherent. It is here that we begin to see how immersion in the field leaves one almost too close to the data themselves to make any broader sense of them.

In the third year of my Ph.D. work, and when the fieldwork period had formally ended, I began to grapple with the task of writing my thesis. It was a daunting prospect to complete the fieldwork and begin the final stage of producing a written thesis for the first time. Moreover, during the fieldwork I had formed deep and personal relationships with the research participants. As a stepmother myself, I was a 'native' to the field of inquiry, with all the incipient dangers that this carries of over-identification with the research participants. Initially I found it impossible to see the research couples as sociological categories. To me they were people with lives and interests that I found fascinating. My study of their lives had included their changing relationships with their stepchildren, which they had experienced in deeply moving and personal ways. It had included problems and concerns about ex-partners and anxiety and joy at having children in a new relationship. These events I had viewed not only as issues about stepparenting but also as part of the total experience of each of their lives. I had spent a period of time with each family and this was experienced by me as a chronology of unfolding events, each inextricably linked and embedded in their past histories. Whilst I can separate these events now, at the end of the fieldwork I could not.

This knowledge of the stepfamilies and my fascination with the minutiae of their lives led me to want to write my data as case studies of the families themselves. My initial drafts focused on the individuals as unedited histories of their lives. The early writing of these chronologies was the beginning of a more formal ordering of data, but within a structure which replicated the personal and individual view I had of each stepparent. Nevertheless, they were an important part of the analytic process as they brought together key ideas in a relatively unstructured way. These drafts, often incomplete, were then packaged and sent on to my supervisor. Although unrefined, they were important as representing a key discourse between my supervisor and myself.

I have written elsewhere about the role and importance of the supervisor in the construction of a Ph.D. (see Hughes and Burgess 1993). It is at this point that I should stress that the development of an analytic framework for my research on the stepfamily owes much to the insight of my supervisor. His crucial intervention at this stage also signified how a detached perspective can offer interpretations which the more involved eye cannot see.

In particular, sections of the drafts, including the one cited above with regard to Jane and Polly, were returned to me with the comments, 'Is this a myth?' or 'Myth seems important here.' Such comments should not have surprised me. The literature on the stepfamily is replete with stories about the wicked stepmother (see for example Brown 1982, Burns 1985, Noble

1977). To the extent that it was so familiar I clearly could not see it. But it was also paradoxical to the extent that my attitude was that as such myths were well known, they were therefore inappropriate for an 'original' Ph.D.

At a general level the need for a Ph.D. to be an 'original' contribution to knowledge may lead the novice researcher to dismiss the known in a search for new theoretical and empirical territory. In my own case, there were certainly elements of this in my approach. Particularly, as the concept 'original' can be so diffuse, one's search for it becomes a quest in itself. Moreover, the extent of my immersion in the lives of the research families created a level of knowledge which had rendered it difficult to disentangle 'what everyone knows' from a more systematic application of concepts when reading data. Thus, at a general knowledge level one could argue that myths about wicked stepmothers are indeed well known, and also that it is generally accepted that society holds various negative stereotypes about stepfamilies. However, examination of the literature indicated that there are key areas which are undeveloped theoretically. What may not be commonly known therefore is the effect that such myths have on the way stepmothers parent stepchildren or how myths become created in stepfamilies about family and ex-family members. Thus the question 'Is this a myth?' was a turning-point in the analytic process. It marked the time when I stopped searching in the dark and began to gain a clear view of the major theme of the research. It was also the point where I began my education in mythology.

FINDING A NEW LITERATURE

One assumes, in a stereotypical way, that a researcher will have at his or her fingertips a broad knowledge base for analysis and theory-building. Certainly, the 'literature review' period in Ph.D. research is when such work is done and I had spent a lot of time reading literature on the stepfamily and family. The concept of myth within the literature on the stepfamily, in particular, is as I have indicated often mentioned but relatively undeveloped. Moreover, key British works on the stepfamily (Burgoyne and Clarke 1984, Ferri 1984) do not focus on a theoretical analysis of mythology at all. As a result, my education in mythology had to begin beyond the disciplinary boundaries of the sociology of the family and stepfamily, and took me into the literature of human resource management and the sociology of education.

Strauss details the process of theoretical sampling where he states that in order to develop grounded formal theory of awareness contexts he looked at 'new data' by reading a range of literature across substantive fields, including work on criminality, celebrities and race (1987: 243–8). The process he describes is self-conscious and directed, as he searches for predetermined categories such as 'rectification phenomena' (pp. 243–8). My own search of other substantive areas was more in the realms of a learning process in itself. My supervisor's background in education had clearly alerted him to the significance of myth in relation to pupils' experience of school transition and in this respect he suggested I read Measor and Wood's (1984) work. My apprenticeship in mythology had begun.

A bibliographic search led me to what turned out to be a key text in developing my knowledge base of the theory of myth (Sykes 1965) and directing the analytic framework for the thesis. Reading this text alerted me to a crucial distinction between one of our everyday uses of the term 'myth' as something which is untrue, and the theoretical underpinnings of an analysis using myth as a key concept. Here, 'the actual truth or falsity of the story is irrelevant; what is important is that the story and the ideas it embodies are accepted and *believed* to be true' (Sykes 1965: 323, emphasis in original). It was the notion that the 'truth' of an issue was irrelevant but belief in its truth all important which enabled me to see the significance of myth as an analytic concept. In this way, my contact with a whole new litera-ture, and consequently new knowledge, informed the final shape of the thesis.

RETURNING TO THE FIELD DATA

The developing insights I had gained from reading widely across substantive fields related to mythology enabled me to return to my field notes with fresh vision. At this stage I clearly needed to re-read my data for this particular significance. It is here therefore that we can begin to see how the analytic process involves both the reading of raw data and the application of concepts which have arisen from outside that data.

Thus, in relation to those events where I had been left with many questions and where I had difficulty in developing an adequate concept for the event, the theoretical underpinnings of mythology were revelatory. For example, the notion that the 'truth' of an issue was irrelevant enabled me to go beyond my own concern at whatever the 'truthfulness' of an event was. Accordingly, my perceptions of seemingly innocent events impacting extraordinarily on stepfamily life led to an understanding that to the participants in them such events were not so 'innocent'.

This kind of understanding was used to develop an analysis with regard to those incidents such as the telephone call described previously when Jane was convinced 'something was afoot'. Whatever the truth of her statement, she *believed* it to be true. This perspective, a belief in the myth, is one that is stressed within the thesis, where I argue that such beliefs influence stepparents' actions and contribute to the way step-parents define their relationships with stepchildren. In terms of the theo-retical underpinnings of myth construction, belief in the truth of one's statements provides the justification for future courses of action (see for example Sykes 1965).

The incident described with regard to Jane and Polly therefore forms at one level part of a wider analysis which centres on the construction of myths about stepchildren. Here I compared the attitudes expressed in statements such as 'something was afoot' with similar statements made not only by Jane but also by other stepparents in the study, as part of a wider analysis of the structuring of attitudes to stepchildren.

My reading of 'something was afoot' suggested mistrust. Similarly, other stepparents' comments indicated their mistrust of their stepchildren through statements such as 'You can't tell by his (her) face that he (she)'s lying' and 'You can never be sure.' Thus, in the thesis I argue, 'In the course of making such statements stepparents would point out behaviour which the stepchild had exhibited or misdemeanours which the stepchild had committed. By so doing, stepparents were building up an image of the child's character in such a way that their own attitudes and feelings would be justified' (Hughes 1991a: 123–4). I labelled such statements as 'harsh judgements' and argue that through the creation of a mythology about children, in which 'harsh judgements' form a central reference point, stepparents are able to cope with their own negative feelings and action towards their stepchildren.

The notion of mythology in relation to analyses of this kind was used to develop an understanding about the way in which myths were constructed about stepchildren and also previous partners. At a conceptual level, therefore, the major aim was to describe and analyze the process of myth construction itself and to put this at the forefront of the analytic task. However, myth was also used to illuminate and develop other key, and more familiar, concepts such as the distinction between stepmotherhood and stepfatherhood and the features of care and love implicit in the parenting task. It is here that we return to the analytic concerns evident in the Theoretical Notes recorded during the fieldwork period.

RETURNING TO EARLY ANALYTIC CONCEPTS

I have noted that my field notes contained, in an embryonic form, an analysis of some of the events I had recorded during the fieldwork period. The notion of 'caring' was one such analytical category where I began to collect and cross-reference incidents which appeared to be of relevance here. Moreover, in contrast to my lack of knowledge about mythology, I was very clearly aware of the feminist literature on motherhood that details the imperative to care selflessly for one's family as a key feature of the good (step)mother. It is at this level of analysis therefore that one sees how one concept, in this case mythology, can be used to illuminate knowledge in other areas of substantive work, in this instance motherhood and caring.

The field notes about Meg and Sandy detailed previously indicate that early in the fieldwork I was alerted to the significance of 'caring' as one way of analyzing the stepmother role. Thus not only had I recorded incidents such as the 'cake', but in the collection of the data in this area my field notes contained many examples of stepmothers taking extra care that their treatment of stepchildren would be seen as loving and absolutely equitable. Thus, stepmothers would keep books of expenditure for all children, step and natural, in the family to prove that they were being fair to all and they would discipline their own natural childen but not their step-children.

The literature on caring predominantly focuses on mothers, not stepmothers (see Rich 1977, Graham 1984), and one could not assume that the caring task for stepmothers was experienced in the same way as by mothers caring for their natural children. Certainly the data indicated that stepmothers had other imperatives beyond that of being a 'source of angelic love' (Rich 1977: 52), which related to concern at being viewed as 'wicked'. The analytic task was to look at the data in these terms and to begin to cate-gorize them.

With the categorization of data under the heading 'caring' began the very messy task of retrieving from my field notes not only those cases where I had previously labelled a TN in terms of 'care' but also other examples of stepmothers' parenting behaviour not previously labelled in this way. The process was not therefore reliant on extracting only those previously coded categories arising from a TN but was in effect again a re-reading of the data. My knowledge of mythology formed the focus of that re-reading and was reflected in the categories chosen. Thus the analysis of stepmothers' caring behaviour also reflected the concept of a mythology of wickedness as a prime focus in stepmothers' lives. The categories in which the data were broadly grouped were: discipline and non-discipline; the stepmother's role in decision-making in relation to stepchildren; stepmothers' perspectives on their role in relation to stepchildren and their actual role; their role in access arrangements; and any data which indicated their perceptions of good and bad parenting.

It was through the collation of these categories that I was able to develop an analysis which indicated that the effects of public attributions of wickedness heightened a stepmother's propensity to public displays of caring. In this way, I argued that such public displays formed one of many strategies stepmothers employed to avoid being viewed, both in their private and their public worlds, as wicked. The use of two key concepts, those of caring and mythology, were therefore brought together to develop an analysis which would illuminate the specific features of a step-mother's role.

CONCLUSION

Strauss comments that when analyzing field data the question '"What's the main story here?" is a kind of motto' (1987: 35), to be repeated often. In this simple format there is an element of truth – it sums up the technical task I experienced when analyzing the stepfamily data. I was searching for a 'main story' and found it in the concept of mythology. However, the process by which this came into being was not only the result of those technical tasks of recording, cross-referencing, reading and keeping analytic records. It was also due to a significant other asking that question and in so doing making a powerful contribution to the analytic process.

The notion of a 'main story', however, unfortunately also serves to reduce the painstaking process which is inevitable in analytical thinking, and to suggest that analyzing data creates no more than a quasi-fictional tale. I would hope that this chapter has given a modicum of insight into the development of analytic categories which do not rely on fiction but are grounded in the data and wider literature, categories which go beyond simple story-telling.

REFERENCES

Brown, D. (1982) *The Step-Family: a Growing Challenge for Social Work*, Social Work Monograph, Norwich: University of East Anglia Social Work Dept.

Burgess, R.G. (1984a) *In the Field: an Introduction to Field Research*, London: Unwin Hyman.

—— (1984b) *The Research Process in Educational Settings: Ten Case Studies*, Lewes: Falmer Press.

Burgoyne, J. and Clark, D. (1984) *Making a Go of It: a Study of Step-families in Sheffield*, London: Routledge & Kegan Paul.

Burns, C. (1985) *Stepmotherhood*, London: Piatkus.

Ferri, E. (1984) *Stepchildren: a National Study*, Windsor: NFER–Nelson.

Glaser, B.G. and Strauss, A.L. (1967) *The Discovery of Grounded Theory: Strategies for Qualitative Research*, Chicago: Aldine.

Graham, H. (1984) *Women, Health and the Family*, Brighton: Wheatsheaf.

Hammersley, M. (1992) *What's Wrong with Ethnography?* London: Routledge.

Hammersley, M. and Atkinson, J. (1983) *Ethnography: Principles in Practice*, London: Tavistock.

Hughes, C.L. (1991a) *Stepparents: Wicked or Wonderful?*, Aldershot: Gower.

—— (1991b) 'A stranger in the house: researching the stepfamily', in R.G. Burgess (ed.) *Learning about Fieldwork: Studies in Qualitative Methodology*, vol. III, London: JAI Press.

Hughes, C.L. and Burgess, R.G. (1993) 'Studying stepfamilies: a project with two tales', in R.G. Burgess (ed.) *Doing Postgraduate Research*, London: Sage.

Measor, L. and Woods, P. (1984) *Changing Schools*, Milton Keynes: Open University Press.

Noble, J. and W. (1977) *How to Win with Other People's Children*, New York: Hawthorn.

Rich, A. (1977) *Of Woman Born*, London: Virago.
Schatzman, L. and Strauss, A.L. (1973) *Field Research: Strategies for a Natural Sociology*, Englewood Cliffs, NJ: Prentice-Hall.
Strauss, A.L. (1987) *Qualitative Analysis for Social Scientists*, Cambridge and New York: Cambridge University Press.
Sykes, A.T.M. (1965) 'Myth and attitude change', *Human Relations* 18(4): 323–37.

Chapter 3

Analyzing Discourse

Jonathan Potter and Margaret Wetherell

The label 'discourse analysis' has been applied in very different ways in the social sciences, and before attempting to explicate discourse analysis as a method it is important to be clear what we mean by it. There are at least four types of work that have commonly been described in this way. The first is influenced by speech act theory and directed at a systematic account of the organization of conversational exchange in settings such as classrooms (e.g. Coulthard and Montgomery 1981). The second is much more psychologically orientated, focusing on so-called discourse processes; for example, the effect of discourse structure on recall and understanding (e.g. van Dijk and Kintch 1983). These two kinds of work are very different from the line of work we will discuss in this chapter, which has much closer links with strands three and four.

The third type of discourse analysis developed within the sociology of scientific knowledge, partly as a response to methodological difficulties with other ways of studying science (e.g. Gilbert and Mulkay 1984). It was concerned less with the traditional sociological question of how 'social factors' influence acts such as theory choice than with exploring how scientists construct their talk and texts to display their acts as rational and warrantable in any particular setting (Mulkay *et al.* 1983). One of the conclusions of this work was that major claims of sociologists and philosophers of science may be simply retellings of scientists' own folk stories.

The fourth and final approach comes from a very different tradition of continental social philosophy and cultural analysis. While most proponents worked with the titles of semiology or post-structuralism, Foucault (1971) is notable for characterizing his 'archeology' of madness and medicine as discourse analysis. Appropriations of this work in psychology, sociology and cultural studies (e.g. Coward 1984, Henriques *et al.* 1984) have tried to show how institutions, practices and even the individual human subject itself can be understood as produced through the workings of a set of discourses. For example, Hollway (1989) has attempted to show how the psychological significance of a decision about avoiding contraception in intercourse is constructed out of a limited number of competing discourses: a male sexual drive discourse; a have and hold traditional Christian discourse; a permissive discourse developed from social changes in the 1960s; and a more recent feminist discourse.

When we use the term discourse analysis in this chapter we are signalling connections to just the latter two of these kinds of work. However, as will become clear, we are also attempting selectively to integrate some of these insights with ideas from conversation analysis (e.g. Atkinson and Heritage 1984) and rhetoric (e.g. Billig 1987). A chapter specifically on the topic of analysis is not the place for a developed survey of the theoretical ins and outs of these claims. Nevertheless, as the analytic aims are so closely tied to the general theoretical concerns in discourse analysis, it is important to give at least a thumb-nail sketch of what we see as the distinguishing features of our particular variant of discourse analysis (for more detail see Edwards and Potter 1992, Potter and Wetherell 1987, Potter *et al.* 1990, Wetherell and Potter, 1992).

Three features of discourse analysis are particularly pertinent for its research practice. First, it is concerned with talk and texts as social practices; and as such it pays close attention to features which would traditionally be classed as linguistic *content* – meanings and topics – as well as attending to features of linguistic *form* such as grammar and cohesion. Indeed, once we adopt a discourse analytic approach, the distinction between content and form becomes problematic; content is seen to develop out of formal features of discourse and vice versa. Put more generally, the discourse analyst is after the answers to social or sociological questions rather than to linguistic ones.

Second, discourse analysis has a triple concern with action, construction and variability (Potter and Wetherell 1987). People perform actions of different kinds through their talk and their writing, and they accomplish the nature of these actions partly through constructing their discourse out of a range of styles, linguistic resources and rhetorical devices. One of the principal aims of discourse studies is to reveal the operation of these constructive processes. Once discourse is conceptualized in this way it becomes clear that there will be significant variation in, for example, descriptions of a phenomenon, as participants perform different kinds of actions. And, as we will show below, these variations can provide an important lever for discourse analytic work.

A third feature of discourse analysis is its concern with the rhetorical or argumentative organization of talk and texts. Rhetorical analysis has been particularly helpful in highlighting the way discursive versions are designed to counter real or potential alternatives (Billig 1991). Put another way, it takes the focus of analysis away from questions of how a version relates to some putative reality and asks instead how this version is designed successfully to compete with an alternative.

Within the style of discourse analytic work we are advocating it is possible to distinguish two broad emphases which are largely complementary to one another. On the one hand, studies have been concerned with the general resources that are used to construct discourse and enable the performance of particular actions. This style of work is most akin to the Foucaultian analysis in that it attempts to map out broad systems or 'interpretative repertoires' which are used to sustain different social practices (Potter *et al.* 1990). For example, studies of scientific discourse have shown the way it is constructed out of the combination of an 'empiricist' and a 'contingent' repertoire, and that *both* are necessary for performing the interpretative tasks that constitute scientific practice (Gilbert and Mulkay 1984; Mulkay 1985; Potter 1984). On the other hand, studies have concentrated more on the detailed procedures through which versions are constructed and made to appear factual. This style of work is closer to the concerns of conversation analysts with the interactional use of members' devices (Pomerantz 1986) and to rhetoricians' concern with the 'witcraft' (Billig 1987) through which an argument is made persuasive.

To some extent this is an artificial distinction, and we would not want to suggest that it can be sustained as much more than a convenient heuristic. Nevertheless, it usefully marks out some shades of emphasis in analysis. In this chapter, we will be concentrating on work which represents the latter tendency and will not be concerning ourselves with the identification and analysis of interpretative repertoires, which have been dealt with in detail elsewhere (Gilbert and Mulkay 1984, Potter and Mulkay 1985, Potter and Wetherell 1987, Wetherell and Potter 1988, 1992). The particular research project that we will use to illustrate our analytic practice is concerned with the way factual versions are produced in a television current affairs programme and, in particular, the ways quantification is used in the manufacture of such versions. In the next two sections we will try to describe how we conducted some of this research, our motivation, and the stages in analysis. Throughout we will focus on the method of analysis and thus will have as a secondary goal the explication of our research findings and conclusions. We refer readers who are interested in our conclusions about quantification in current affairs documentaries to the paper describing this work (Potter *et al.* 1991).

A QUALITATIVE ANALYSIS OF QUANTIFICATION

The research project we will draw on was an intensive case study focused on the making and reception of a television current affairs programme about the effectiveness of cancer charities. The programme, called *Cancer: Your Money or Your Life*, was transmitted in 1988 as part of Channel 4's 'flagship' *Dispatches* series. The programme was described as an exposé of the way donations to cancer charities have been directed into basic research projects which have only the most tenuous links with cancer; it also made the argument that cancer charities were using hard-hitting advertising to scare people into donating money in the face of very little evidence that charity-funded cancer research has made any difference to the recovery rates for the major cancers.

One of the features of the project was that we were able to collect a number of different types of material related to the programme. Obviously we had a video of the programme itself. We also collaborated with one of the team of programme-makers, who acted as a participant observer during the entire period of its making. This enabled us to collect a range of relevant discursive materials: for example, various drafts of the script, shooting schedules and, most important, recordings of the sessions in which certain sections of the programme were edited together. We also had access to the programme-makers' interviews with the various parties who were shown on the programme (cancer scientists, charity heads, advertisers, alternative or holistic therapists); we later interviewed some of these people ourselves and recorded their reactions to the film and the way their own interviews had been edited. Finally, we interviewed some people who had worked on the programme and for the production company. The analytic value of being able to collect this range of different types of material will become clear below.

Our general interest was in current affairs television as an institutionalized arena for the construction of factual accounts, comparable to science, television news, court-rooms and various kinds of less formal everyday talk. As such our study is part of a broader concern with the way factuality can be understood as a situated product of a range of social practices, some general and some specific (Edwards and Potter 1992, Potter and Edwards 1990). In our original grant proposal to the UK Economic and Social Research Council we suggested that our study might try to accomplish for a television film what Latour and Woolgar (1986) had done for peptide research in a biochemistry laboratory, that is, to look at the procedures through which some part of reality is made to seem stable, neutral and objectively there.

This general focus and set of aims encouraged the more specific interest in the practices of quantification in television documentaries. Quantification in one form or another is one of the most important devices used in the manufacture of authoritative factual versions. Numerical accounts are often contrasted explicitly with 'vaguer', 'less precise', 'more subjective', qualitative versions of events. But should quantitative accounts be given this status? We wanted to question and explore the ideal or received image of quantification and examine how numbers are actually used in practice. This conceptualization – the questioning of an ideal or taken-for-granted story – is often very helpful in focusing one's analysis. It generates a set of questions and issues for interrogating the analytic materials. Our interest in quantification also had a *reflexive* aim. Quantification is at least as important in social scientific research as in television documentaries; and this is particularly true of the research by psychologists and those other social scientists who have modelled their activities closely on images of the natural sciences. We hoped our investigations would provide a basis for intervention in methodological disputes within social science itself.

There is a relatively small amount of analytic work on this topic, although there are some ground-breaking studies of economics (Ashmore *et al.* 1989, McCloskey 1985), market trading (Clark and Pinch 1988) and 'ethnostatistics' more generally (Gephart 1988). The lack of attention to quantification in the existing literature is a double-edged sword, however. On the one hand, it suggests that a study of quantification in media settings has a guaranteed originality. On the other, the specific studies which can provide analytic start-points or be used as contrast cases are not available. As with any form of analysis or investigation, it is helpful in discourse analysis to be able to fend off and react to well-established positions based on other kinds of theoretical perspective.

Our final motivation for selecting quantification as a topic concerned the nature of the specific materials we collected, and this was probably the over-riding determinant of our interest. A quantified argument was central to what was widely seen as one of the most crucial and controversial sequences in the film we wished to study. In this sequence, cancer charity claims about their significant success in curing cancer are contrasted with the 'fact' that there has been remarkably little progress, given the huge financial outlay. This argument was picked out for attack by representatives of the cancer charities we interviewed, and it also contrasts with versions of cancer success offered in the charities' interviews with the film-makers and in their promo-tional materials. Importantly, we also had a complete record of the editing sessions in which this sequence was put together. The presence of a number of radically competing versions suggested that this would be a good start-point: comparison of differences between versions would be a central analytic heuristic.

We should note that, of course, all these motivations are to a greater or lesser extent *post hoc* reconstructions. We could tell the story of our research in other ways and refer, for example, to a host of contingent, subjective factors, such as parts of the film we had found interesting, our recent discussions with the author of one of the major studies of quantification (Ashmore), and the feeling that there was 'something there' that would make a good narrative. It is conventional to talk about motivations in methods chapters, but it would be counter to our practice as discourse analysts not to be self-conscious about our own methods of constructing a factual account (Ashmore 1989).

THE FACTS OF CANCER DEATH

The sequence reproduced in Extract One and the table that went with it (Figure 3.1), were thus our raw materials. We had the whole film in transcribed form as well as on video, so our initial approach was both to watch the sequence and pore over its transcript. At the same time, we tried to map the themes raised in the sequence through the rest of our materials. We could have done this quite adequately by reading all of our transcribed materials and selecting out what was relevant. To do this carefully, however, would have been a very time-consuming and laborious task – it is hard to keep the subtle analytic issues to the forefront of one's mind for hour after hour in this way. To circumvent this we took advantage of the fact that all our materials were transcribed on to a personal computer. We made a list of about a dozen keywords and phrases that related to the sequence – percentage, cure rates, death rates, 1 per cent, etc. – and ran through each of the interview and interaction files looking for them with the standard word-processor (which happened to be 'Microsoft Word').

Whenever we got a 'hit' we would read the surrounding text to see if it had relevance to our target sequence. When it did we would copy it across to an already opened coding file (using the windowing facilities of the word-processor), noting the transcript page numbers at the same time. If we were not sure if the sequence was relevant we copied it anyway, for, unlike the sorts of coding that take place in traditional content analysis, the coding is not the analysis itself but a preliminary to make the task of analysis manageable. This activity resulted in a coding file of fifty-eight double-spaced pages.

Our next step was to go back to the original tapes and check the transcript for all the sections on the coding file. This not only improved the transcript but also tuned us into the sorts of voice features and sense of dynamic interaction that are not easy to render into transcript. Furthermore, by noting the appropriate sections of tape we could move between transcript and tape easily in the course of analysis to check our interpretations against the sound rather than just the words on paper. This was particularly important for the film sequence, of course, where the visuals (crucially the table of annual cancer incidence) were delicately meshed with the spoken words.

Finally, we went back to the film-makers' own interview with the charity head, which forms part of the sequence, and copied the surrounding text. This allowed us to consider some of the constructive work that went into putting the target sequence together and to compare the version in the film with sections of the talk that were not transmitted. So at the point at which we started on 'analysis proper' (and again this is a clarifying fiction rather than a fully accurate chronology) we had a manageable archive of materials: the target sequence, a section of film-makers' transcript, five sequences from our own interviews and a sequence from recordings made during editing that ran to over forty pages. We will start with the target sequence and then consider some of the ways in which we went about analyzing it.

The sequence comes about half-way through the film, following interviews with scientists who question the relation of their charity-funded work to cancer treatment success.

Extract One

COMMENTARY: The message from these scientists is clear – exactly like the public – they hope their basic research will lead to cures in the future

– although at the moment they can't say how this will happen. In the mean-time their aim is to increase scientific knowledge on a broad front and they're certainly achieving this. But do their results justify them getting so much of the money that has been given to help fight cancer? When faced with this challenge the first thing the charities point to are the small number of cancers which are now effectively curable.

[on screen: DR NIGEL KEMP, CANCER RESEARCH CAMPAIGN]

KEMP: The outlook for individuals suffering from a number of types of cancer has been totally revolutionized. I mean for example – children suffering from acute leukaemia – in old days if they lived six months they were lucky – now more than half the children with leukaemia are cured. And the same applies to a number of other cancers – Hodgkin's Disease in young people, testicular tumours in young men, and we all know about Bob Champion's success.

Scrolling table starts at this point.

COMMENTARY: But those three curable types are amongst the rarest cancers – they represent around 1 per cent of a quarter of a million cases of cancers diagnosed each year. Most deaths are caused by a small number of very common cancers.

KEMP: We are well aware of the fact that erm once people develop lung cancer or stomach cancer or cancer of the bowel sometimes – the outlook is very bad and aaa obviously one is frustrated by the sss relatively slow rate of progress on the one hand but equally I think there are a lot of real opportunities and and positive signs that advances can be made – even in the more intractable cancers.

As indicated, the spoken words are accompanied by the scrolling table labelled 'Annual incidence of cancer' (see Figure 3.1); the film-makers referred to this as a 'roller'. The table starts scrolling across the screen while Dr Kemp is first speaking and is complete at the words 'the outlook is very bad'.

One of the difficulties in writing about the process of discourse analysis is that the very category 'analysis' comes from a discourse developed for quan-titative, positivist methodologies such as experiments and surveys. Analysis in those settings consists in a distinct set of procedures; aggregating scores, categorizing instances, performing various sorts of statistical analysis and so on. It is sometimes tempting to think that in discourse work there is some analogous set of codified procedures that can be put into effect and which will lead to another set of entities known as 'the results'. To see things in this way would be very misleading, although, given the authority which accrues to these procedures, it is tempting to try. We are aware that this chapter is peppered with disclaimers about what we are *not* doing; this is because, to

ANNUAL INCIDENCE OF CANCER

PLACENTA	20
CHILDHOOD LEUKAEMIA	350 ←
EYE	400
SMALL INTESTINE	400
PLEURA	500
BONE	550
MOUTH	900
CONNECTIVE TISSUE	900
THYROID	950
TESTIS	1,000 ←
PHARYNX	1,000
LIVER	1,200
GALL BLADDER	1,300
HODGKIN'S DISEASE	1,400 ←
LARYNX	2,000
MYELOMA	2,300
MELANOMA	2,600
BRAIN	3,200
KIDNEY	3,500
UTERUS	3,700
CERVIX	4,400
LEUKAEMIA	4,400
HODGKIN'S LYMPHOMA	4,600
OESOPHAGUS	4,800
OVARY	5,100
PANCREAS	6,400
PROSTATE	10,400
BLADDER	10,500
RECTUM	10,600
STOMACH	13,100
COLON	16,800
BREAST	24,600
SKIN	25,000
LUNG	41,400
TOTAL	243,000

Lines marked by arrows appeared in yellow (in contrast to white) on screen to mark 'curable' cancers. The figures are said in the commentary to denote cases of cancer diagnosed in a single year.

Figure 3.1 Scrolling table of cancer incidence

some extent, we are writing *against* prevalent expectations about analysis (cf. Billig 1988).

Another point of departure from the way analysis is understood in more traditional studies concerns the procedures through which claims about the data and the research conclusions are justified. In much traditional work, to be seen to carry out the procedure of analysis correctly and comprehensively is itself part of the justification of results. Thus the impression of the solidity of a finding is reinforced through the operationalization of the variables, the appropriate stratification of the sampling, the appropriateness of the statistical analysis and so on. In discourse analysis, in contrast, the analytic procedure is largely separate from the warranting of claims. How you arrive at some view about what is going on in a piece of text may be quite different from how you justify that interpretation.

Much of the work of discourse analysis is a craft skill, something like bike riding or chicken sexing, which is not easy to render or describe in an explicit or codified manner. Indeed, as the analyst becomes more practised it becomes harder and harder to identify explicit procedures that could be called analysis. Nevertheless, there are a number of considerations that recur in the process of analysis. We have picked out five types of analytic consideration, from a potentially longer list, to highlight here. They can be summarized as:

1 using variation as a lever;
2 reading the detail;
3 looking for rhetorical organization;
4 looking for accountability;
5 cross-referring discourse studies.

We will take them in turn, trying to illustrate how they operate in the analysis of quantification in Extract One. Before we do this we should note that they are not all of the same status. Some, such as looking for accountability, refer to features of texts that are highlighted as important by discourse theorizing (Edwards and Potter 1992, Heritage 1984); others, such as reading the detail, refer more to craft skills or analytic frames of mind. Nor are they distinct from one another; they are often overlapping concerns, and as the analyst becomes more skilled their separation becomes less and less clear-cut.

Using variation as a lever

We have already noted the idea that discourse is constructed in the service of particular activities which lead to variation, and that variation can, in turn, be used to help identify features of construction. This is probably the single most important analytic principle in doing discourse analysis. Attention to variation works on a range of different levels and senses. One thing it does is to focus the analyst's attention on differences within a particular text: variations within the talk of a single speaker on a single occasion (e.g. Potter and Wetherell 1988), or within a single document (e.g. Yearley 1981). For example, if we consider just the numerical formulations in the commentary sections in Extract One we read the following description of the amount of cancers that are curable: '1 per cent of a quarter of a million'. The variation here is minimal. There is not a difference between versions in a single text but merely a change in the type of quantification used in a single description: it mixes a relational description (the percentage) with an absolute quantity (*x* many cases). For discourse analysts, even variation as minimal as this can be used to explore questions of how the discourse is orientated to action, how it is doing different work in the text. Why does the commentary move between different kinds of quantity terms in constructing this version?

Now in this study, elucidating the sorts of activities that were going on was not the main goal. Indeed, one of the features of these materials is that, in general, activities are relatively clear-cut: cancer charity representatives are concerned to show that their work is valuable, while the film is explicitly criticizing the worth of the charity-funded work. Thus, while not taking for granted that any *specific* stretch of discourse can be characterized in this way, these different sorts of orientations provide a helpful frame for interpreting the detail. So, if we assume that the film-makers' work is here to show the lack of success of the charities, we can read the variations in numerical formulations as contributing to a description which accomplishes 'lack of success'. Following this line of thinking, we suggested that the *relational quantity* ('around 1 per cent') was used because it has an almost definitive smallness to it. It is as small a non-zero percentage as you can get without using fractions or decimals, while the *absolute quantity* ('a quarter of a million') was used because it evokes largeness; it is 'millions talk'. The *combination* of the two provides a contrast which is used as a document of failure.

We can note two things about this conclusion. First, our analytic claim concerning the numerical presentation is not a result of any mechanical procedure; it is an interpretation backed up by reference to the materials which is open to dispute by another analyst on the basis of these or other materials. Identifying this variation is not the same as making a viable interpretation of it. Second, as well as paying attention to variation in the text the analyst needs to be alive to the question of difference: why is the text this way and not that way? Why do these words or phrases appear rather than others? So we are not only comparing actual variation but also potential variation. For example, part of seeing the effectiveness of the description that appears is a result of comparing it to potential alternatives such as 'two thousand eight hundred out of two hundred and forty three thousand'. The general point is to sustain the idea that the discourse is a contingent, manufactured entity; there is nothing natural or absolute about its particular form.

In practice, variation between texts is often much more striking than variation within texts, although variations within a single text or a single speaker's talk are often more analytically revealing. Not surprisingly, people often attend to the consistency of their discourse more carefully when it is delivered in a single passage of talk or writing, while different speakers regularly produce very different constructions of the world. Something of the extent of potential variability can be seen if we consider the following untransmitted segment from Dr Kemp's interview with the film-makers, which follows directly after the passage transmitted in Extract One:

Extract Two

> KEMP: Er, one way that I find useful to look at this is that er, each year in the United Kingdom two, roughly two hundred and forty thousand people get cancer. Each year er, roughly a hundred and sixty thousand people die from cancer, so there's a difference of eighty thousand, and eighty thousand is one third of two hundred and forty thousand which is the number of people who get the disease, so one could say that one's a sort of third of the way there. It's not a totally useless way of looking at it and sometimes quite helpful. So there has been progress but we're probably not half way there yet.

If we compare the 'bottom line' figures for progress in treating cancer we can see the film-makers' figure is 'around 1 per cent' while the cancer head's figure is approaching 'half way there'.

We used the difference between this version and that in Extract One to explicate further some of the quantification practices used to justify particular claims of success and failure. The sheer scale of the contrast between these versions suggested that we needed to look for something radically different in the quantification practices of the film-makers and the cancer charities. One device we used to help reveal these different practices was to use participants themselves to get at them. In effect, we used our interviews with participants in the programme who were critical of the programme's account to perform their own analyses; we put their *interest* in rebutting it to work. The idea is not that they will provide some sort of neutral analytic account, but that they will illustrate further variability between versions, but in a particularly explicit manner.

For example, the public relations officer for the largest British cancer charity, the Imperial Cancer Research Fund, particularly objected to the construction of the table of cancer incidence used to calculate the 'around 1 per cent' statistic. In fact she characterized the table of cancer deaths (Figure 3.1) as 'utterly irresponsible' because many people recover from breast cancer or even lung cancer:

Extract Three

> WILKINS: I'm very angry about that [. . .] there isn't a form of cancer (.2) for which (.) no one gets cured [. . .] if you were sitting at home with breast cancer [. . .] and you saw that the only curable cancer was in yellow but breast cancer was in white (WETHERELL: Yeah) you'd think your doctor's been lying to you.[1]

This and other passages encouraged us to think of the notions of 'cure' and 'curable cancer' as fundamental to the quantification practice of making progress in treatment appear good or bad. For example, we saw moves between technical notions of 'curable cancers', which are decided by using some criterion such as 80 per cent survival for five years, and everyday notions, which might for example allow that a cancer is curable if some people can be said to be completely rid of it. We also saw flexibility over whether someone who survives cancer has been actually *cured* of cancer (as opposed to 'spontaneous recovery' or simply having a non-fatal cancer) and over whether a cure is dependent on cancer-funded research or other factors such as craft advances amongst surgeons. By taking curable cancer in its technical sense, ignoring survivals from other cancers, and taking the total of curable cancers as a percentage of those diagnosed, the programme-makers were able to generate a small figure. In contrast, by simply taking the difference between diagnosed cancers and deaths for a particular year (and thus avoiding the issue of what is a curable or incurable cancer) the charity head could produce a much bigger figure (but one which ignores questions about spontaneous recovery and craft advance).

Reading the detail

One of the things that should be eminently clear from our discussion of variation is that the analyst needs to be attentive to the fine details of discourse. Indeed, precisely the sort of detail that is lost in more traditional quantitative analytic techniques such as content analysis, and may be obscured in forms of qualitative analysis such as participant observation or interpretive studies of interviews, is often crucial in discourse analytic studies (Potter and Wetherell 1987). This work has been strongly influenced by the insights of Harvey Sacks, developed through many studies of conversation (e.g. Atkinson and Heritage 1984, Button and Lee 1987). His argument was that all the details in a stretch of discourse – the pauses, repairs, word choice and so on – are potentially there for a purpose; they are potentially part of the performance of some act or are consequential in some way for the outcome of the interaction (Wooffitt 1990). It is worth noting, however, that our description – 'the detail' – is itself part of a set of social science presuppositions about what are 'big things' and what 'mere details'. As the researcher starts to get into the right 'analytic mentality' (Schenkein 1978) the notion of detail, at least in its trivializing sense, becomes increasingly redundant. What were details start to seem like the big things, the consequential things for making sense of actions through talk.

Our example of variation within numerical descriptions of cure rates in the previous section illustrates the value of an analytic attention to detail. We were able to show that there was a potential orderliness to the selection of 'quarter of a million' rather than, say, 'two hundred and forty three thousand'. Almost any other feature of the study would provide another example of the value of attention to detail; let us take one of the non-numerical quantifications from Extract One in which 'curable cancers' are formulated as 'amongst the rarest cancers'. The selection of the description 'rarest' for curable cancers could be seen as merely a statistical commonplace (the majority of people get other kinds of cancer); yet in addition to this there are specific inferences available from this category 'rare', which may also invoke notions such as 'unusual' or 'atypical' and which in this context may raise questions about the generalizability of research success from these cases to the more 'common' ones. That is, rather than see this term as merely a felicitous stylistic variation we can see it as subtly providing another element in the programme-makers' case. There is no formula for reading for detail; and it is surprisingly difficult to overcome years of academic training in which the goal of reading is to produce some gist or unitary summary. The process of analysis is often a long struggle with one's own tendency to read in this way (Potter 1988).

Looking for rhetorical organization

As we noted at the start, one of the central features of our approach to discourse is a concern with rhetoric. Again, this is best thought of as an orientation built into the analytic mentality through practice rather than the basis for any specific procedure. Nevertheless, this orientation leads us to inspect discourse both for the way it is organized to make argumentative cases and for the way it is designed to undermine alternative cases (Billig 1991). Put another way, the rhetorical orientation draws our attention away from questions about how a version relates to some putative reality (which is anyway a problematic question within discourse analysis) and focuses it on how a version relates to competing alternatives.

A concern with rhetoric in this way is often, in practice, our previous concern with variation in another guise. A comparison of differences between and within versions is frequently the best way to start to unpick their rhetorical organization. Extract One is an example where alternative versions are presented in a single construction. That is, the programme-makers are reporting the cancer charities' case for their success and undermining this version through developing their alternative. In our original study, we considered a range of devices through which the commentary version was privileged over that of the head of the cancer charity (not the least of which is the selection from Kemp's interview of the section about three cancer successes while ignoring descriptions of success with common cancers such as breast cancer and the general argument about progress given in Extract Two).

The rhetorical orientation can be seen clearly in the discourse of the programme-makers during their editing of the film. This involved developing the final form of words for the commentary and combining the words with film and graphics. These sessions presented manifest examples of the way the programme-makers were trying to make strong argumentative points with the material. For example, in the passages where they constructed the roller showing 'annual incidence of cancer' we see the team working to heighten the contrast between the (small) numbers of curable cancers and the (big) figure for total cancers diagnosed. Extract Four is from transcripts of recorded talk between the programme-makers as they edit the final version of the film; we have added emphasis to indicate those sections where this orientation is most explicit.

Extract Four

BILLINGER: The er all the rest wipe off and total just comes up into the middle and stops by itself (.2) or (.2) conversely (.) what if you don't put total on that at all but lung – just so that (.) they all just go up and roll right off and *then I mix total up in the middle* (.2) *slightly bigger* (.8) *as if you know – as if you were doing executive producer* ....

FINNIS: Oh there's other bits in the programme where sort of (.) one in three people get (.) one in four people get so (.) it's not meant to demonstrate how erm (.) many people get any sort of cancer *it's meant to demonstrate that the three its just said are uncurable are a tiny (.) proportion of the lot.*

BILLINGER: *Ye:ah it just makes – it's more impact isn't it if you if you notice that the other one going by was five and the total of all of them is two hundred and forty-five.*

The extract catches the practical film-makers' work of trying to accomplish the *bigness* of the figure for cancer diagnoses and the *smallness* of the figure for cancers which are curable.

Looking for accountability

Concern with rhetoric is closely linked to concern with accountabilty. Indeed, in some respects they can be viewed as two sides of the same coin. Making one's actions and claims accountable can be viewed as constructing them in ways which make them hard to rebut or undermine, ways which make them seem fair or objective. This is perhaps a rather obvious consideration for a current affairs television programme, which has at least some institutional requirements of objectivity (Clayman 1988); however, ethnomethodologists have argued that accountability is an essential character of the design and understanding of human conduct generally (Heritage 1984, Watson and Sharrock 1991).

The analytic point that arises out of this is an important one. Traditionally, work in both sociology and social psychology has often concentrated on accounts as a discrete class of activity (Scott and Lyman 1968, Semin and Manstead 1983). From this perspective, talk is thus examined specifically for passages which contain excuses or justifications. However, the ethno-methodological perspective suggests we look for accountability as a dimension of any stretch of discourse.

If we consider our target passage, Extract One, it can be viewed as a version designed to stand up to scrutiny; its factual status is accountable (note: whether it succeeds in this is a participant's judgement; the analyst is concentrating on how accountability is done, not how well). The editing sessions show the programme-makers rehearsing various criticisms that might be made against the film and of the lines they could take arguing against them. For example, they consider whether their '1 per cent' figure can be justified as they rehearse the commentary.

Extract Five

FINNIS: So of the quarter of a million annual cancer cases

BILLINGER: nearly quarter million

FINNIS: yeah cancer research can lay claim to – eighty years of cancer research can lay can – claim to having found cures for just one per cent (.2)

CHITTY: you really want to make it that strong?

FINNIS: I I I If one can make it that strong(.) I'd like to make it that strong (.) it's the most surprising thing that's shown (.2)

CHITTY: Okay what if they say that err

FINNIS: breast cancer

CHITTY: breast cancer Tomoxifen treatment has extended lives (.) has increased five-year survivals by 10 per cent.

FINNIS: They wouldn't say that they could <u>cure</u> breast cancer (.2)

CHITTY: But actually they're <u>might</u> (.) [*Chitty outlines a potential counter-argument.*]

Whoo God I can't think of any others that really (.2) possible –

FINNIS: Screening the cervix.

CHITTY: Screening – screening the cervix they've dropped deaths by two thousand (.) 50 per cent erm –

FINNIS: Can we say that was cancer research though?

CHITTY: Well it certainly was.

FINNIS: Was it?

CHITTY: Yeah I mean but the pep em cervical cytology test (.) is really (.) it's not <u>Brit</u>ish cancer research (.) it's American thing.

FINNIS: So that's pushing it too far.

BILLINGER: <u>Mamm</u>ography would be the same (.) they say that – (.4) and only be detailed analysis of X-rays – [inaudible] they haven't <u>done</u> it yet but they –

FINNIS: Right right

BILLINGER: Yeah I think all we can say is they say these are curable (.) and these are the big <u>claims</u> that they make (.) for these three and yet (.2) those three are such a minute percentage of cancers.

FINNIS: So we have to keep it on the basis of their publicity as it were.

Here we see the programme-makers exploring a range of potential arguments against the claim that cancer research has had only a small (1 per cent) success. Breast cancer improvements are treated as extending life rather than actually curing (again, we see the importance for the film-makers' version of the category 'cure'). Improvements from screening for cancer of the cervix are treated as a product of American research (the film was directed at British cancer charities). Yet they decide to bypass these potential worries by focusing on 'curable cancers' and the claims the charities make about them. This is not to say that there is no concern with the 'precision' or 'truth' of the figure; rather it is that 'precision' and 'truth' are not being understood in the abstract but in the context of *arguments* where specific sorts of issues will arise. Again, this shows how collecting the right kinds of materials can make the task of analysis more straightforward.

Cross-referring discourse studies

The final analytic consideration that we will address concerns the way discourse studies are themselves drawn on as an analytic resource. Although discourse analysts have not been interested in the production of general laws in the more traditional social scientific sense, they have been concerned with features of discourse construction and interaction that might apply across different contexts. Indeed, conversation analysis in particular has been notable for the cumulative nature of its insights and how what were often viewed as rather trivial or uninteresting early findings have borne fruit in the analysis of subtle phenomena or complex institutional situations (Heritage and Greatbatch 1986, Levinson 1983).

Again, there is no mechanical procedure for applying prior studies in a way which will bear fruit in the current situation. Nevertheless a wide familiarity with conversation analytic and more general discourse work is undoubtedly a major resource in being able to make workable interpretations of a set of materials. At its most general level, reading other work is one of the ways of developing the analytic mentality. Indeed, it can be a very useful practice exercise simply to try to reproduce a finding with a new set of data, for this will force hidden assumptions to be confronted and provide a feel for the analytic decisions that have to be made. More specifically, earlier studies can throw light on phenomena appearing in current materials.

We can illustrate this with two examples of quantification research. The first one we used was a study of market traders (Pinch and Clark 1986). Pinch and Clark had examined the devices that traders used in making their goods appear to be bargains. The relevance of this is that it is a realm of quantification (in this case financial) where particular kinds of contrast are being produced. One technique was particularly striking, and that was the building up of the worth of some goods by selling them in a collection (a pen is sold with a pencil, a case and so on). By building up this list it seems like there are a lot of goods in comparison to the selling price; by listing the goods in this way they are constituted as a bargain. We suggested that something similar was going on in the construction of the roller (Figure 3.1). Here the very long list of cancers, and the very big end total, serve to emphasize the smallness of the number of curable cancers.

The second example was a study of 'ontological gerrymandering' in sociologists' discourse by Woolgar and Pawluch (1985). Their argument is that in addressing the solution to 'social problems' the conclusions are often dependent on unexplicated assumptions about what is and is not a relevant realm of objects and ideas. Put another way, when conducting an argument part of the rhetorical work is to bring a particular terrain for dispute into existence and ignore or eliminate other potential terrains. Using this notion we were able to make more sense of the very wide disparities between the claims in the programme and by the cancer charities about progress. In particular, we argued that the programme-makers had selected the issue of curing cancer as a major focus of their critique while avoiding or reworking two other important issues: prevention and palliation. This helped us see how the programme-makers' 'around 1 per cent' bottom line for charity success could be seen as the product of a set of contingent decisions: to make an argument based on curing cancers, to take curabilty of cancers as the criterion rather than overall numbers of cured people, to calculate the number of curable cancers as a particular kind of proportion.

CONCLUSION

Throughout this chapter we have tried to emphasize the craft aspects of doing discourse analysis. In doing this we have not wanted to say that there are not some mechanical procedures that are often particularly helpful in doing analysis. Rather we have been wanting to undermine the idea that by simply using these procedures interesting 'results' will fall out in some way. The quality of analysis is dependent on how particular analytic interpretations can be warranted, and this depends on a whole range of factors: how well they account for the detail in material, how well potential alternatives can be discounted, how plausible the overall account seems, whether it meshes with other studies, and so on.

More than in many other kinds of social research, the evaluation of discourse analytic studies depends on the quality of the write-up. Obviously we cannot reproduce our write-up of our analysis here (see Potter *et al.* 1991) and at this point must stop our explication of method. If you are interested in our 'final' conclusions about quantification practices it is up to you to examine the published version of our work; in a sense you will need to perform your own discourse analysis to judge its persuasiveness as a critical investigation of quantification. Readers of discourse analytic studies need to be able, to an important extent, to perform their own evaluations of the analytic conclusions.

Perhaps for this reason it is difficult to make a clear-cut distinction between the process of analysis and the process of writing up. Often it is only when the discipline of presenting a study publicly necessitates filling in all the steps that flaws and problems appear. We have commonly had the experience of finding that things fall apart in one way or another in the process of formal writing and we have had to go back to the materials. Because of this we have found that collaboration in analysis can be extremely advantageous: the regular attempt to make interpretations stand up publicly is a very useful discipline.

NOTES

We would like to acknowledge the UK Economic and Social Research Council's support for this research (grant no. R000231439).

1 The standard transcription scheme of conversation analysis has been used here, and in following extracts:
[. . .] denotes omitted material;
(.2) denotes pauses timed to a tenth of a second;
(.) denotes a noticeable pause, too short to time;
British: underlining denotes emphasis;
Ye:ah Colon denotes a lengthening of the previous vowel sound;
claim to– A dash marks a sharp cut-off in the speech.

REFERENCES

Ashmore, M. (1989) *The Reflexive Thesis: Wrighting Sociology of Scientific Knowledge*, Chicago: University of Chicago Press.
Ashmore, M., Mulkay, M. and Pinch, T. (1989) *Health and Efficiency: a Sociological Study of Health Economics*, Milton Keynes: Open University Press.
Atkinson, J.M. and Heritage, J. (eds) (1984) *Structures of Social Action: Studies in Conversation Analysis*, Cambridge: Cambridge University Press.
Billig, M. (1987) *Arguing and Thinking: a Rhetorical Approach to Social Psychology*, Cambridge: Cambridge University Press.
—— (1988) 'Methodology and scholarship in understanding ideological explanation', in C. Antaki (ed.) *Analysing Lay Explanation: a Case Book*, London: Sage.
—— (1991) *Ideologies and Beliefs*, London: Sage.
Button, G. and Lee, J.R.E. (1987) *Talk and Social Organization*, Clevedon, Avon: Multilingual Matters.
Clark, C. and Pinch, T. (1988) 'Micro-sociology and micro-economics: selling by social control', in N. Fielding (ed.) *Actions and Structure*, London: Sage.
Clayman, S.E. (1988) 'Displaying neutrality in television news interviews', *Social Problems* 35: 474–92.
Coulthard, M. and Montgomery, M. (eds) (1981) *Studies in Discourse Analysis*, London: Routledge & Kegan Paul.
Coward, R. (1984) *Female Desire*, London: Paladin.
Edwards, D. and Potter, J. (1992) *Discursive Psychology*, London: Sage.
Foucault, M. (1971) 'Orders of discourse', *Social Science Information* 10: 7–30.
Gephart, R.P. (1988) *Ethnostatistics: Qualitative Foundations for Quantitative Research*, London: Sage.
Gilbert, G.N. and Mulkay, M. (1984) *Opening Pandora's Box: a Sociological*

Analysis of Scientists' Discourse, Cambridge: Cambridge University Press.

Henriques, J., Hollway, W., Irwin, C., Couze, V. and Walkerdine, V. (1984) *Changing the Subject: Psychology, Social Regulation and Subjectivity*, London: Methuen.

Heritage, J. (1984) *Garfinkel and Ethnomethodology*, Cambridge: Polity Press.

Heritage, J. and Greatbatch, D. (1986) 'Generating applause: a study of rhetoric and response at party political conferences', *American Journal of Sociology* 92: 110–57.

Hollway, W. (1989) *Subjectivity and Method in Psychology: Gender, Meaning and Science*, London: Sage.

Latour, B. and Woolgar, S. (1986) *Laboratory Life: the Social Construction of Scientific Facts*, 2nd edn, Princeton, NJ: Princeton University Press.

Levinson, S.C. (1983) *Pragmatics*, Cambridge: Cambridge University Press.

McCloskey, D. (1985) *The Rhetoric of Economics*, Brighton: Wheatsheaf.

Mulkay, M. (1985) *The Word and the World: Explorations in the Form of Sociological Analysis*, London: Allen & Unwin.

Mulkay, M., Potter, J. and Yearley, S. (1983) 'Why an analysis of scientists' discourse is needed', in K. Knorr-Cetina and M. Mulkay (eds) *Science Observed: Perspectives in the Social Study of Science*, London: Sage.

Pinch, T. and Clark, C. (1986) 'The hard sell: patter-merchanting and the strategic (re)production and local management of economic reasoning in the sales routines of market pitchers', *Sociology* 20: 169–91.

Pomerantz, A.M. (1986) 'Extreme case formulations: a new way of legitimating claims', *Human Studies* 9: 219–30.

Potter, J. (1984) 'Testability, flexibilty: Kuhnian values in psychologists' discourse concerning theory choice', *Philosophy of the Social Sciences* 14: 303–30.

—— (1988) 'What is reflexive about discourse analysis? The case of reading readings', in S. Woolgar (ed.) *Knowledge and Reflexivity: New Frontiers in the Sociology of Knowledge*, London: Sage.

Potter, J. and Edwards, D. (1990) 'Nigel Lawson's tent: discourse analysis, attribution theory and the social psychology of fact', *European Journal of Social Psychology* 20: 405–24.

Potter, J. and Mulkay, M. (1985) 'Scientists' interview talk: interviews as a technique for revealing participants' interpretative practices', in M. Brenner, J. Brown and D. Canter (eds) *The Research Interview: Uses and Approaches*, London: Academic Press.

Potter, J. and Wetherell, M. (1987) *Discourse and Social Psychology: Beyond Attitudes and Behaviour*, London: Sage.

—— (1988) 'Accomplishing attitudes: fact and evaluation in racist discourse', *Text* 8: 51–68.

Potter, J., Wetherell, M. and Chitty, A. (1991) 'Quantification rhetoric: cancer on television', *Discourse and Society* 2: 333–65.

Potter, J., Wetherell, M., Gill, R. and Edwards, D. (1990) 'Discourse: noun, verb or social practice?' *Philosophical Psychology* 3: 205–17.

Schenkein, J. (1978) 'Sketch of an analytic mentality for the study of conversational interaction', in J. Schenkein (ed.) *Studies in the Organization of Conversational Interaction*, New York: Academic Press.

Scott, M.B. and Lyman, S.M. (1968) 'Accounts', *American Sociological Review* 33: 46–62.

Semin, G.R. and Manstead, A.S.R. (1983) *The Accountability of Conduct: a Social Psychological Analysis*, London: Academic Press.

van Dijk, T.A. and Kintch, W. (1983) *Strategies of Discourse Comprehension*, London: Academic Press.

Watson, D.R. and Sharrock, W.W. (1991) 'Something on accounts', *The Discourse Analysis Research Group Newsletter* 7: 3–12.

Wetherell, M. and Potter, J. (1988) 'Discourse analysis and the identification of interpretative repertoires', in C. Antaki (ed.) *Analysing Lay Explanation: a Case Book*, London: Sage.

—— (1992) *Mapping the Language of Racism: Discourse and the Legitimation of Exploitation*, Hemel Hempstead: Harvester/Wheatsheaf.

Wooffitt, R.C. (1990) 'On the analysis of interaction: an introduction to conversation analysis', in P. Luff, G.N. Gilbert and D. Frohlich (eds) *Computers and Conversation*, New York: Academic Press.

Woolgar, S. and Pawluch, D. (1985) 'Ontological gerrymandering: the anatomy of social problems explanations', *Social Problems* 32: 214–27.

Yearley, S. (1981) 'Textual persuasion: the role of social accounting in the construction of scientific arguments', *Philosophy of the Social Sciences* 11: 409–35.

Chapter 4

'Second-hand ethnography'
Some problems in analyzing a feminist project

Marilyn Porter

INTRODUCTION: ON THE PERILS OF NOT LOOKING BEFORE LEAPING

In May 1988 I embarked on a large and well-funded research project intended to explore 'Women's economic lives in Newfoundland, Canada'. It was both the first such study on any scale to be carried out in the province, and the first Strategic Grant (SSHRC) project in the field of 'Women and work', to be focused on Newfoundland.[1]

At the time that I applied (a full year earlier) the reasons to do so – both political and theoretical – seemed compelling. My own work had reached the point where I was frustrated by the lack of data of any kind on women in the province, including province-wide generalizations and statistical data. There was also sustained pressure from the feminist community in St John's on women in the university to do studies that would provide 'really useful knowledge'. Women, involved in various kinds of feminist activism – from the Women's Policy Office to anti-poverty groups – wanted 'facts' in order to bring pressure on government and other official agencies. What more useful 'fact' than a university-accredited 'statistic' demonstrating the point? It was also, I was persuaded, my feminist duty to access academic research funding, provide employment for qualified feminist research assistants and produce the kind of academically respectable material that was made possible by my position in the university.

A year later, when I actually began the study, things looked different. The original potential research assistants had long since been snatched up by other employers or had left the province; my encouraging colleagues (while still encouraging) were too busy to do more. I was on my own, facing a large sum of money, an ambitious proposal, a university bureaucracy that seemed more than usually obtuse and some previously unconsidered factors. These included practical matters, such as the time and exhaustion involved in driving to the study communities, especially in normal Newfoundland winter conditions of snow, fog, rain, ice, gales as well as some theoretical, methodological and moral problems I had previously skirted.

The project was a large-scale one, and as such, its organization seemed to drift inevitably into hierarchical structures. It employed a variety of methods, and, as well as intellectual motivations, it had a feminist political purpose. All these aspects turned out to be problematic. In this chapter I want to examine some of those that have a particular bearing on whether, and how, it is possible to extend feminist ethnographic methods to larger-scale projects. The increasing feminist commitment to small-scale qualitative methods poses serious problems for the steady accumulation of knowledge.[2] Qualitative feminists or sociologists tend to concentrate either on tiny 'ungeneralizable' cameos or on high-level theory. Research that focuses on middle-range data tends to employ quantitative methods. There has been a tendency, then, for feminists to exclude themselves from the acquisition of middle-range data, including the 'useful facts', demanded by activists. In the project I report on here, I took the option of including quantitative methods, but as a result of that experience, I want to argue for other ways of expanding the range of qualitative methods.

The approach I have taken, in this chapter, is to retrace the methodological decisions I took, the (apparent) reasons for them at the time, and their consequences. In the course of doing this, I found that what my reflections were uncovering were not only shortcomings and errors, but a richer way of interrogating the relationships between the members of my research team and the data we produced and worked on: a process I have come to call 'second-hand ethnography'.

It was a 'feminist project', in the sense that the declared allegiance, theoretically, methodologically and politically was feminist. Certainly, each stage of the project was enforced by a desire to develop a feminist piece of research. But if I was sure what that meant at the outset, I am much less sure now. It is a topic I will return to throughout the chapter.

A CHOICE OF METHODS?

I shall look, first, at the original theoretical basis for the project, especially for the methodology I proposed. In particular, I want to examine some of the slippages and assumptions I uncovered as the study progressed.

The proposal to SSHRC included the use of a variety of methods, but concentrated on the qualitative ones I felt most comfortable with. The bulk of the study was to be a comparison of three very different communities, and the focus of each was to be an ethnography carried out by a research assistant. I had recognized that three ethnographies tacked together would not make a study, so I had added a number of other elements that would, I argued in the proposal, both provide a basis for province-wide comparisons and 'triangulate' the evidence from the ethnographies. They included historical work (such as the collection of oral histories), interviews with 'significant informants' of a conventional sociological type (union officials, social workers, teachers, etc.), a labour market study, an institutional ethnography of a hospital and a survey based loosely on the one used by R. Pahl in Sheppey (Courtney 1982), as amended after a pilot project carried out in one of the three communities.

My defence for this mix of methodologies was drawn from varied and, to some extent, contradictory arguments. I rehearsed the criticisms of survey methodology and quantitative data that have been raised by feminists among others (e.g. Eichler 1988, Fonow and Cook 1991, Kirby and McKenna 1989, Klein 1983, Oakley 1981, Stanley and Wise 1983). Most of this work is directed at attacking both traditional quantitative methods and the social relations in sociology that embody them (see especially Smith 1987). Feminist writers, in particular, have been inclined to equate 'feminist' with 'qualitative' methods as a result, a point I want to return to later.

I defended my continuing use of quantitative methods partly by referring to the ongoing debates, and especially those that have either attempted to rehabilitate their use, or are working on some synthesis between two types of methods previously regarded as hostile to one another.[3] I also made reference to 'triangulation', and the implicit assumption that 'more is better', a concept I will take up again below.

None of the literature I consulted addressed the problem of using *different* methods in the *same* project. In particular, I could not find any discussion about whether the use of one method would have an adverse effect on the data produced by others or how one would choose which set of data to believe if they turned up contradictory evidence. The standard texts encouraged a kind of methodological pluralism, though they offered no defence of it. Yet at least some conflict is implied by the epistemological underpinnings of quantitative and qualitative data. A number of writers have dichotomized quantitative and qualitative methods as 'objective' versus 'subjective', 'scientific and value free' versus 'empathetic', 'interpretive' and 'politically involved'. Anderson (1987), in particular, makes clear the incompatible roles of the researcher in quantitative and qualitative methods, yet at the very end of his book he suggests a possible synthesis between the two, based on an honest acceptance of the criticisms of them – something that seems quite at odds with his earlier dichotomizing description.

BUT WHAT IF THE 'FIELD' IS FULL OF POTHOLES?

While I was quite open about my misgivings about survey methodology, I proposed it partly on the grounds that it would enable me to compare my communities with data collected by two male colleagues who had a strong quantitative bias and who were carrying out a study of economic and social adaptations on the Great Northern Peninsula, and partly because I wanted to examine Pahl's Sheppey findings in a different context.[4] This begs two important questions. How much would asking the same questions as (or similar ones to) Pahl's actually tell us about the validity of his concepts of household strategies, the domestic division of labour, forms of work and sources of labour in the very different context of Newfoundland?

We had already discovered from our pilot study that many of the questions in Pahl's interview schedule were meaningless or inappropriate in a New-foundland context. Virtually all the questions probing material possessions and self-provisioning activities had to be rewritten. Home ownership is much higher in Newfoundland and public housing is limited to welfare ghettos in St John's and a few of the larger towns, so questions relating to tenancy are simply confusing. Similarly, any documentation on self-provisioning in Newfoundland that fails to allow for hunting, or to check the availability of moose licences, for example, or which ignores the possession of a skiddoo (motorized sledge) or all-terrain vehicles for woodcutting, would be useless. But even where the questions drawn from Pahl's schedule seemed to make sense, that didn't guarantee that the *answers* would be comparable. And how would data collected using such an instrument relate to, never mind 'triangulate with' material collected in quite other ways?

The concept of 'triangulation' (see Denzin 1970) is borrowed from surveying and navigation. The navigation analogy is more accurate, referring to the process whereby a position is 'fixed' using, preferably, different *kinds* of measures, for example compass bearings, depth soundings and radio bearings or at least 'position lines' drawn from different positions. The underlying idea is that the wider the variety of evidence you can bring to bear, the smaller the area of doubt about your position. The concept is much more problematic when applied to epistemology. In any case, the concept of triangulation in sociological studies operates differently. It is less a case of checking a 'fact' collected by one method, using another method, than using one method and then justifying the results by means of another. Usually, it is the survey that is the primary method. Data from informal interviews, or open-ended questions tacked on to the questionnaire or data from other kinds of sources are then used either as illustrations of the 'fact' or as an explanation. For example, a recent report on a study of women and labour market poverty in Canada is written essentially around quantitative data presented in tables and figures and discussed in the text. But every few pages a different kind of data, drawn from interviews with poor working women, appears, boxed off and in a different type-face. These are either little cameos, potted biographies or direct quotes, and they are organized to support the dominant text. As the authors say in their introduction, 'The interviews were conducted as part of the study and provided useful qualitative data, the human face, *in addition to* [my emphasis] the statistical treatment of the problem' (Gunderson and Muszynski 1990: 4).

My own approach was, in a sense, the reverse of this, though no less suspect. The study was exploratory. I was genuinely looking for information of as many kinds as possible that would help me understand how women's economic lives were constituted and sustained: what factors affected them, and how, and so on. Such a sweeping approach is probably valid in itself; the difficulty lies in assessing the relative validity of different sources of information, especially when they seem to be in contradiction.

I encountered several examples of the difficulty of evaluating contradictions between different kinds of information in the course of the study. For example, in the largest community – Grand Falls – we held regular meetings with the local interviewers who were carrying out the household survey. Sometimes these meetings helped to clarify details that had been recorded in a confusing way, but quite often the interviewers would challenge the veracity of the answers given in the survey on the basis of their specific local knowledge. This was especially the case in matters of income and material possessions but it also arose over other matters. For example, an interviewer would comment, 'She *said* her son contributed to his board, but I know he spends it on beer', or 'She didn't say, but what about her Aunt up in Springdale, I know she visits?' Not only does this kind of exchange cast doubt on the rest of the data generated by the survey, but it also undercuts the whole notion of the 'impersonal', 'objective' interviewer, and whether or not she could be persuaded not to modify her entries on the schedule, to say nothing of the problem of anonymity.

We also had interesting discussions, from which we learnt a great deal, when the interviewers explored their own feelings about the interviews and their interpretation of what they were told. They were meeting people outside their usual social circles, which was challenging their 'common-sense' assumptions about their community. They were often horrified by the evidence of poverty, stress and overwork they found. But they were also highly sceptical of what they were told. This was especially the case when they suspected the respondent of giving a 'proper' or 'correct' answer instead of 'the truth'. They would become angry especially when they suspected their informants of 'covering up' for unhelpful, or even violent husbands.

We found that the transcripts of these discussions provided us with some of the richest *qualitative* data on the community, and I did not hesitate to use the information in my report *even if it contradicted the survey findings*. Over and above my bias towards such data, there are two good reasons for this. The first is that where the data were in direct contradiction, it was either because the interviewee may have purposely not provided the 'correct' information, or because the design of the questionnaire allowed some ambiguity. The second reason was that because we were working in the community as ethnographers for a considerable time, we were able to check the interviewer's account against other people's accounts and other evidence. It thus became part of an accumulation of knowledge about the community, rather than about individuals.

There were other ways in which the use of different methods raised problems. The most important of these was the growing conviction each of the research assistants felt that their administration of the survey compromised their role as ethnographers. They all found that the administration of the survey devoured a disproportionate amount of their time, but more important, they felt that it adversely affected their relations with respondents. The survey was much more visible in the communities than the other methods, and the research assistants frequently had to explain and defend it. How was the sample drawn? How could we guarantee anonymity, etc.? Especially in Grand Falls, the most affluent families were often reluctant to complete the survey if it involved revealing their income. As this was the hardest group for the ethnographer to penetrate she felt that the survey made this process much more difficult. She also felt that the fact that the survey concentrated on certain kinds of information (mainly about household resources and forms of work) made it harder for her to enquire about other subjects – health care, for example. It was as if asking about health was less legitimate because it wasn't in the survey. When the research assistants carried out the surveys themselves, they appreciated the access but disliked the false relationship they felt it created (I will discuss the most extreme case of this a bit later).

On the other hand, when I visited the communities I would often conduct some interviews and found the experience positive. It was partly that I had greater experience, but it was much more that I actually *wanted* to know the answers to the questions, even if I doubted the format of a structured interview. As a result I would find myself turning the occasion into an informal interview, pursuing loose ends and leads in a way not used by the research assistants, and certainly not by the interviewers we employed in Grand Falls. That there was so much unevenness in the quality of the data different interviewers could derive from the survey did not reassure me about the method. On the other hand, as an infrequent visitor to the community, conducting surveys myself gave me a form of access I would not otherwise have had.

DOES STRETCHING A METHOD MAKE IT ANY BIGGER?

There were two main ways in which I attempted to extend ethnographic methods in the project. The first was to 'add on' other methods, especially the survey. The second was to expand the scale of ethnography, by placing three ethnographers in three communities. We chose the communities to represent various characteristics that we wanted to compare, and the intention was to build up the comparison so as to achieve a level of generality based on qualitative data. I now want to examine how this worked out, and especially how the process revealed the underlying methodological problems.

The root of some of these problems lies in the hierarchical model of research held by SSHRC and other funding agencies, a model that is in profound contradiction to the principles of feminist research as I was attempting to practise them.[5] In this model the principal investigator, who normally holds a full-time teaching position in a university, is responsible for the theoretical formulation of the project, for its administration and for writing the reports, but not for actually carrying out the research. The principal investigator is expected to devote his or her 'research time' (time left over from normal teaching and administration duties) to the project, but it is assumed that he or she will not undertake the data collection or fieldwork. While SSHRC does have a category of 'research stipend', which allows full-time academics to apply for time off, it is explicitly discouraged and very rarely granted. Instead, the principal investigator is expected to hire research assistants, interviewers, and even more lowly, transcribers, coders and secretaries. The assumption that the research assistants will be at the beginning of their careers or less qualified than the principal investigator is built into the conditions under which research assistants may be hired, and especially into the rates at which they can be paid, which are very low.[6]

This model appears to be derived from the 'hard sciences', where much research is carried out in labs, set up and controlled by senior academics, in which most of the painstaking but relatively low-level procedures are carried out by their 'teams'. Such a model is fairly easily transferable to survey research, which also depends on large quantities of fairly routine tasks, but I would argue that it is neither appropriate nor conducive to ethnographic projects, especially feminist ones, for at least three reasons: one practical and two theoretical.

The practical reason is geographic distance. Some science projects and all surveys depend on fieldwork which may be located some way away from the university. But even if the data are collected elsewhere, that part of the process is fairly rapid, and much more time is spent in preparing the data and then performing various manipulations with it. This is not the case with ethnographic studies, where the bulk of the work takes place in the field and where the processes of data collection and analysis are hopelessly interwoven. In my case, all three of my communities were at least four hours away from St John's and one required the best part of a day to reach. I could not, as a physicist might, drop into the lab between classes. Instead, I had to carve a few days here, a week there, to pay flying visits to my fieldworkers in the communities. The upshot was, inevitably, that I was divorced from the major part of the data collection. More important, I could not collect my *own* data as I have been used to doing. This was not merely an inconvenience, as I shall argue later.

One of the theoretical problems was due to the hierarchical structure of SSHRC, which I have already mentioned. The grant was in my name. I was ultimately responsible for the project and the money; I had considerable power and authority over other members of the research 'team'. No matter how we disguised it, or how far we tried to achieve more equal relations and more democratic procedures, the inescapable fact was that I had more power than my 'assistant' and, ultimately, it was my reputation that was at stake. As feminists we found this situation intolerable. By and large we worked within it, and dealt with the inevitable anger and frustration as best we could. But it is farcical to suggest that we achieved anything close to the feminist ideals of a co-operative of equals engaged in the research process.

And that was just among the 'researchers'. In SSHRC's collective mind there is a very clear notion of the division between 'researchers' and 'researched', a clear responsibility on the former to 'do research', with few rights of reply or participation accorded to the 'researched'. It is notoriously difficult to get funds to return the research to the community in any sense, and certainly not to engage the community in the research.[7] Another consequence of SSHRC's hierarchical model was the pitifully low pay scales allowed for research assistants.[8] In my case, I felt I needed research assistants who would be mature and developed researchers (at or near Ph.D. level), who were excellent ethnographers, and who shared at least some of my own background in feminism, Marxism and sociology. Such people would be well able to work independently and to develop their own research agenda within the main study. I hoped to build a team of as near equals as possible who would be able to work in conjunction with one another, especially on the comparative aspects of the study. While I stated all this in the proposal, I had not fully recognized how vital it would be to acquire such research assistants. Newfoundland is a remote province within Canada, and the communities I selected were remote within it. The one university in the province has only just begun a Ph.D. programme in sociology. There are, thus, no 'locally-grown' Ph.D. students in sociology. The people I was looking for would, almost by definition, be older than their early twenties and would probably have various domestic and personal ties and commitments. Fine people, of exactly the character and qualifications I sought, certainly existed in central Canada, but they could simply not afford to relocate to a remote community for eighteen months for a bare subsistence wage. The hierarchical model, therefore, imposed on me a working group very different from the one I had envisaged.

THE RESEARCH ASSISTANTS: BOTH RESEARCHERS AND RESEARCHED

The three research assistants I finally hired all lived in Newfoundland, although two were immigrants: one from central Canada, one from Germany. Gunda, who did most of the work in Grand Falls, was a woman in her early forties. She had left Germany twenty years before (though she retained a slight German accent) and had a varied career in the USA and Canada before coming to Newfoundland to do a Ph.D. in folklore. Her main interest was in tourism. She had no sociology or Marxism and she came to feminism during the course of the study. She had however been trained in ethnographic methods and had a fine, organized, scholarly mind. Sandy, who worked in Grand Falls and was responsible for the South East Bight study, was an extraordinarily talented young Newfoundland woman in her late twenties. She had an arts (BA) degree (which did not include sociology). She had, however, worked as a research assistant on various projects including the Royal Commission on Employment and Unemployment. She had long been involved in political and feminist activity in St John's, although she had not read widely in the theoretical literature. She was one of Newfoundland's more promising young poets and had also edited both poetry journals and biographies.[9] She seemed to have natural ethnographic skills and was an astonishingly sensitive and intelligent observer.

Cathy, who administered the survey and worked in Catalina, was the only one with a child. She had a background in social work (twenty years earlier). Immensely energetic, she had since had a long and varied career as a political activist involved in a range of social concerns. Like Gunda she became more engaged with feminism during the project. Cathy had a wide range of reading and a practical commitment to social change, but she had no formal sociology and little in-depth theoretical reading. She was also the one who suffered the most frustration about the division between 'academic' work and practical activism.

All three women were talented, vigorous and intelligent. While none of them had the skills and background I was looking for, all of them brought positive and valuable characteristics to the study. Nevertheless, it meant that I could not do the study as I first intended.

I have just presented you, the reader, with thumb-nail sketches of the three women who worked as research assistants on the project. Relying on points I want to develop subsequently and on what I conjecture is your background, I have made a selection of features of their characters and biographies. Both the selection and the way I have presented it reflect my own interpretation. Undoubtedly, if they were to write a paragraph on what they thought they had contributed to the project something very different would emerge. But you, as reader, are dependent on me for your 'knowledge' of these three women.

This is an obvious, but crucially important point because of the way the study developed. I could not do my own ethnography. Essentially I had to depend on my research assistants to do it for me. On my field visits, I did some interviews and as much watching and listening as I could arrange. Much of this was directed at 'training' the research assistants, trying to get them to see the things I was seeing and ask the questions I would ask. What I soon found I was doing was studying my own ethnographers. Only by understanding how they saw and heard the community could I 'interpret' 'their' 'data'.

Even had I been working with the ideal ethnographers I had in mind this same process would have taken place. I would still have been dependent on *their* eyes and ears, their social experience and their interpretation of it. The process may have been blurred because we would have had a larger common theoretical framework and vocabulary with which to exchange information, but it would still have been 'second-hand ethnography'. I became acutely aware of the problems and limitations of using other people to 'do' one's own ethnography because of their diverse and less than comparable academic backgrounds. But I would argue that the same methodological and epistemological problems arise in any study set up on these lines. What I am attempting in this chapter is to make explicit the processes that were set in train and the consequences they had for the 'results' of the study.

When the fieldwork was complete, the data out of which I wrote the report were of various kinds: data collected by the surveys, written material of different kinds, 'facts' and figures we had culled from informants, etc. However, the richest and, to me, most valuable sources were the reports, tapes and field notes of the research assistants and my own field notes and tapes, which included interviews I had conducted, but also notes on conversations I had had with the research assistants. In the rest of this chapter I am going to present some of this 'second-hand ethnographic data', which is also, of course, data *on* the method of using such data.

'SECOND-HAND ETHNOGRAPHY'

I have already explained that I did not treat the quantitative and qualitative data equally. When I interpreted the data I gave a greater weight to qualitative data if any existed. When I carry out my own ethnography I rely on my own material. Where survey or other quantitative material supports it, so much the better. But if the material appears to be contradictory I will explore it on the basis that in the last resort I will trust my ethnographic eye over any other source. I am making this explicit, because it raises different problems when one is trusting *someone else*'s eyes. When I write about the study, I am asking the reader to trust not my ethnographic understanding of the communities, but my interpretation of my research assistants' ethnographic understanding of the communities.

Let us uncover some of the processes involved in this 'second-hand ethnography'. All the research assistants contributed written sections of the final report as well as other papers and articles. We also presented a number of joint workshops. But they also provided me with field notes while they were living in the communities. These were half-way between their own personal jottings and their finished work. They were direct communications with me. In them they tried to express their developing impressions and they also tried to give me the information they thought I wanted, that is, they also contain *their* interpretation of me.

I have chosen to use these 'texts' to illustrate the process of 'second-hand ethnography' precisely because of their reflexive, self-aware character. In particular, I want to make as explicit as possible the way in which one selects one 'truth' over another, and how one decides whether and how far to 'trust' an account.

Of the research assistants, Cathy was the most explicit about her role as an ethnographer, the role of the study and my role as the principal investigator and as 'boss':

Went drinking with MP last night. The second bar was good for playing pool. A woman I'd interviewed turned out to be the best pool player around except for her buddy I met in the bathroom. Sue, the woman I'd seen before, whirled and danced, subtly, around the table. Men would offer them advice but then they would reject it, which felt good after listening to women go on and on about a woman's place is in the home if she has small children or is 'Needed There', or that she is a natural secretary, and shouldn't be out getting dirty or lifting heavy objects. MP was being very observant and pointing at people rather too obviously, I thought.

When I stopped wincing at this criticism I thought back to that smoke-filled bar. We must both have stuck out like sore thumbs, as all strangers in small communities do. And we were plainly, both by accent and dress, not 'from here' (i.e. Newfoundlanders). But it had seemed to me as if we had been accepted round that pool table, and I was prepared to trust my judgement of what was 'happening' there. This was partly because it tallied with Cathy's, who had a very different approach. We'd talked at length that evening about the people, and what Cathy had learned about how they fitted together. It was no accident we'd gone drinking. We both felt happy in such places. As Cathy wrote later, 'People here are divided into strict addiction categories and I think my category became obvious last night, hic.' At the time I had been concerned that neither of us should do anything that would make us 'unacceptable' to other parts of the community and also that by doing anything as positive as 'going drinking' we would 'intervene' in the society we were observing, that we would become less 'all-seeing' than the wallpaper of participant observer fantasy – common worries in ethnography. Cathy had no such inhibitions, and as a result she uncovered significant levels of alcoholism and other 'deviant' behaviour in the community. People trusted her and confided 'hidden behaviour' to her. She also discovered dense and complex helping networks among the women she knew. None of this, of course, emerged from the surveys she was also collecting.

I was thrown out of one house in Catalina by the son of the older woman I was interviewing. The older woman hardly got to say Boo to the goose, because her daughter-in-law tried to answer the questions for her, in spite of my non-verbal cues such as leaning towards the older woman, looking only at her, and calling her by name. I had been very careful to advise the household members, three generations of whom were sitting at the kitchen table with me, that they could refuse to answer any questions and also ask me to leave any time during the survey.

As we discussed who did the household chores, the daughter-in-law claimed she did chores which later several other people in the community told me the older woman did. The daughter-in-law claimed that men never did any housework, so I told her that I knew a few men who did half the housework. She asked me 'Why don't you send some of those men down then? Nobody like that around here.' Then we got to the income section. 'Estimate all income from all sources per week in the household', I twittered.

All of a sudden I heard an incoherent blast of sound from the room off a hall leading from the kitchen. The daughter-in-law looked confused, and hurried to see what was happening. At first I thought somebody had lost leave of their senses . . . but then I realized this was a roar of rage because of me. The son of the respondent was yelling 'Tell Mrs. to get her fucking ass out of this house' and 'all that damn foolishness' and this went on for several minutes. 'Do you mean me?' I yelled. 'Yes' he screamed. 'Yes, SIR' I yelled. 'Don't get lippy' he screeched. I asked the respondent if she wanted me to leave. She nodded, speechless. I left, after apologising to her for making trouble.

Apart from Cathy's growing unhappiness with conducting the survey interviews (and with their eventual usefulness) part of the interest in this passage lies in the differences between this version (which appeared in Cathy's report on methodology) and the original account in her field diary, which is much more vivid, and much more revealing about the inequality and scarcely disguised violence in the household.[10]

This account, supported by other conversations with Cathy, caused me to suspect that not only my survey, but others, underestimated intra-household inequality and potential or actual domestic violence that was taking place. In this case, I encouraged Cathy to focus on those issues when she was spending time in households. It also caused us to question the local doctors, nurses and social workers about their perceptions of these issues. In this case then, Cathy's report had the effect of moving the focus of the inquiry and alerting us to other kinds of evidence.

By the end of the fieldwork, Cathy was disillusioned with the research process and more than anxious to get back to her daughter and St John's.

I am beginning to dislike intensely my position here. I go to the PO to get a stupid survey and they all snicker. Paranoia? No, reality. Most of the respondents were people who I would never choose to spend any time with. That part is good. But it's awfully unfriendly.

When Cathy got back to St John's, her feelings were as mixed as those of most ethnographers.

Seven hours in a snowstorm at 30–50 km per hour all the way home. I miss my landlady. She says I'm not allowed to talk about her, so I won't. I'm exhausted from nervous storm energy and no sleep and the homecoming.

Catalina is a great place, and I like the people I met. (Next day) I am home, in my Privatised Space, as MP reminded me on the phone (is that the pot calling the kettle black or wot?), and it *is* a luxury not to live in a boarding house where the cigarette smoke is predominant. But I miss my landlady . . . . You can't really start talking about what any place is like after a few weeks there, or even a few years. You only know about it if you are going to stay there . . . . Goodbye Catalina. I miss my landlady.

Cathy's field diary is a remarkable account, and it shows her creating her experience of Catalina and struggling to understand it. Yet it was clearly Cathy's experience and Cathy's interpretation of it. Had Gunda or Sandy worked in Catalina I (and other readers) might very well have got a different picture of the community.

While I encouraged all the research assistants to visit each other and each other's communities it was only in Grand Falls that two research assistants actually worked in the community. Grand Falls was the largest community, and with 10,000 people it is hard to tell if Gunda and Sandy were seeing different parts of the town, or the same parts differently. However, when two such different research assistants 'saw' the same thing it became powerful testimony. Only a few days after she got there Sandy wrote,

Social class, it seems, has always been a big thing in Grand Falls. When the original company started the town, the company decided who could live there. Those who couldn't lived in Windsor or other surrounding communities. Ida described growing up 'out on the Botwood road' and having 'no status at all'. The town was planned such that houses for different classes of mill workers were built on different streets, i.e. the labourers got one street and mill wrights got another, and on up to the top. The company did the landscaping, providing different neighbourhoods with trees for their yards, a different tree for each. So you can walk around Grand Falls and see small houses on one street with one kind of tree; the next street will have larger houses and another type of tree.

With her poet's eye, Sandy has picked out an image to explain to me a perception about the community that she can't yet 'prove' in sociological terms.

When Gunda got to Grand Falls, she soon uncovered quantities of evidence both about the split between Grand Falls and the despised Windsor – the town across the tracks – and about the severity of social class divisions within Grand Falls. Gunda wrote,

Grand Falls is a good place to live for the affluent and for old established families, who are members of the various groups and cliques. However, this 'closed', status- and class-conscious town is a hard place to like for 'outsiders' i.e. the less well-to-do, newcomers, single women. Even married women, whose husbands come to Grand Falls to make careers as doctors or mill engineers, often find themselves lonely and frustrated. After a year in Grand Falls, the outgoing wife of the mill engineer who had been transferred from the Abitibi Price plant in Stephenville, complained that she had not once 'been invited for a cup of coffee'.

In this case, the fact that Gunda and Sandy supported each other's accounts allowed me to 'believe' them. This was, initially, difficult because of the widespread conviction in Newfoundland, supported by other ethnographers, that it is a relatively egalitarian and 'classless' society.[11]

Gunda talked a lot about this problem, and it was clear that she was finding it easier to make contacts among single (especially professional) women and among the middle-income couples. She could not penetrate the self-declared 'elite', nor could she get them to complete surveys. But, at the same time, Gunda began to uncover the social ills that lay beneath the smug exterior of Grand Falls. She found levels of domestic violence and nervous and psychological disorders, which were not surprising in themselves, although the degree to which they were hidden did surprise us. Gunda followed the attempt to found a Transition House (for battered women) in some detail and recorded informal resistance as well as the open and official position, much of which was based on a flat refusal to encounter the idea that domestic violence could happen in Grand Falls. Psychologists in the next town, Gander, referred to the 'Grand Falls syndrome', meaning women who would not reveal their problems to professionals in their own town. Gunda also became involved in the problems of working women, especially those working as clerks in the banks. In one case, she helped a victim prepare an extensive dossier for the Human Rights Commission. Gunda also documented the exhausting schedule followed by women who worked for wages and kept TV-ad perfect homes as well as keeping up a punishing social round.

But Gunda was herself a single woman, and a German. I started to wonder how far it was her social persona that was leading to her exclusion from the elite circles and colouring her view of the community. When I visited Grand Falls her view of the community seemed to be confirmed at social gatherings we attended, in conversations we had, and by other evidence. I aired the problem of the 'closed', 'cliquish' and 'snobbish' structure of Grand Falls society with the informants I met. We discussed it with our interviewers and with the community advisory group we had set up. Grand Falls sends a disproportionate number of its youngsters to university and to work in St John's. I would raise it with Grand Falls natives I met, and even in my classes. The answer was consistent. Yes, Grand Falls was like that – and more so. The stories other people told me were far more critical than Gunda's gentle, reasonable account. It became clear that Grand Falls was atypical of Newfoundland communities in its greater prosperity, its sharp social divisions, the degree to which conventional dreams were remorselessly pursued and the ferocity of its exclusion of anyone who did not or could not conform to the established patterns.

This, coupled with an increasing interest in health and caring issues, led Gunda and me into long discussions as we tried to make sense of a complex and to some extent, unexpected situation. Gunda lived in Grand Falls for over a year. Both her notes and mine reflect a growing consensus in our interpretations. Was this because I was imposing a theoretical framework on Gunda, or was it because I was increasingly experiencing Grand Falls through Gunda and learning to trust her judgement? It soon became very hard to disentangle. However, while this means that our accounts ceased to cross-check each other, they did build an increasingly rich account of the community, based on two converging perspectives and a variety of information.

Gunda remained intensely self-critical of her own fieldwork, continually trying to reach new sections of the community or broaden her participation in various activities. She was also aware both of the falseness of the distinction between researcher and researched and the need to return the research to the community in a usable form. I have already mentioned that we set up an advisory group of local women in Grand Falls. The intention was that we could 'feed back' what we found to the group on a regular basis and learn from their interpretation of it. We also hoped that such a group would be able to make use of what we found in their own work. In the event, Gunda found herself increasingly drawn into various activist projects in the town. She worried about how her involvement in such activities would 'compromise' her role as a researcher, and solved the problem by passing the mantle of 'responsibility' on to me. As the 'professor' from the university I found myself dressing in my smartest clothes and attending functions and interviewing people that Gunda felt would be alienated by her. It was a curious process and led both of us to examine what kind of information each of us could get from different sources, and where in all that might the truth lie.

South East Bight offers a startling contrast to Grand Falls. It is a tiny community of a hundred people lying half-way up Placentia Bay and reachable only by boat. The people depend entirely on the inshore fishery, various subsistence activities and transfer payments. It is remote, wild and idyllically beautiful. Here are extracts from the opening section of Sandy's field notes.

> The boat moved through dense fog, through intervals of yellow-grey light suddenly illuminating the sea. A whale breached, and no one but the 'strangers' paid any attention. Close to an island a loon sang out. The boat trailed a quiet wake. I spent most of the time on deck.
> An elderly man drank beer; it was eleven a.m.
> 'Where're you headed?' he asked, 'Petitforte?'
> 'South East Bight.'
> 'From there?'
> 'No.'
> 'Just visiting are you, yes?'
> 'Yes.'

'Oh'. He was at a loss for anything else to say.

All through the trip he drank beer, and looked as if he didn't know what else to do. Other men were drinking too, walking fore and aft, talking, then drifting off in groups again. Women, some of them young girls, carried babies about and tried to keep track of assorted youngsters. Men conferred on deck about weather and fishing. Merasheen, resettled empty home of wistful and romantic dreams, shone through the fog. First stop, Paradise .... As we left Paradise, I was struck by the houses. Two in particular had a curious effect on me. There were traditional houses, tall and narrow with long symmetrical windows; these are the houses which let you know where on earth you are. I watched the light shine through empty windows in the ruined gardens beyond, tottery paling fences defining a wild tangle of native grasses. The skeletons of dories sat on decayed slipways. And then new houses – fishing shacks, modern bungalows, cabin-like structures, and big houses with aluminium sliding like houses in Mount Pearl.

When the government resettled Paradise no one stayed. They trickled back, and the place became a summer fishing station. Things that were abandoned were not used again, but left to rot. New houses, new boats appeared. This made me wonder about the Bight; would its past be visible, or had it been left to rot?

In the Bight, people had resisted resettlement. Six families stayed; their members began to organize, and they began to get the services the government had threatened to deny them ...

Instinctively, I 'trusted' Sandy's account of South East Bight. Why? Because she wrote beautifully? Because she was raised in the next bay? Because what she said confirmed ideas I already had? Because South East Bight was less a community than a cause? It was probably all of these things. I was aware, as I analyzed Sandy's account, and incorporated it into the final report, of the dangers of seduction. Writers such as Atkinson (1990) and Clifford and Marcus (1986) have pointed out that *all* ethnographic accounts use 'poetics' (as Anderson (1987) calls it) to present themselves, and have begun to develop more sophisticated ways of understanding how it is done. If, as they aver, 'Sociology is a rhetorical activity' (Atkinson 1990: 10) then there is no reason to disbelieve an account *because* it is successful in its appeal.[12]

Sandy's sensitive use of her own background shows in this brief reference to merchants.

I'm interested in the status Marg has in the community. Where I grew up, the merchant wielded a great deal of power because they could extend and withdraw credit. The children of the merchant next door beat and bullied us frequently; we had a bill run up there. I must find out what power these merchants – Marg and Martin – have. I know they extend credit.

But I discovered there is a sign in Martin's store now: 'As of Aug. 1, there will be no more credit from this store. All bills should be paid in full.' What is going on here?

This accords with previous ethnographic and historical discussions of the place of the merchant in small communities, and raises new questions in the context of South East Bight.

My acceptance of Sandy's account did not make the interpretive problems easier. South East Bight has fought hard to continue to exist, and has found a complex way of surviving economically. It is under threat, not only from a world that has long since rejected small-scale rural solutions, but from the particular difficulties confronting the Atlantic fishery and the Newfoundland economy. South East Bight might not be there in another year or two. All of us on the project found we cared about this passionately. After much discussion we were all agreed that of the three communities we had studied, the women of South East Bight lived the most complete and satisfying economic lives, and were most positively attached to the way of life they led. Furthermore, we thought that the situation of the women of South East Bight had much to teach other women in other communities. I had felt some awkwardness about criticizing the way of life in Grand Falls and Catalina, arising from the feminist conviction that research should be 'for' women. South East Bight seemed to offer a more direct and 'useful' role for the research, which comforted me politically, at least.

So we cared politically about South East Bight's vulnerability, and we cared theoretically about what we thought we were learning from the community. The argument is too lengthy to summarize here. Suffice it to say, that as soon as we expressed it we were open to charges of 'rural romanticism', 'anthropological navel-gazing' and wanting to deprive women of the benefits of hospitals, supermarkets and high speed cars. All this can be rebutted, but the point I am making here is that the main basis for our argument was the material Sandy collected and some observation of my own. I trust her judgement – but should you, and how could we use it to convince the sceptics? The argument I want to make about South East Bight is an important one. What other kind of evidence could a feminist project collect to support it? Would we, inevitably, have to resort to more 'objective' quantitative data?

WAS THIS A 'FEMINIST' PROJECT?

I have tried, in the last few pages, to show how 'second-hand ethnography' is carried out and some of the inherent weaknesses in the practice. I have implied throughout that this was a 'feminist' project but the only ways in which I have made that explicit are in terms of its original goal to produce 'useful knowledge' for the feminist community. I also discussed my concern that if ethnography is a distinctively feminist method and if there are feminist reasons for being suspicious of quantitative methods then we must grapple with the problem of scale if feminist knowledge is to continue to grow.

There is increasing interest in 'feminist methodology' and I looked to this literature to guide me both in the initial conception of the project and to overcome its shortcomings as they emerged. Some recent contributors to the problem include Smith (1987, 1990), Stanley and Wise (1983), Stanley (1990), Fonow and Cook (1991) and Eichler (1988). Between them they have gone far beyond criticizing the established practices, especially of quantitative research, to developing a new epistemology. In Smith's words, 'A sociology for women preserves the presence of subjects on knowers and actors. It does not transform subjects into the objects of study or make use of conceptual devices for eliminating the active presence of subjects' (1987: 105). But as Cook and Fonow point out, 'feminist epistemology and methodology arise from a critique of each field's biases and distortions in the study of women', rather than creating anew. The result, they argue, is that feminism has incorporated several underlying assumptions, among which they discuss 'reflexivity, an action orientation; attention to the affective components of the research; and the use of the situation-at-hand' (Fonow and Cook 1991: 2).

I would argue that these then take on the guise of explicitly and exclusively feminist characteristics and become mandatory for all feminist projects. This, among other things, is how ethnography has acquired its prominent place as 'the' feminist method. This is encapsulated in the synopsis of a recent article on feminist ethnography:

> Many feminist scholars have identified ethnographic methods as ideally suited to feminist research because its contextual, experimental approach to knowledge eschews the false dualism of positivism and, drawing upon such traditionally female strengths as empathy and human concern, allows for an egalitarian reciprocal relationship between knower and known.
>
> (Stacey 1988:21)

But while this sets up a political and ethical expectation that feminists *ought* to do ethnography it does not seem to me to establish a separate, distinctive 'feminist methodology'. By applying and developing the vigorous standards feminists set themselves we may arrive at *better* methods, but this only guarantees better sociology rather than a new kind of 'feminist sociology'.

While, in this sense, this seems to be accepting the denigrations of Clifford and Marcus, that would be a misreading. Feminist research is both a delicate blending of political imperatives and theoretical insights *and* a dynamic and rapidly developing discourse. To say that the end result of this is to create a better sociology rather than a distinctive *feminist* methodology does not detract from its continuing role.

CONCLUSION: TOWARDS 'LINKED ETHNOGRAPHIES'

Meanwhile, we are left with the problem of scale, with the deficiencies of quantitative methods and with the need to develop methods appropriate to every level of generality and scale. While it is fraught with methodological, epistemological and ethical danger, ethnography seems to me to continue to provide one of the satisfying ways of conducting research as a feminist. I have exposed some of the dangers and difficulties of trying to conduct second-hand ethnography, but I have also shown how the examination of colleagues' field experience and field notes can be a source of knowledge itself. What is necessary is for the process to become more equal and more explicit. Let us imagine three ethnographers working together to establish a common theoretical framework and approach and then going to separate communities or other 'fields'. As they collected their material and wrote their field notes, they would exchange them with their colleagues (at least every week; maybe by computer). They would meet frequently and interrogate each other's accounts using all the sophisticated and sensitive tools that have been developed for such interrogation within feminist practice. They would report back to their 'subjects' and be subjected to interrogation of their interpretation by them. They would visit each other in the field; they would construct joint accounts. To some extent, this is simply an extension of what we did. But it would take place in conditions of academic equality and with a clearsighted understanding by the researchers of what they were trying to achieve.

These 'linked ethnographies' seem to me to be both a possible and a sound way of expanding single ethnographies. The focus would inevitably be as much on the researchers and the process of the research as on the original 'subject', but that is not, in itself, a weakness. In fact, it may repair some of the damage caused by our lack of self-awareness in the past. It accords with feminist methodological expectations of traditional ethnography. Our experience, limited though it was, of discussing each other's material and working through to shared conclusions was one of the most positive aspects of the study.

I said at the outset that the project 'Women's economic lives in New-foundland' was exploratory. I meant that so few studies had been conducted and so few data had been collected that I could not know precisely what sort of material I wanted or how it would be collected. In methodological terms, I tried to build on existing methods to meet my own needs, and, particularly, to meet the needs of a feminist agenda. Feminism carries with it a sense of urgency and an intense desire to know, in order to change, women's experience. If the kind of failures and mistakes I have explored have speeded this process, then they must be welcomed as an equal contribution to the awkward and exciting project of building feminist knowledge.

In conclusion, let me return to the thorny question of what, if anything, is specifically feminist about the project I have described. At one level, I have called it feminist because I was a feminist and a large part of its political and theoretical purpose was feminist, i.e. to explore and analyze women's economic lives within a feminist theoretical perspective, with the explicit intention of enhancing those lives. When I came to select my research team, my research methods and the other choices I made in setting up and conducting the research I referred to a body of established feminist practice. For example, I chose to use certain methods in full awareness of criticisms that had been made of them of misrepresenting women's experience, and tried to improve them.

The particular problem and its partial solution that I have highlighted in this paper, that of what I have called 'second-hand ethnography', derives from feminist concerns, and I have described both the problem and its solution in terms of feminist literature. However, neither the problem, nor its solution, are *exclusively* feminist. It is inextricably entwined from origin to conclusion with other strands of sociological thought. As it should be. There would be very little point in my contributing to this collection if my project did not have a more general applicability to the project of social science. It is thus that feminism has come of age. Our commitment remains feminist and aspects of our work can be clearly identified as feminist but the boundaries are neither so impermeable nor so limiting as they were. It was, in fact, a feminist-sociological project.

NOTES

1 The Social Science and Humanities Research Council (SSHRC) is the major source of academic funding for the disciplines in its purview in Canada. It is the direct, although not exact, equivalent of the Economic and Social Research Council (ESRC). Strategic Grants target particular areas of research and tend to be particularly well funded.
2 While not all feminist researchers are exclusively qualitative in their approach, there is certainly a heavy emphasis on the virtues of qualitative methods in the literature. See Eichler 1988, Fonow and Cook 1991, Harding 1987, Stanley and Wise 1983.
3 The ground has been shifting recently, with attempts to modify the practice and theoretical application of quantitative methods so as to make them more compatible with the principles of subjectivity. The jury is still out on the matter but interesting (if inconclusive) recent contributions include Cain and Finch 1981, Stanley 1991, Section B, Strauss and Corbin 1990.
4 P. Sinclair and L. Felt's study of Social and Economic Adaptation on the Great Northern Peninsula (1992) was also based on Pahl's work on household strategies, and they were also using some adaptations of his questions.
5 I am examining SSHRC in some detail, because it funded this study. I have no reason to think other funding agencies, such as ESRC, are any different, especially over the conduct of a large-scale project.
6 SSHRC has since responded to this kind of criticism and now has a much more flexible, and generous, pay scale for research assistants. At the same time, it has virtually eliminated the research stipend, as well as the category of 'private scholar', both of which increase both the degree of hierarchy and the involvement of formal academic institutions in SSHRC-funded research.

7 These principles are now well-established tenets of feminist research; see Kirby and McKenna 1989, CRIAW 1986, Kleiber and Light 1978. It is also well established in politically engaged research, notably in Newfoundland, where D. Snowden and Memorial University of Newfoundland (MUN) Extension developed a combination of social research, political activism and film-making to help rural communities resist resettlement in the 1960s – a process known as 'the Fogo process'.

8 The maximum I could pay an RA with a Ph.D. was $23,000. Such a person at the time of the project would command $32,000 as an Assistant Professor at MUN and much more as a research assistant for the government or the private sector.

9 It is some indication of her talent that she received a grant from Canada Council to write poetry for six months, which entailed her leaving the project for that period.

10 When Cathy left the project she was both angry and disillusioned with the whole research process and with the structure of the project. She was also extremely concerned about the confidentiality of her material. She wrote some of the best field notes I have ever seen: vivid about both her material and her own responses to the (to her) new experience of fieldwork. Unfortunately, she has not released these for quotation.

11 This is especially true of the ethnographies published by the Institute of Social and Economic Research in St John's in the early 1970s, e.g. Faris 1972, Firestone 1978.

12 These, and other anthropologists, have recently developed what they call the 'new ethnography'. In many cases, this seems to entail using the insights of postmodern and other contemporary discourses to develop more sophisticated validations of established ethnographic practice. The Clifford and Marcus collection is remarkable for its explicit denial of the contribution of feminist theory to recent developments in ethnography despite its 'great potential significance for rethinking ethnographic writing' (Clifford and Marcus 1986: 19).

REFERENCES

Anderson, J. (1987) *Communication Research: Issues and Methods*, New York: McGraw Hill.

Atkinson, P. (1990) *The Ethnographic Imagination*, London: Routledge.

Cain, M. and Finch, J. (1981) 'Towards a rehabilitation of data', in P. Abrams, R. Deem, J. Finch and P. Rock (eds) *Practice and Progress: British Sociology 1950–1980*, London: Allen & Unwin.

Canadian Research Institute for the Advancement of Women (CRIAW) (1986) *Women's Involvement in Political Life*, Ottawa: CRIAW.

Clifford, J. and Marcus, G. (eds) (1986) *Writing Culture*, Berkeley, Calif.: University of California Press.

Courtney, G. (1982) *Isle of Sheppey Study: Technical Report*, London: Social and Community Planning Research.

Denzin, N. (1970) *The Research Act: a Theoretical Introduction to Social Research*, Chicago: Aldine.

Eichler, M. (1988) 'The relationship between sexist, non-sexist, woman-centred and feminist research', in A. McLaren (ed.) *Gender and Society: Creating a Canadian Women's Sociology*, Toronto: Copp, Clark, Pitman.

Faris, J. (1972) *Cat Harbour*, St John's: Institute of Social and Economic Research.

Felt, L. and Sinclair, P. (1992) 'Everyone does it: unpaid work in a rural peripheral region', *Work, Employment and Society* March: 43–64.

Firestone, M. (1978) *Brothers and Rivals*, St John's: Institute of Social and Economic Research.

Fonow, M. and Cook, J. (eds) (1991) *Beyond Methodology: Feminist Scholarship as Lived Research*, Indianapolis, Ind.: Indiana University Press.

Gunderson, M. and Muszynski, L. (1990) *Women and Labour Market Poverty*, Ottawa: Canadian Advisory Council on the Status of Women.

Harding, S. (1987) *Feminism and Methodology*, Indianapolis, Ind.: Indiana University Press.

Kirby, A. and McKenna, K. (1989) *Experience, Research, Social Change: Methods from the Margins*, Toronto: Garamond Press.

Kleiber, N. and Light, L. (1978) *Caring for Ourselves*, Vancouver: University of British Columbia Press.

Klein, D. (1983) 'How to do what we want to do: thoughts about feminist methodology', in G. Bowles and D. Klein (eds) *Theories of Women's Studies*, London: Routledge.

Oakley, A. (1981) 'Interviewing women: a contradiction in terms', in H. Roberts (ed.) *Doing Feminist Research*, London: Routledge.

Porter, M. with Brown, B., Dettmar, E. and McGrath, C. (1990) *Women's Economic Lives in Newfoundland: Three Case Studies: Final Report to SSHRC*, Ottawa: Social Science and Humanities Research Council.

Sinclair, P. and Felt, L. (1992) 'Separate worlds: gender and domestic labour in an isolated fishing region', *Canadian Review of Sociology and Anthropology*, Winter.

Smith, D. (1990) *Texts, Fact and Femininity: Exploring the Relations of Ruling*, London: Routledge.

Smith, D. (1987) *The Everyday World as Problematic*, Boston, Mass.: North Eastern Press.

Stacey, J. (1988) 'Can there be a feminist ethnography?', *Women's Studies International Forum* 11 (1): 21-8.

Stanley, L. (1991) *Feminist Praxis: Research, Theory and Epistemology in Feminist Sociology*, London: Routledge.

Stanley, L. and Wise, S. (1983) *Breaking Out: Feminist Consciousness and Feminist Research*, London: Routledge.

Strauss, A. and Corbin, T. (1990) *Basics of Qualitative Research: Grounded Theory Procedures and Techniques*, Newbury Park, Calif.: Sage.

Chapter 5

Linking qualitative and quantitative data analysis

Jennifer Mason

INTRODUCTION

Analyzing qualitative data can sometimes be a complicated business, and is always a time-consuming one. In this chapter I am going to discuss some of the analytical procedures and techniques that Janet Finch and I developed and used in the research project we recently conducted on family obligations.[1] The discussion will range quite widely, from very practical concerns about managing large qualitative data sets, to more epistemological issues about the meaning and status of different kinds of data, and the limits and possibilities with which we grapple when deciding how best to make theoretical or general claims on their basis.

As well as looking at techniques for analyzing qualitative data, I am going to focus on their linking or integration with quantitative data in the analytical process. This raises, in a sharp form, epistemological concerns about the meaning and status of data, and requires the working through of intellectual questions about what we think we are doing conceptually when we integrate different types of data, as well as technical questions about how, in practical terms, such integration might be achieved.

AN INTRODUCTION TO THE FAMILY OBLIGATIONS PROJECT

I want to begin by giving a brief account of the aims of our project, and the methods we employed to achieve them, because these have implications for my discussion of data analysis. Overall, we were setting out to investigate the nature of relationships between adult kin (outside the 'nuclear family') and, specifically, to examine the nature and operation of obligations and responsibilities to provide practical and material assistance between them. Additionally, we wanted to compare how obligations operate in reality with 'public' assumptions made about them in, for example, social policies.

We used both qualitative and quantitative methods to achieve these aims, built into a two-stage research design.

The first stage was a large-scale interview survey (978 respondents), using a statistically representative sample of the population of Greater Manchester, achieved through random cluster sampling. In the survey respondents were asked questions about what they thought people should do for their relatives in a variety of hypothetical circumstances. We used the vignette technique, where respondents are given imaginary people in imaginary situations and asked to decide what those people should do (Finch 1987). An example of one of our vignettes is given in Table 5.1.

Table 5.1 Example of a survey vignette

(a)	Suppose an elderly couple need money to redecorate their home. Do you think that relatives should *offer* to pay to have the work done?
(b)	Assuming they could all afford to help, which, if any, relatives should offer money?
(c)	(If more than one relative given) Which relative should be the first to offer the money?
(d)	If the elderly couple cannot do the decorating themselves, do you think they should *ask* relatives for the money to have it done?
(e)	(If *no* to (d)) Why should they not ask?

Some vignettes were a little shorter than this, and some were a good deal longer, taking the respondents through a sequence of events perhaps occurring over many hypothetical years. Our aim in this part of the study was to discover whether, and to what extent, there was a consensus in the general population about 'the proper thing to do' for relatives in a variety of given circumstances. Our focus was on public statements and general levels of agreement. We did not try to get at what people actually did for their own relatives nor how they felt about them in this part of the study.

The second stage of the project involved a more qualitative study, where we conducted 120 in-depth, semi-structured, tape-recorded interviews with 88 people. Fifty-eight of these people had kin who were also in the study, and we have a total of 11 'kin groups' where we interviewed between three and eight members of the same family. In this part of the study we *were* trying to discover what people actually did in practice for their own relatives, and also the processes by which they came to do it and make sense of it: did a sense of obligation or responsibility have a role in the process? How did people in practice work out what to do for their kin, or ask of their kin? We wanted to understand how commitments and obligations built up over time between relatives.

From the beginning, then, we were using the two parts of our study to ask distinct sets of questions about family obligations. Not only were we employing different methods to generate different types of data, but we anticipated that these would tell us about different aspects of family obligations. We were explicitly *not* following the more conventional model of using a survey to provide a broad picture of a phenomenon, and a qualitative study to cover a more limited area of the same ground but in more depth. However, our view was that an understanding of kin obligatedness *in practice* would require an analysis of the relationship between the two data sets and the social processes they expressed.

MAKING QUALITATIVE DATA MANAGEABLE

My discussion of data analysis begins by drawing a distinction between the processes of making data manageable – or amenable to analysis – on the one hand, and actually developing an analysis on the other. The first set of activities usually involves a variety of indexing and retrieval systems which researchers develop to help them get a handle on their data set. The second set of activities is more likely to entail going on to do some further creative work on the products of the first, in order to develop the analysis. In practice, the distinction between the two sets of activities becomes blurred, not least because devising indexing systems and deciding how to index different parts of the data set require the researcher to engage in analytical and creative thinking. But it is useful to treat the two sets of activities as distinct because this helps to underline the important point that, although techniques like indexing and retrieval provide materials with which an analysis can be created and crafted, they do not represent the analysis in and of themselves.

In this section I focus on our version of the first set of activities. Our qualitative data set consisted of verbatim typed transcripts and field notes, and we used a number of techniques to organize and understand them.

Analytical categories

The first of these techniques was to search the data set for themes, to develop analytical categories, and to index the data accordingly. This is probably the most familiar technique – in some form or other – to qualitative researchers (Glaser and Strauss 1967, Miles and Huberman 1984, Strauss 1987), and is a good way of starting to get to grips with qualitative data systematically. In the 'Family obligations' study we devised two sets of analytical categories to help us make sense of our data: descriptive and conceptual.

The descriptive categories were very straightforward: simply a list of the key substantive topics in which we were interested. Some example are given in Table 5.2.

We developed about thirty-five of these descriptive categories, and used them to index our transcripts and field notes so that all mentions of any of the topics were eadily retrievable. Of course, deciding when someone is talking about a particular topic is often a matter of interpretation, even with straightforwardly descriptive categories like these. People in everyday discourse very rarely use the precise words with which researchers have chosen to label their analytical categories.

Table 5.2 Examples of descriptive categories

Types of support which pass between kin, such as:
     accommodation,
     personal care,
     financial support.
Social characteristics and experiences of people such as:
     education,
     employment.
Kin categories and relationships such as:
     parent,
     sibling,
     mother–daughter.

If identifying and indexing descriptive categories is not a straightforward clerical job, then repeating the process for conceptual categories is even less so. Our conceptual categories were aimed at teasing out, across the board in our qualitative data set, aspects of kin relationships relevant to our research questions. They were grounded in the theoretical perspectives which we brought to the study, in the sense that they were themes which we felt would help us to marshall data enabling us to address those questions from a variety of angles. But the categories were also grounded in the data, and devised in part through our growing familiarity with the data. We engaged in several 'pilot categorizing exercises', which involved trying out categories on batches of transcripts, developing new categories and refining existing ones in the light of these trials, swapping ideas and assumptions between ourselves about what we were doing, and so on.

We developed over eighty conceptual categories in our study. In retrospect, we agreed that this was probably too many, since we would have found it more useful to begin with very broad categories which could be refined and subdivided at a later stage in the analytical process, when our theories were more advanced. Ironically, from past experience we knew this, and we were not *intending* to produce very finely tuned categories at the beginning, but in practice I think we found the creation of more and more interesting conceptual categories rather seductive. Notwithstanding that, we still managed to do quite a lot of subdividing and amalgamating of categories later on, in the light of our developing theoretical ideas.

As with the descriptive categories, we used these systematically to categorize and index the whole of our qualitative data set. Conceptual categories were indexed as a separate exercise from descriptive categories, and we divided the labour between us: I did the conceptual categories and Janet Finch did the descriptive ones. All of our transcripts had been typed on to computer disks, so that we were able to use a PC to assist with the administrative functions of indexing and retrieval.

Tables 5.3 and 5.4 illustrate the way we applied conceptual categories to a piece of transcribed text.

The extract in Table 5.3 forms a small part of a long sequence of dialogue in which the interviewee is describing her relationship with her parents-in-law. Some years ago, her parents-in-law moved from another part of the country to live nearby, and shortly after that there was an argument which resulted in contact ceasing between them and our interviewee. The extract – as with almost any section in our data – therefore makes sense really only as part of something bigger. But the decision about exactly *what* that something bigger is will vary for different purposes or – in terms of the present discussion – for different categories. For example, a focus on 'negotiations' will imply slicing the data differently from a focus on 'family relationships as distinctive'. What degree of additional text consequently needs to be indexed with this chunk in order to locate it in an appropriate category context is always going to be a matter of interpretation.

Our decisions about these issues are of course reflected in the way categories were indexed. In the extract, categories written on the right of the text all

Table 5.3 Conceptual categories in an extract of transcribed text

The point at which each category started and finished was marked in pencil on hard copies of the transcripts, ready for further processing on the computer. See Table 5.4 for the meaning of the category codes used here.

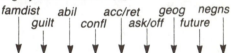

famdist   *abil*   *acc/ret*   *geog*   *negns*
       guilt   *confl*   *ask/off* *future*

Interviewer: Yes, so until that point you'd been quite involved in giving your parents-in-law support? You'd done other sorts of things like that for them had you?

Interviewee: Yes, yes. Um driving them around you know. They hadn't accepted much when they lived in Norfolk. I'd occasionally drive them down to the shops. But they preferred to walk, well fair enough, that was their habit. But I, I didn't really do very much, wasn't really very much use to them. And my children were younger so I was more involved with them, yes. They didn't want to put me out. They didn't want to give me any status as a member of their family, any acknowledgement.

applied to varying amounts of the immediately preceding text as well as to the paragraph by the interviewee, whereas the relevance of those on the left started at this point. As long as a system is devised which allows the easy identification of the beginning and the end of every category, then indexing is a straightforward procedure.

Table 5.3 shows that we decided that nine of our conceptual categories applied to this paragraph (descriptive categories, indexed in a separate exercise, are not shown here). The coexistence of quite large numbers of categories was not unusual, and indeed many paragraphs were indexed with many more categories than this.

The category files which we produced by this method were the starting-points for various forms of analysis, and at the very least we went on to generate analytical commentaries and notes based on the material in the files. Thus although the process of indexing involved us in analytical thinking, the categories themselves only provided us with a way into the data rather than

Table 5.4 What the categories mean and why they are applicable

famdist: Family relationships as distinctive, particular, or different from other relationships.
In this case the interviewee is talking about being excluded (both symbolically, and in practice) from her in-laws' family.

abil: Ability to provide support, and factors which apparently create ability or inability.
In this case, her comment about having young children could be interpreted as influencing her ability to help her parents-in-law.

negns: Negotiations about kin support and kin relationships.
This paragraph is part of a longer sequence about the way in which support, and the relationships themselves, were being negotiated.

geog: Geographical distance.
This is part of a longer discussion of the impact of her in-laws moving closer.

acc/ref: Accepting and refusing in kin relationships.
The paragraph itself is largely about this.

ask/off: Asking, offering and hinting in kin relationships.
This is part of a longer sequence about how this interviewee and her in-laws were going about asking for support, and offering support.

confl: Conflict in kin relationships.
This is part of this interviewee's account of her experience of family conflict.

guilt: Guilt in kin relationships.
This interviewee told us that she feels guilty for currently being unable to offer her in-laws support, as a result of their argument. This paragraph is part of her explanation of that.

future: Perceptions of the future in kin relationships.
The long sequence of which this forms a part was prompted by the interviewee contemplating what she would do, in future, should her in-laws need more support.

representing analytical end-products. The picture of the data set which the categories helped us to develop was a cross-sectional one – like slicing the data set horizontally and looking at topics or themes across it. For example, if I look in our 'generosity in kin relationships' file I will find it to contain excerpts from many transcripts across the data set relating to the issue of generosity in kin relationships. This is the main purpose and strength of categorizing data in this way. But there is also a limitation here: these excerpts, although having some meaning in themselves, have been removed from the contexts from which they originated. Yet for qualitative researchers the context – whether that is viewed as the social interaction of the interview itself, or interviews with other kin, or the biography of the interviewee, or something else – is usually highly relevant both to understanding what is going on, and to validating analytical claims. For almost any purpose the researcher will want to do some contextualizing, especially where she or he is investigating the nature of social processes, and that will mean bringing to bear other data to make sense of, and make the most of, the cross-sectional themes. *How* to contextualize, *which* other data to draw upon, and how to understand relationships between themes in the data, are of course matters of intellectual judgement which form part of the process of developing the analysis.

Administrative techniques can be developed to enable the pulling together of categorized data in various ways, and the main requirement is that these are anticipated at the indexing stage. For example, as well as being interested in examining particular themes for our whole data set, we also wanted to be able to pull together and compare thematic material from members of each of our kin groups, so that we could develop kin group case-studies if we wished. We therefore made sure that our indexing system was flexible enough to be able to cope with that option. In general, a very basic and straightforward technique which can aid all sorts of more complex procedures is always to label chunks of categorized dialogue with their 'address', that is, the interview and interviewee numbers and pseudonyms, the page or paragraph number, and so on. This can be done automatically by some computer packages for the analysis of qualitative data (Richards and Richards 1991; see also Richards and Richards, this volume). By doing this at least the excerpt can then easily be traced back to the interviewee and to the interview context which produced it.

Producing good indexing and retrieval systems like this is very labour- and time-intensive, and herein lies a dilemma. It is important – and not always easy – to maintain the energy to be painstakingly thorough in the categorizing process whilst not overemphasizing the inherent value of its products. The balance of time and effort involved in categorizing and, to an extent, the systematic and neat appearance of the products, can be quite seductive. It is tempting in this context to feel that the analysis is finished once the category files are complete, and it can be quite difficult to force oneself to recognize that there is a lot more intellectual work to do.

Nevertheless, the importance of the activity of categorizing and indexing cannot be understated. It provided essential building blocks for a great deal of our analysis, and the systematically categorized version of the data often gave us surprises which forced us to challenge our early impressions. What is more, if well indexed and organized, the category system continues to be a useful resource long after fieldwork is done and the first products written up. For example, from our data set, I can still pull out files on any categorized theme in which I am interested and start to germinate further analytical ideas, to look at the data set from different angles, and to find other ways into understanding it.

Charting the contours of the study group

We wanted to know something about the contours of our study group, not only for our analysis, but also to help us in the ongoing process of theoretical sampling (which ultimately becomes a crucial component of the analysis, as I will argue later). This involved making lists of – and sometimes tabulating – the social and personal characteristics of our interviewees, and also their experiences of kin support. For some purposes we wanted to count and aggregate these in simple ways, and also to be able to produce kin group characteristics by collating the data from related individuals. All of this probably seems very obvious, yet the purposes of this kind of counting and aggregation are commonly misunderstood. The object of this exercise was emphatically *not* to produce variables which could be used in some kind of quasi-statistical analysis, and neither was it an attempt to produce a study group which we could claim was representative of the wider population. Instead the exercise was intended to help us to appreciate some of the contours and the range of characteristics and experiences of our study group.

As a consequence, our counting procedures were *necessarily* crude in this part of our process. There are a number of reasons for this. Most important was that our interviews had focused on the life stories and experiences of particular interviewees, because our aim was to understand how family responsibilities operated in each person's life. For this reason we had rejected the idea of working through a structured list of questions about different types of kin support or whatever with each person, in favour of discussing issues and events relevant to particular individuals in a sequence meaningful to them. One of the implications of this decision was that there was not a neat self-contained section within every interview where this type of information would always be located. Instead, relevant sections of dialogue were invariably dotted around all over the interview, and needed to be extracted from the transcripts at a later stage (indeed one of the jobs of the descriptive categories was to help us pull out this material). Neither was the amount of data on different experiences comparable between interviewees. Some might talk at length about lending money to a relative, whilst others might mention this only briefly.

Another implication was that, although we would be able to count how many experiences of, for example, particular types of support *had* been reported to us, we could not confidently claim that *all* those people who had not given such reports had actually not had those types of experiences, unless we had specifically asked them that question. Clearly, if the researcher's intention is to create variables for quasi-statistical analysis on the basis of such data, this is a major flaw. For our purposes it was not a flaw, but it *was* important for us to remember when we were counting and aggregating this material that this was one of the implications of our interviewing strategy.

Another key reason why our procedures had to be crude relates to the nature of the phenomena we were trying to document and count. Although we wanted to get a broad idea of the range of experiences of kin support reported to us by our study group, our view was that the operation and negotiation of kin support is a complex business, often taking place over long periods of time, with a multitude of different meanings for different people in different contexts. It would therefore have been nonsensical to count up instances of support and use those as variables in our analysis. First, that would have meant erroneously assuming some kind of equivalence between all stated experiences of certain types of kin support, as though their quantity and quality were either all the same, or were quantifiably different.

Second, it would have implied that reported experiences could be assumed straightforwardly to represent objective realities or facts. However, we have suggested elsewhere that it is quite possible that some people do not count as 'kin support' – and therefore do not mention – experiences which other people would very definitely put into that category (Finch and Mason 1993). People do not just objectively have or not have experiences of kin support which they report to us; the experiences themselves are partly a product of the way people make sense of them.

For example, consider what we might make of responses to a question such as 'Have you ever lent a relative money, or received a loan from a relative?' Imagine the case of a young adult who has received £300 from a parent. Whether or not this is a gift or a loan may be unclear, and a matter for interpretation and negotiation between them. The young adult may assertively claim that this is a loan which will be repaid, whilst his or her parent may on the face of it agree that this is the case, yet simultaneously 'know' that the financial assistance was actually a gift, not expecting the young adult to repay, or not intending to accept the offer of repayment when it is made. The difference in their viewpoints may reflect their different positions with regard to the balance between dependence and independence in their relationship, and in fact that balance may actually currently be in the process of renegotiation – the financial transaction being one expression of that. Whether or at what stage we could surmise that this transaction actually *had* been a loan would depend on a number of other factors, for example, what would 'count' as repayment of this loan? Would it have to be the exact sum of money? Would interest have to be added? Would a repayment in kind be allowable? Would helping out a third party to whom the parent felt obligated confirm the status of the transaction as a loan? And how soon after the transaction would repayment have to be made before this status was put in jeopardy? These are the kinds of factors which are likely to inform people's explanations of their experiences, and people may well have particular interests in defining transactions in which they have been involved in specific ways. This of course is the stuff of our qualitative data and analysis. Returning to the question about lending money, or receiving a loan from a relative, the young adult and the parent in this example might both give different answers and explanations about the status of the same financial transaction. Neither would be objectively right or wrong, and to look for the 'right' answer is to miss the point. We needed to use more sensitive and conventionally qualitative approaches to understand these aspects than the counting and aggregating of reported experience could provide.

I am not putting these provisos forward as failings or gaps in our data set which should have been filled, but rather as inevitable consequences of earlier decisions about research design and strategy, or as features of the phenomena under investigation, or of the data themselves, which needed to be borne in mind in the process of counting and aggregating. Only by reflecting on these could we ensure that we knew exactly what we were doing when we were counting and aggregating. These are good reasons why we regarded our aggregations of this kind of material as important, but limited. We treated the products of this exercise accordingly, for example, as guides to understanding, as contextual information, as indicators of whom to sample next using principles of theoretical sampling, or to give us ideas for potential paths of analysis.

Diagrams and charts

Family trees and life story charts were our key diagrammatic aids to analysis. As with our analytical categories and with documenting social characteristics and experiences, the work of creating family trees and life stories was carried out by pulling the appropriate material out of the transcripts (or directly from the tapes in some cases) after the interview, collating it and putting it into a different form. As with the other exercises, this was material which could be buried at any point in the transcripts.

Family trees provided an invaluable way of mapping out the broad pattern of relatedness between groups of kin. They could be constructed from one person's account, or from a consolidation of the accounts of a number of members of a kin group. In these latter cases we were able to build up quite complex and detailed family trees.

Life story charts worked in a similar way. We constructed charts for individuals, and built up group charts where we had more than one interviewee in a kin group. These contained summarized information about life events, charted in chronological order. They enabled us quickly to examine the pattern and sequence of key events over a person's life, and also – where we had interviews with other members of a kin group – the intersections between the life stories and events in the lives of a number of relatives.

We used these diagrams and charts primarily to help us in the process of analysis, for example to speed up contextualization of other types of data such as categorized chunks of text, or to help us to build up kin group case studies. Unlike the products of the other data management techniques which I have described, they can also be very useful end-products in the sense that they can be used as context providers in the presentation of our analysis to an audience. Family trees were found to be particularly suitable for this purpose.

DEVELOPING AN ANALYSIS: LINKING DATA FROM DIFFERENT SOURCES

These techniques helped us to get our qualitative data set ready and amenable for the development of our analysis. However, I stated earlier that we need to push our thinking even further when considering how to *use* data to develop an analysis, and in this section I want to suggest that in doing this it is necessary to work out the answers to three main sets of questions. These are:

1 Data on what? *What* do these data tell me about and, crucially, what can they *not* tell me about?
2 Strength of claim. *How well* do these data tell me this? How convincing are claims I want to make on the basis of the data? How can I make the strongest claims possible, without pushing the data 'too far' by making claims which are beyond their capacity?
3 Integration of data. How best can I integrate and make sense of different forms of qualitative data? How can I integrate quantitative and qualitative material? The answer to this must take full account of, and be consistent with, the researcher's answers to (1) and (2).

Questions (1) and (2), of course, have their basis in the familiar concern with validity, generality and representativeness. Question (3) presents the intellectual and practical dilemma of how to integrate data sets which may provide different answers to these crucial epistemological questions.

1. Data on what?

We began our study with the assumption that different methodological techniques could yield data on different aspects of family obligations, and this was written into our research design and data collection strategy. One way of answering the 'data on what?' question was therefore to re-examine and hold up to critical scrutiny the logic of our research design.

For the first stage of our research, we had chosen to use a large survey, with a structured questionnaire, which we analyzed using statistical techniques. The reasoning behind this was that we wanted to assess whether people in general would agree on a set of appropriate family responsibilities. If asked in an interview situation, would most people concur that relatives have certain specified responsibilities towards each other? Could we document a set of moral norms, rules or principles of kinship based on these 'public statements', which most people in contemporary Britain would recognize? We were very clear throughout the research that we were *not*, in this part of the study, trying to understand what people actually do or feel in their own kin relationships, nor the (probably) complex processes through which they decide what to do, nor the role of the concept of obligation in people's own actions and feelings. We believed that none of these types of questions can be answered with structured questionnaire or interview techniques. The more limited questions about what people say third parties in hypothetical situations should do for their relatives were – in terms of the 'data on what?' questions – far less ambitious, and more amenable to survey techniques.

These were our aims. How far did the data reflect these? In our survey we asked normative questions, for example, what *should* a specified person do in a particular given situation. The intention was that these types of questions would elicit normative answers, for example, that the person *should* do this, and that we could measure levels of agreement and disagreement to build up a general picture of publicly expressed norms.

Of course, it is possible that a respondent would select a course of action for one of these hypothetical people, without *necessarily* viewing that in a normative way, for example they might be giving a prediction of what such a person *would probably do*; they might even be recounting what *they themselves did* in a similar situation; or they might be offering what they suppose is *the most acceptable answer* to give to an interviewer; and so on. We had to work through these, and other, possibilities and the issues they raised for the 'data on what?' question. Did they jeopardize the normative status of the data? Our view was that they did not. We considered, in any case, that norms are complex and situational; we certainly do not support a view that norms exist in some rigid or structural way, or as static underlying attitudes or beliefs, and we would expect people to engage in a variety of forms of reasoning in order to produce even an apparently straightforward answer to a normative question. In the survey, we were less interested in the reasoning process, than in whether people were giving replies which could be taken to represent their sense of *appropriate* answers (however they reached that conclusion). We concluded that it was reasonable to interpret our data as – at the very least – reflecting what people saw as appropriate in this way. So, being able to document what percentage of a survey population said that a particular line of action was appropriate is, in our view, one facet of understanding the normative elements of family obligations. Again, the point for us to remember was that this was only one facet, and we would have to decide what its relationship was to other parts of the process, reflected in other parts of our data sets.

Our qualitative study was intended to approach family obligations from a different direction, and to get at those other parts of the process. Therefore, in the second part of our project we chose to use a smaller, in-depth study, using qualitative techniques of data collection and analysis. Our reasoning here was different from the survey: we had different questions and expected different kinds of answers. At this stage we were interested in the *processes* through which support and help gets given and received in families. We wanted to know how people work out what to do for their kin, how they experience these processes, and to what extent they make sense of their family relationships using ideas like 'obligation' or 'responsibility'. We were, therefore, much more explicitly concerned with people's reasoning processes, and with the way in which their experiences of kin support had developed and changed over time. Survey methods are not very amenable to answering such questions.

Therefore, the division between the two stages of our study did not straightforwardly reflect what is probably the most commonly supposed division between qualitative and quantitative work: that is, between structure (quantitative) and meaning (qualitative) (Fielding and Fielding 1986: 34). Instead, *both* stages of our study were designed to ask questions about, amongst other things, different levels of meaning. However, we were relying on our qualitative study to tell us about *process*, and in some senses to give us the key to understanding how different levels of meaning, structure and constraint actually fit together and work in practice in people's lives.

2. Strength of claims

Just as the different parts of our study yielded data on different aspects of family obligations, so too there were essential differences in the way we would make claims on their basis, and the techniques we would use to strengthen and make rigorous these claims. We had chosen a large-scale approach for the first stage of our research because we wanted to make claims about levels of agreement or disagreement concerning aspects of family obligations amongst the general population. The underlying logic was that random sampling would produce a population whose social characteristics would mirror those of a larger population. On that basis, we would be able to use statistical calculations to assess the probability with which our sample's pattern of responses to our questions would be reproduced in similar proportions if we were to conduct a census of the whole population. That way we would be able to make predictions about *how commonly* would certain sets of responsibilities to kin be acknowledged as appropriate. The strength of these claims would depend upon the rigour – in statistical terms – of our techniques of sampling and analysis, as well as the statistical integrity of the sample we ended up with. However, claims made on the basis of the survey, although we hoped they were well founded, would remain limited in *scope*, because data from the survey – however rigorous in statistical terms – represented only one facet of the way in which family obligations should be understood.

By contrast, we had chosen a smaller, in-depth study, using qualitative techniques of data collection and analysis because at that stage we were more interested in claiming that we were producing a credible argument about the social processes involved in the operation of family obligations. We could then make general theoretical or analytical claims on the basis of having produced a valid account of those processes. The concern would be to produce a rounded and convincing analysis of, for example, the ways in which family responsibilities are negotiated in a variety of circumstances. The strength of these claims therefore would involve demonstrating – as far as possible – that we had identified a full set of contours of the process, and understood at least some of the circumstances under which that process operated in certain ways. This is quite different from the more enumerative or statistical logic of the survey.

We had embarked upon various strategies to develop our analysis and strengthen our claims. What we wanted to achieve was analytical roundedness and rigour, which for us entailed asking: what are all the components necessary for generating a viable and convincing explanation and how do we get to that point? The answers to these questions lay in both processes of data collection and of analysis.

For example, in data collection we had used strategies and techniques which we felt would be most likely to give us all the components of the analysis we would wish to build. An example is our strategy of including 'kin groups' within the study, where we would get the perspectives and accounts of a number of relatives within one family, thus helping us to develop a rounded picture. Another example was a strategy which was intended to produce an analysis sensitive to the changes and developments in family responsibilities which take place over people's lifetimes. Although our study was not longitudinal, we focused our interviews around the histories of people's experiences of family responsibilities. These and other aspects of our data collection strategy were very much informed by our view of the form and type of analysis we would want to develop, and the parts of the picture we would need to generate and strengthen this analysis. This meant that in the early stages of designing the qualitative study, we were thinking very much in terms of *principles* of analysis (although not the precise practice of it), and that throughout the study we worked hard to achieve a two-way interrelationship between each stage of analysis, design and data collection.

Another example of this emphasis involves our strategy of theoretical sampling, which we have described in some detail elsewhere (Finch and Mason 1990a). Our sampling strategy for the qualitative study was guided by theoretical principles, and our express intention was to use it to help to develop a sound theoretical analysis of our data, rather than to produce a representative sample of the population. Amongst other things, this implied making decisions about sampling in an ongoing way, whilst the fieldwork was in progress, rather than in a once-and-for-all way at the start. Our sampling decisions were informed by 'stock-taking' exercises which helped us to sketch out a picture of what types of experiences, or people, or kin groups, or 'instances of support' had already been included in our sample, and what gaps needed to be filled in order to push our analysis further. But in identifying them as gaps we were guided by theoretical considerations about what was needed to build up and to test our developing analysis, rather than statistical ones about the social characteristics of our interviewees *vis-à-vis* the general population.

This can all be seen as part of a process of analytic induction, involving the generation of theory from data and the use of strategic sampling to assist in the refinement and strengthening of the theory. It is in this sense that theoretical sampling should be seen as integral to the process of analysis, although its relationship to qualitative analysis is distinct from the relationship of statistical sampling to statistical analysis. Nevertheless, both may be equally important in validating their respective analytical products. It is easy to assume that principles of sampling are less important in qualitative than in quantitative research, yet as Jennifer Platt so cogently argues, this is to overlook the very potent role that rigorous theoretical sampling can play in strengthening claims made on the basis of qualitative data (Platt 1988).

When the fieldwork is complete, a similar logic and set of principles can be used to make comparisons within the data set. Again, the guiding principle is to search the data set for comparisons which help not only to flesh out the theory, but also to sharpen and test it. This can be done by asking relevant questions such as: on the basis of the data examined so far, what are the credible or likely explanations for what is going on? What is the full range of influences at work here? What makes the process work in the way it does? What are the constraints? It is usually not possible to answer all such questions, although at the very least the researcher will be able to produce an account of what is *possible* under the conditions observed so far, and then to make an informed decision about how to move out from there, to broaden or deepen the analysis. At some stage, as in theoretical sampling, it is vital to engage in a search for counter-evidence, or in other words to try to find an example which contradicts the emerging explanation. The result of this search, coupled with rigorous theoretical sampling done at an earlier stage, may be that the explanation can be strengthened, or that it must be modified.

In our project we used the technique of drawing comparisons to build up explanations in various ways. One of these was to use case study methods of analysis. For example, for some purposes we developed kin group case studies, where we drew on the accounts of several relatives to understand certain aspects of family obligations in a specific family. We began our analysis of the way in which commitments develop over time in this way. Our aim was to produce a detailed analysis of the processes involved in this aspect of family obligations for the particular case study we had chosen. Once we felt we had achieved that as far as we could, we began to look for and understand the basis of similarities and differences of process in further kin group case studies, with the aim of enhancing or modifying the original analysis which we had begun to develop for the first case study. It is possible to use this procedure to compare all case studies in a data set, or just selected ones, and it is also possible to begin with a case study and subsequently draw in more cross-sectional material for comparison (see Finch and Mason 1990c). Other strategies may not involve case studies at all but, whichever approach is used, the logic of selection for comparison always needs to be governed by analytical and theoretical concerns.

Asking oneself quite simple questions may help to keep this procedure on the right track. For example: 'how am I going to demonstrate to others – and myself – the validity of this particular analysis as against an alternative analysis?'; 'what other evidence do I need to do this?'; 'how can I demonstrate that I have tested and challenged this analysis?'

Given the centrality to qualitative analysis of techniques such as these which are emphatically not statistical, can we assume that numbers and aggregation are of no consequence at all? For example, does it matter *how many* examples can be gathered to support a particular part of the analysis? For me, the answer is that numbers do matter, but that we need to work out and demonstrate just what their salience is in our analyses. Numbers cannot be assumed to have either equivalence, or neutrality. For example, one kin group case study showing a lack of reciprocity in relationships between certain relatives might be very significant indeed if the developing theory and analysis suggest that reciprocity is particularly likely to develop there. Similarly, in reverse, one case might be highly relevant if the circumstances did not appear conducive to reciprocity, but yet there was a strong reciprocal relationship between some relatives. A case like this may enable the researcher to make the claim that 'even here, in these unlikely conditions, reciprocity seemed to be at work', and to move forward to begin to understand what it is about that particular case study, or the relationships within it, which means that this is so. The significance of numbers of examples is therefore not a given, nor can it be deduced or treated in a purely statistical manner, nor is it always the most relevant aspect of the analysis. These are matters of analytical interpretation which need to be worked out and understood afresh each time.

3. Integration of data

It should be clear by now that in the 'Family obligations' study, we were not using our two-stage research design as a method of 'triangulation', at least not in the sense of using one part of the study simply to check the validity of the other part. Given that each part yielded data on different phenomena, we could not have done that in any case. However, our two-stage design certainly was intended to enhance the validity of the overall analysis, precisely by producing data on different aspects of family obligations so that we could build up a rounded and credible overall picture. Table 5.5 summarizes the distinctive features of our two data sets in terms of the key questions about status of data and strength of claim which I have discussed so far.

Table 5.5 Status of data and strength of claims

	Survey	Qualitative study
Data on what?	Public normative statements	Processes of family responsibility, involving norms and negotiations
Claims based on?	Enumerative or statistical logic. Representative sample	Inductive or qualitative logic. Valid analysis of process

The challenge of integrating these data sets involved two elements. First it involved dealing with the intellectual questions about how the different aspects of family obligations represented by the data sets actually operated together in practice (if they did). I pointed out that in our study we saw the two methodologies as giving us data on different things. The intellectual task for us was to formulate an account of how we thought those things were related, that is, how public statements about 'the proper thing to do' (derived from the survey) related to how people worked out what to do in practice in their own families and how they made sense of this (derived from the qualitative study). The answer to this question is not straightforwardly a technical one, but is much more to do with the philosophy of our overall analysis and theoretical position, what we see our different data sets as representing (that is, which parts of the picture), and how we see those parts as fitting together.

The second element involved dealing with the more technical questions about how actually to do the integrating, that is, how to 'glue together' data which have been produced by methods with different logical principles. This could only really be accomplished after the first element, the intellectual questions, had been worked through. Both elements, incidentally, apply to integrating different forms of qualitative data – for example categorized chunks of text, case studies – as well as to qualitative and quantitative data integration.

We used a number of strategies to achieve what we saw as an appropriate integration of our data, combining these two elements. I give just a few examples.

The first involves the principle of following up similar themes in the different data sets as a way of linking the data. We did this by trying to ask questions of each of our data sets that would problematize the relationship between them; this is not the same as asking identical questions of each. In the survey, one way in which we did this was to generate 'propositions' which could then be tested out against the data. This meant producing a statement about a conceptual issue which might lie behind a number of the vignettes used in the survey. An example might be: 'People are less ready to agree that relatives should provide help where the person needing help *asks* for it than where the donor *offers* it.' We did not ask this question directly in the survey, but we did weave the theme of 'asking and offering in kin relationships' into a number of the vignettes, including the one given as an example in Table 5.1. All our propositions were couched in terms which were relevant to the enumerative logic of the survey and to the normative status of its data, as in this example: '*people* . . . agree', 'relatives *should* . . .'. This type of proposition would not be valid for our qualitative data. Yet we could use the same 'asking and offering' theme to ask questions of a different order of the qualitative data set. Here, we did not put forward propositions to be tested, but asked questions which would help us to open up processes of family responsibility. So, for example: 'do our interviewees ask for the help which they need, or do they wait for it to be offered?'; 'how does asking and offering actually get done in practice?'; 'how far is the *way* that support is negotiated, and specifically whether support is asked for or offered, an important element in whether or not support is given?' For the qualitative study, we would generate many interwoven questions like these, not all of which we would be able to answer categorically, but looking for the 'answers' would help us to begin to understand the processes of family responsibility. We could use case study material, or categorized chunks of text on 'asking and offering' and related themes, to do this (see Finch and Mason 1993).

Testing propositions and asking questions in this way would enable us to explore themes like asking and offering from a variety of angles, including what a representative sample of the adult population said about normative principles of asking and offering, and what sense people made of experiences and feelings about asking and offering in their own lives.

Another method of linking our data sets involved using them to address a particular topic (rather than a conceptual theme) from a variety of angles. This might involve developing quite an extensive set of propositions and questions which all related to that topic. An example is the topic of 'relationships between parents and their adult children'. We have written about one aspect of this: how far a notion of kin obligation underscores the assistance which may be given to elderly parents by their adult children (Finch and Mason 1990b). To do this we used survey data to look at a variety of dimensions of public norms about filial obligations, then a kin group case study to look at processes of filial obligations 'close up' in one family. We used both data sets side by side, and endeavoured to explore the relationship between them. For example, we used the survey to ask whether people seem to acknowledge publicly, at the normative level, clear 'rules' about filial obligations. We used the case study to ask, in practice, whether people do have the idea that there are well-understood rules about how you should behave towards your parents. When faced with the actual needs of their parents, is it obvious to children what is the 'proper thing to do'? Or is it more complex than that? We could then use our categories to look more cross-sectionally in our data set, to see how far similar or different themes emerged there.

For some purposes in our analysis we used only one of the data sets, chiefly because the other one could not provide the relevant type of data on that issue. This happened most often where we were examining social processes in depth, and we perceived that the survey did not have a lot to offer specifically. However, we have also used the survey data on its own, to debate the point about whether or not there is a public 'normative consensus' about family responsibilities (Finch and Mason 1991). But even where one data set has apparently little to contribute, it can often still provide an important added dimension. For example, we have developed in some detail an analysis of the way in which *commitments* to kin develop over time (Finch and Mason 1993). This analysis is based principally on our qualitative data, where we can examine the build-up of commitments in families often over many years. But our survey can add to this picture by showing how far people say that the idea that commitments *should* be cumulative, or the idea that past help should be reciprocated, are appropriate ones.

These are a few of the ways in which we have integrated and linked the different parts of our qualitative data set, and the qualitative and quantitative data sets. Where we could, our guiding principle was to present different forms of data side by side and to explore the relationships between them. The intellectual task was deciding upon which questions each data set, or type of data, could address, and what mix of data was appropriate to particular issues.

CONCLUSION

There are, of course, a number of challenges – and some difficulties – in integrating or linking data, and I conclude with a few general points on this theme.

A key challenge, especially where the integration is between qualitative and quantitative data, is developing the necessary technical competences to deal with data that have different logical principles. It becomes very important to be able to move easily between one logic and set of assumptions and another, yet most of us feel more comfortable in placing ourselves on one side or other of the so-called qualitative–quantitative divide. In the 'Family obligations' study we designed, conducted and analyzed the qualitative part of the study ourselves. However, we had the valuable assistance of Mick Green, of Lancaster's Centre for Applied Statistics, with the survey data statistical analysis, and of Gill Courtenay and Social and Community Planning Research with the survey design and data collection. But we could not straightforwardly 'subcontract' those parts of our study. Not least, we needed to be able to build an integrated analysis and we had to develop and consolidate in ourselves the appropriate expertise to use and move between the different parts of our study and data sets. This raises the question of the division of labour and how far it is possible to ensure an appropriate balance of skills and expertise in a research team by choosing people with different specialisms (if that is desired), yet at the same time establishing and maintaining a common language.

Another issue – and perhaps it is also a challenge – is to be circumspect about the role that computers can play in the process of qualitative analysis and data integration. Computers can undoubtedly help in the indexing and retrieval functions of qualitative data management, and some packages can go further in assisting the exploration of relationships between categories or even whole data sets (Richards and Richards, this volume). But computers cannot perform the creative and intellectual task of devising categories, or of deciding which categories or types of data are relevant to the process being investigated, or what is a meaningful comparison, or of generating appropriate research questions and propositions with which to interrogate the data, and so on. Recognizing the limitations of computers in this respect is, I believe, as important as appreciating their benefits.

Another challenge which emerged rather unexpectedly in our project involved recognizing that we may periodically have to explain to our funders, to the research community, and sometimes to ourselves, that each part of our study produced only one facet of the overall picture we wished to develop. The survey in particular, although representing a major commitment of time and resources, was necessarily limited in its scope in the sense that it could only yield data on one – albeit vital – dimension of family obligations. This could have produced misunderstandings about publication and dissemination, since the assumption was that each part of the project could be disseminated separately and stand on its own. Yet we made an early decision not to publish any survey data (although we had gathered that first), until we had the qualitative data to complete the picture, and with one important exception which, ironically, was delayed in the publication process, we have not done so (Finch and Mason 1991). However, it is important to recognize that the many and varied pressures on researchers to publish their research material at regular intervals make the adherence to these kinds of intellectual principles rather difficult to uphold in practice.

Finally I think the most important challenge in integrating quantitative and qualitative data analysis involves developing mechanisms to ensure that you are asking sensible, meaningful and appropriately limited questions of your data sets. In a sense, that is what much of this chapter has been about. Critical scrutiny of one's own decisions and, in team research such as the

'Family obligations' project, the maintenance of a stimulating and effective dialogue between researchers, can be very helpful in this respect. But a further difficulty involves being asked the 'wrong questions' about the data by other people. In a sense, all qualitative researchers encounter this problem in that they are often asked questions which assume that they can make statistical inferences on the basis of their data (see Mason 1989). But the issue is further complicated where a variety of logical principles under-pins the different elements of one study. For example, we have often been asked if the findings of our qualitative study 'contradict' our survey data. That is the wrong question in the sense that the two parts of the study were not designed to validate each other. They give data on different things, so the relationship between them cannot be one of confirmation or contradic-tion, although they may contain themes which are similar or distinct. The problem is usually that the question is intended to be about the substance, or the 'findings', of the research project, and not about its epistemology or methodology. The challenge, as I see it, is to be able to construct a mean-ingful response on both counts.

NOTE

The study 'Family obligations: social construction and social policy' was funded by the Economic and Social Research Council between 1985 and 1989 (Grant No. Goo 232197).

REFERENCES

Fielding, N.G. and Fielding, J.L. (1986) *Linking Data*, London: Sage.
Finch, J. (1987) 'The vignette technique in survey research', *Sociology* 21(1): 105–14.
Finch, J. and Mason, J. (1990a) 'Decision-taking in the fieldwork process: theo-retical sampling and collaborative writing', in R.G. Burgess (ed.) *Studies in Qualitative Methodology*, vol. 2, *Reflections on Field Experience*, London: JAI Press.
—— (1990b) 'Filial obligations and kin support for elderly people', *Ageing and Society* 10: 151–75.
—— (1990c) 'Divorce, remarriage and family obligations', *The Sociological Review* 38(2): 219–46.
—— (1991) 'Obligations of kinship in contemporary Britain: is there normative agreement?', *British Journal of Sociology* 42(3): 345–67.
—— (1993) *Negotiating Family Responsibilities*, London: Routledge.
Glaser, B.G. and Strauss, A.L. (1967) *The Discovery of Grounded Theory: Strategies for Qualitative Research*, Chicago: Aldine.
Mason, J. (1989) '"No peace for the wicked": older married women and leisure', in M. Talbot and E. Wimbush (eds) *Relative Freedoms*, Milton Keynes: Open University Press.
Miles, M.B. and Huberman, A. (1984) *Qualitative Data Analysis: a Sourcebook of New Methods*, Beverley Hills, Calif.: Sage.

Platt, J. (1988) 'What can case studies do?', in R.G. Burgess (ed.) *Studies in Qualitative Methodology*, London: JAI Press.

Richards, L. and Richards, T. (1991) 'The transformation of qualitative method: computational paradigms and research processes', in N.G. Fielding and R.M. Lee (eds) *Using Computers in Qualitative Research*, London: Sage.

Strauss, A.L. (1987) *Qualitative Analysis for Social Scientists*, Cambridge and New York: Cambridge University Press.

Chapter 6

Analyzing together: recollections of a team approach

Virginia Olesen, Nellie Droes, Diane Hatton, Nan Chico and Leonard Schatzman

Critics of qualitative research have frequently argued that accounts of findings often fail to provide sufficient detail on how researchers analyzed their data. Even reports with vivid details on data gathering sometimes gloss the analytic manœuvres with a ritualistic and uninformative reference to a style of analysis, such as grounded theory (Glaser and Strauss 1967), domain analysis (Spradley 1979), unit analysis (Lofland and Lofland 1984), without specific details on how findings and conceptualizations were shaped. Nowhere is this more the case than in team research, a notable exception being Finch and Mason's account of theoretical sampling, an analytic as well as a sampling tactic, in their 'Family obligations' study (1990). There are, of course, good reasons for sparse accounts. Details of every analytic decision in even a small project could well swamp the findings.

Here we report team analysis of interview data done in the late phases of an ongoing study of self-care practices. We describe how we utilized generic concepts derived from our earlier studies (Wiseman 1987). We outline how we analyzed collectively and systematically in order to try to establish plausibility and consistency. We show how we utilized various analytic styles, primarily constant comparative analysis (Glaser and Strauss 1967: 101–16), domain analysis (Spradley 1979: 92–3) and dimensional analysis (Schatzman 1990).

This chapter also briefly discusses a little-explored topic in qualitative analysis, namely, the need for researchers in certain contexts to have technical knowledge in order to grasp specific issues and to frame or modify the findings. Though this can be particularly critical for qualitative work on health and illness, studies of other realms e.g. construction projects (Bresnen 1988), laboratory science (Latour and Woolgar 1986), police work (Van Maanen 1991), and elite decision-makers (Stacey 1986) have also commented on the importance of such knowledge for data gathering and analysis.

To reconstruct our analytic structures and manœuvres, we analyzed some twenty documents, our own memos, summaries, notes of team meetings based on verbatim transcriptions of audiotaped team meetings and the chronological methodological sections of our final reports to our sponsor. Our extensive notes are related to the taping and transcription of team meetings which captured the team's cognitive processes, the 'thinking out loud' and the synergistic interaction of the team analysis. Some of these documents were rewardingly rich in analytic detail; others less so. For the sake of clarity we present our account chronologically, thus invoking linearity and smoothness that did not always characterize the hard work of analysis. Where we experienced drifts and starts, delays and depression, anxiety and exhilaration, we try to capture those.

THE SELF-CARE STUDIES

Two of us, Olesen and Schatzman, had started qualitative study of self-care of mundane ailments (headaches, upset stomach, colds, etc.) in the early 1980s to try to move away from the dominant emphasis in sociological studies of health and illness on dramatic health problems, e.g. heart disease, stroke. We believed such emphasis neglects the types of problems most people experience every day. Those more mundane experiences, we thought, provide one context in which people assess their bodies, their symptoms, assign meanings and do or do not take action. Mundanity, in conception, allows for an examination of whether or how people decide an ailment 'belongs' in the domain of illness as against nuisance. It was our view then and now that better understanding of how lay people interpret and deal with critical illnesses can be achieved if we know how they understand and manage mundane ailments. These are not mutually exclusive domains of human interpretation and behaviour, but, rather, intersect and mutually influence one another. In retrospect we did not set out to develop a theory of self-care of the mundane ailment. Rather, our interests lay in delineating this realm of social-cultural life, in charting an ethnographic description of the conditions and circumstances under which people define and manage this particular experience.

However, more abstract and theoretical issues quickly emerged. Being symbolic interactionists, we were early drawn to theoretical issues about self. We began to wonder if or how the meaning of such trivial ailments plays a part in shaping self in interaction and consultation with others, lay and professional and, importantly, in self-reflective processes (Olesen *et al.* 1989). The data spoke to the part embodiment plays in these assessments and views of self, leading us to recognize and emphasize the body, a neglected element in Meadian social psychology (Olesen and Schatzman 1982, Hatton and Droes 1987, Olesen 1992). Our work therefore moved between a descriptive exploration of the self-care of mundane ailments and these more theoretically articulated concepts. In this account we draw on both streams of analysis. To provide the background on how the team emerged and our analysis developed we briefly describe the earlier phases of our work, which led to the study which is the focus of this paper.

EARLY ANALYSIS

We began our studies with a small pilot study of 25 men and women who were interviewed in an open-ended interview on how they defined, experienced and managed mundane ailments. (These respondents were in their twenties and thirties and of Caucasian, middle-class, college-educated backgrounds.) We and our graduate student interviewers held lengthy debriefing and brainstorming sessions to pull out first-order statements from respondents' reports of how individuals defined, managed and consulted. Then we sifted through these substantive statements to assign properties or dimensions that we saw in the statements, such as familiarity, duration of the ailment, perception of risk, intensity, etc. (Schatzman 1990). For example, the statement, 'The sore throat was so painful I could barely speak; it was frightening because it lasted three days. In our family that kind of sore throat can easily turn into a "strep" (streptococcus) throat', would contain dimensions of intensity ('so painful'), duration ('three days'), and risk ('turn to strep'). The dimensions move up a level from the respondents' first-order statements.

We then compiled what we agreed were related dimensions into two analytic schema: (1) naming and locating the discomfort or ailment (including the dimensions of sensitivity, tolerance, options, risk, stake) and (2) situated conditions (incorporating the dimensions of biography, understanding, social context, social supports, environmental–cultural supports). Readers familiar with domain analysis will recognize similarities to manœuvres in that analytic style: the search for component parts of a phenomenon (the experience with the mundane ailment) and the subsequent attempts to work out relationships among the parts and their relationship to a whole (Spradley 1979: 92–3). In both dimensional and domain analysis, respondents' specification of the parts is a critical element. Compiling the parts and specifying their relationships becomes the analyst's work, a first step in the 'triple mediation' involved in the creation of findings (Olesen 1988).

Utilizing the analytic frameworks from the pilot study which centred on individuals' perceptions of mundane ailments, we framed a second, federally-funded study focused on a specific group whose members shared a common characteristic. These were persons who had undergone abdominal ostomy (a surgical procedure to provide an opening in the abdominal wall for release of body wastes). We selected this group because we had access through a local chapter of the United Ostomy Association. In keeping with our views about the importance of mundane ailments, we were not concerned with studying them as persons with the serious diseases some had, though we could scarcely overlook these conditions as they influenced mundanity. Rather, we were interested in their experience of mundane ailments, especially in the transformation of meanings around such ailments.

The funding regularized research positions for two doctoral students in nursing who had been participating (Droes and Hatton) and solidified loosely framed team arrangements from the earlier pilot phase. More importantly, their assured continuing participation enhanced the integration of technical, professional knowledge into our analytic discussions. Although the sociology faculty (Olesen and Schatzman) and graduate student (Chico) on the project could sociologically interpret respondents' accounts of mundane ailments, often more precise clinical knowledge was critical, e.g. the potential risks if a sore throat went unattended and became a strep throat, how rapidly a neglected cut could become infected, etc. When we began to gather data from the ostomates, the nurse graduate students' technical knowledge became central in understanding and interpreting the ostomates' reports of mundane ailments and their strategies. Reflecting later on this, Hatton (1990) wrote,

> Based on clinical knowledge of the natural history of disease and multiple experiences in caring for patients, the nurse members of the research team discerned subtle variations in respondents' descriptions of their pre- and post-surgical experiences that were not as readily apparent or deemed significant by the sociologists. Early in the analytic work, the nurses developed tentative findings about the meaning of illness for various types of ostomy patients .... The sociologists viewed illness from the abstract perspective of 'trajectory of illness'. The nurses' clinical perspective interacted with the sociologists' interpretive perspective to enlarge the idea of trajectory, for the findings revealed that trajectories for each of the ostomy groups varied considerably. These analytic differences emerged from the interactions among team members and their disciplinary and professional perspectives.

As the doctoral students in nursing came to acquire the techniques of sociological qualitative analysis and sociological concepts, the sociologists began to learn necessary technical knowledge of ills and ailments which recast sociological concepts. Growing mutual understanding of the data and team members' altering knowledge bases shifted roles. Instead of being two faculty and three students, we became a quintet of analytic equals. That transition was fully realized when we undertook further work on self-care, mundane ailments and use of health care services. Indeed, it was precisely because we were emerging as a team that we had the resources and talent to compete successfully for the modest funds that supported our next study. The story of the analysis in that study is the heart of this chapter.

THE HMO STUDY: A COMPARATIVE ANALYSIS

Characteristics of the HMO (health maintenance organizations) study promoted growth of our analytic collaboration. We had to work at both a descriptive level to provide information for our sponsor and an abstract level to yield concepts for our professional presentations and papers. Further, this inquiry required us to analyze and compare two groups of people rather than to analyze a single group as we had previously. This resembles survey design, but differs because survey design compares samples on rigidly set categories. In our study this meant looking at two samples, analyzing each independently in light of earlier concepts to ascertain differences in the concepts and then altering the concepts as necessary before a comparison was made between the two samples. Thus there were more demands on the team.

We undertook this study because much of the US health care literature claimed that persons who bring in mundane ailments over-utilize health care services and add to the escalating cost problems. We proposed to Maxi-Care Foundation, a foundation concerned with HMOs, that we explore whether this was true for HMO members. (For non-US readers who are unfamiliar with health maintenance organizations, these provide members with health care services free at the point of service.) The key issue was whether the HMO members, having access to such low-cost care, would over-use the services for these trivial ailments. Thus, relationships to types of services became a key element to be added to the concepts and dimensions that had emerged in the earlier phases.

To answer our question we designed the HMO study in a comparative format. We drew a random sample of thirty-two persons from the membership roster of a Bay Area HMO which agreed to co-operate with us. We selected eight men and eight women who had policies that covered themselves and others and eight men and eight women whose policies covered only themselves.

To obtain a comparison sample of non-HMO members, we advertised in a local 'alternative life-style' newspaper and used the networks of graduate students in sociology and nursing to recruit a sample of six men and nineteen women. (We took these approaches because of research 'fatigue' among available populations in the heavily researched Bay Area and because individuals without insurance are typically not employed, hence difficult to reach.) This sample included thirteen individuals who had fee-for-service insurance and twelve who, in the vernacular, were 'going bare' (without insurance). Other than the predominance of women in the non-HMO sample, an attribute our analyses did not show to be significant, the HMO and non-HMO samples were comparable in age, employment and domestic arrangements, e.g. with whom the respondents were living.

Using a wide-ranging, open-ended interview schedule which had been developed in the earlier phases, we interviewed the HMO sample first since access was so much easier than it was to the scattered individuals who would become the non-HMO sample. We worked intensively on the HMO category and completed interviewing quite quickly, hence could analyze it as a group. The slower receipt of the non-HMO interviews meant that we analyzed many of them as they came in.

COLLABORATION USING MIXED ANALYTIC STRATEGIES

Several researchers have outlined features of credible qualitative accounts (Burgess 1984: 209–20), Strauss and Corbin 1990: 249–58). Briefly, they show that all qualitative analysis must: (1) Demonstrate optimum use of the data: were all cases, incidents, events included and analyzed from all possible angles? (2) Fully describe the conventions selected to achieve plausibility and consistency: did the researcher attempt to refute his or her own findings with negative cases?

We did not have a prior, highly rational, deliberate set of strategies to realize these analytic goals. Rather, they evolved as various elements shaped our situation: cordial working relationships carried over from the earlier phases of the study, a tight time-frame imposed by a very modest budget, our other obligations as faculty and students, the necessity to link our work conceptually to our earlier analyses whilst providing our sponsor relevant and appropriate non-academic findings. More often than we in qualitative analysis report, these everyday matters influenced the course of analysis. These practical factors prompted us to parcel the analysis among us in order to share the work, as well as to achieve some consensus, consistency, or in the words of survey researchers, reliability. Within the parcelling we played ourselves off against one another in order to maximize comparison and contrast and to highlight attempts to refute and confirm that which we thought we knew. These strategies proved useful for the entire analysis.

ANALYSIS OF THE HMO MEMBERS' INTERVIEWS

Bearing in mind our central concern about the use of services in the self-care of a mundane ailment, we reviewed the data with two purposes: (1) to affirm, alter, negate or add to the previously delineated dimensions and schema (noted in the section on early analysis) and (2) to discover how these related to the context of use. We went through five phases: we linked and compared sectors of new and old data, we reviewed all HMO member data, we analyzed by categories of respondents, we analyzed by questions, and we integrated a final analysis. These steps are now given in detail.

Linking and comparing new data with previous data

We agreed that our starting-point would be to utilize our previous data and conceptualizations. Several questions arose. Which earlier dimensions should we select to see whether these would hold up in the HMO member data? Would the HMO member responses fall along these dimensions so that we could see distinct groupings? How many dimensions should we use in the comparison in order to see distinct groupings in the new data? This latter question was not a numeric issue, but rather one relating to patterning. The dimensions mentioned here are style of managing the mundane ailment and 'trust in the body', a subjective assessment of the body's capacities and of the self as sufferer of a particular mundane complaint. 'Trust' also involved the factor of risk, another dimension used earlier. Transcribed team meeting notes for 22 May 1984 show how we began this analysis of the HMO member data.

LS: In no way here can we create groups that are distinct along more than one or two dimensions.

VO: Your point a week ago, Lennie, is that a more interesting issue is to –

LS: – follow a bunch of dimensions and see where people fall.

VO: In order not to drive ourselves nutty with this next step of our analysis, why don't we take just our ideas of managing and management styles and work on those (to see where people fall) and then see how they link up with other dimensions like trust in the body, and risk, both physical and social.

LS: So, we're looking for management styles and the conditions that might explain them.

VO: Shall we each take an HMO member, an ostomate and a non-ostomate to see how this works out?

So our starting-point was to check our previously delineated ideas using a comparative and linking mode with a limited number of old and new cases. We undertook an inductive exercise analyzing incoming data to alter and amend previously held conceptualizations. Readers here will recognize some familiar sectors of constant comparative analysis (Glaser and Strauss 1967: 101–16) and inductive analysis (Denzin 1978: 192). This comparative and linking exercise complete, we turned to the whole set of HMO member interviews.

General review of HMO member data

Acting as a group of five and using leads from the linking exercise, we each read all HMO member interviews as they became available to see if new dimensions emerged, if old ones held, or if we had to change our concepts of context (the second schema) in light of the respondents' access to readily available, modestly priced health care. This familiarization exercise, discussed at numerous team meetings, began to sensitize us to the ways in which the members used the HMO for care of these ailments. That sensitivity derived from attention to the earlier dimensions of risk, etc. We concluded in our 19 June 1986 team meeting,

The same dimensions that characterized our earlier respondents' decision to seek care, e.g. *duration, severity, persistence, symptom intolerance*, or some *sense of risk* characterize the HMO members' decisions to search for care of the mundane ailment.

Analysis by respondent categories

Though previously delineated dimensions seemed to appear in the new data, in July 1984 we faced the critical question of how abstract our analysis should be. We saw that we needed general codes that would cut across all eight cases in each of the four groups of respondents (eight men and women with insurance on themselves and others, eight men and women with insurance only on themselves), using gender as an obvious dimension. On 23 July our team conference focused on these issues:

> How formal should we get? Is our goal simply to describe the groups of men and women in the sample? For our report to Maxi-Care [our sponsor] we can fall out somewhere between completely formal codes and an overly discursive kind of thing. In other words a general description of each of these groups versus analysis across and within our analytic dimensions or categories. The strategy that emerged is that we will delineate a couple of descriptors for each group and then see if we can blend them at a higher level above the raw data. The agenda for next time then is to characterize the four groups by certain questions (health history, taking care of self) using dimensions we've dealt with for years like persistence, risk, etc. We don't have to invent new categories.

A week later, when we gathered to review this exercise, our team meeting notes acknowledged that it was easier to describe what respondents do than to characterize them more abstractly. At that meeting our report of our exercise shows a very descriptive set of statements for the groups, but not the abstract conceptualizations we sought. This prompted a more thorough reading of each of the four groups (eight men with, eight men without coverage for others, eight women with and eight women without coverage for others).

To do this each team member took one of these groups and read each interview for that group of eight in its entirety, again looking for alteration of older dimensions or emergence of new. Each team member then wrote a memo on his or her respective group, summarizing the group question by question. Here is part of Droes's summary on the women with policies for self and others, showing the interplay of previously delineated dimensions in their reports of physician use:

> Respondents' assessment of *consequences* of self-care, preventive care, *tolerance* or *persistence* of symptoms influence their use of the physician.

In another summary on the men with policies only for themselves Olesen reported a new dimension – links to serious disease – a variation on the risk dimension and an addition to the respondents' biography as a part of the context schema:

> There is, however, a significant factor . . . the possibility that the mundane ailment might *portend* or be *linked* to Aids. A common ailment

linked to this dreaded disease would, as one man put it, 'quickly send me screaming to the doctor'.

Perhaps our sponsor would have been satisfied with these summaries, which described various types of policy-holders. We, however, looking ahead to the analysis of the non-HMO data, believed that it was necessary to achieve a higher order set of statements. We were also working on a series of papers for academic and professional audiences, using our entire data set, these and previous interviews. For that task we needed to step up from sheer description to conceptualization.

Analysis by question

We therefore undertook a more intensive analysis of our dimensions and schema. To this end, we logically clustered questions from the interview form and divided these clusters among the team members. Each member analyzed his or her cluster of questions in all thirty-two interviews and prepared what we called a 'co-ordinated summary'. Writing such a summary on questions related to HMO membership, persistent physical conditions, childhood health history and recent health history, Schatzman noted a new dimension or property, namely adjunctiveness, which refers to parallel use of self-care and health service care:

> for persistent problems there is intermittent medical and parallel or independent self-care . . . . In the overall process the respondents learn what doctors can do and what they themselves can do . . . given the failure of cure, the limitations of medicine and the relative success of self-management, this population places medicine in an *adjunctive* frame.

Here at last we had reached a higher-order abstraction which related to both self-care of the mundane ailment and use of services. This dimension, adjunctiveness, would later become critical in the analysis of the non-HMO members and the comparison of the members and non-members.

Final analysis of the HMO sample

At this point we exchanged our co-ordinated summaries and argued with one another regarding what each of us thought was affirmed, altered, undermined or added. Frequently, these lengthy team meetings involved pulling questions out of interviews and re-analyzing together as a group in order to reach agreement. This meant that we opted not for the descriptive mode of recounting how each of the four groups handled themselves, but for a more abstract, theoretical presentation. As a final step we gave each other writing assignments for sections of the report on the HMO members which related to our dimensions and schema (Olesen, Schatzman, Droes, Hatton and Chico 1985).

Here we utilized three dimensions of the efficacy of self-care which we had seen repeated in the data (limitations of respondents' expertise, technology available for self-care, tolerance of symptoms and consequentiality of self-care efforts). We also drew on several dimensions of the efficacy of medical care (benefits of early detection of underlying pathology, early management of conditions and the efficacy of medical therapeutics). The report answered the study's central question about HMO members' use or over-use of services:

> These men and women assess (1) efficacy of self-care and (2) the capability of medical science in deciding whether or not to use physician services. In none of the episodes which took the individual to the doctor, however, is there the slightest indication that they sought medical care instantly upon not feeling well. Quite to the contrary. If there is a single dramatic finding, it is that they tend to rely on their own judgements of their particular conditions and their self-care strategies. What brought them to the physician were conditions which they could no longer handle with their own self-care strategies or conditions which were unfamiliar, hence not easily managed.

The report also signalled some key attributes – personal responsibility and adjunctive use of services – which had emerged from the analysis:

> Once under care they used medicine in an adjunctive framework, mostly following the doctor's orders, but with some supplementing .... Their ethnotheories seemed to incorporate the idea that they were individually responsible for their health or illness and for attempting to manage ailments, but once within the medical care system, they saw themselves responsible for following orders in order to return to health.

In summary, in this phase at various points we analyzed as a group and then as individuals. The analytic strategies included two comparisons, across and within groups of respondents, and across and within groups of questions. These strategies entailed struggles over how descriptive or abstract our findings should be. The findings, oriented to a policy-minded sponsor, reflected both description and abstraction, but were also conceptualized to facilitate contribution to the social science and theoretically oriented nursing literature.

COLLABORATIVE ANALYSIS CONTINUED: THE NON-HMO SAMPLE

Slowly, much more slowly than we would have liked, the non-HMO interviews trickled in. To speed up the flow we inserted new advertisements for more respondents, renewed our efforts to be sure each contact generated an interview and urged our interviewers to move expeditiously on appointments for interviews. Because qualitative analysis encourages working back and forth between newly received and previously analyzed data, we began to analyze the non-HMO data as they came in, even as we were completing the HMO report for our sponsors. Our manœuvres were a general review of all non-HMO interviews, further analysis by questions, an attempt to break a stalemate, cluster analysis of dimensions and final comparisons. Here are the details on these steps:

General review

As they flowed in, we each read all available non-HMO interviews to see what, if any, general differences we could discern between the HMO and non-HMO samples on various dimensions and schemas generated earlier. Though few differences could be detected at first, some hints began to emerge, as reflected in this exchange among Chico, Droes and Olesen at a team meeting on 8 April 1985:

ND: I have a sense of a different flavor. I think we are talking about distinct groups of people. The use of alternative approaches in this group is more pronounced than in any so far.

NC: I wonder if that is tied in with the lack of insurance. Most of these non-HMOs don't have any insurance.

VO: ... people who would volunteer for this kind of study have an interest in self-care. Perhaps we're tapping the residues of the 1960s health movement.

NC: A reflection of our sampling?

VO: I think these people are even more of what we saw in the HMO members: they are monitoring constantly and are constantly aware of their care strategies.

ND: Is the awareness there because it is money out of their pocket to seek care?

VO: Cost is not all of it. One of our non-insured respondents said she could afford to go to the doctor, but still didn't do it .... I am now re-stating Nellie's point, that there is this incredible sense of responsibility in monitoring ailments that derives from a fundamental sense of responsibility, but also from the economic thing.

Our initial conceptualization of responsibility would later alter drastically as our analysis delved further into the non-HMO members' accounts to support or refute this finding. This is a good example of how themes or concepts which are viable at one point change when comparisons are made with later data. (See the following section, 'Further analysis by questions').

We then discussed at length the next analytic strategies to bring out these differences, questioning whether we should summarize by categories of respondents or by questions. We decided to cluster the questions as we had before, because the clusters provided points of comparison between the non-HMO and HMO member data. Each member read a cluster for the female non-HMO respondents, then compared those impressions with the co-ordinated summaries done for females on the same questions in the HMO analysis. This was later done for male respondents as well. Lest our efforts seem all too smooth, here is an extract from the notes of one team member who vividly described our anticipation and frustration as we began to work with the non-HMO data:

> I always have this reaction when approaching data, how in hell are we going to make sense? How do we ever get to the place we were with the analysis of the HMO members? It's always somewhat discouraging to approach the raw data initially.

At our 29 April meeting on this exercise we began to sharpen the comparisons between the HMO and non-HMO samples:

> Comparing them (the non-HMO respondents) to the HMO members on the dimension of self-care and the efficacy of medical science, there is not a sense that they are like the HMOs. They still rely on self-care. However, their calculus of risk is not the same .... One does not get the sense of advantage of early intervention that one does with the HMO group .... Is this related to lack of insurance? We need to break the non-HMOs into groups of those with fee-for-service insurance and those without insurance and compare those groups.

Further analysis by questions

Acting on our hunch at the 29 April meeting that we needed to look more closely at the non-HMOs in terms of whether they did or did not have insurance, we again clustered the questions as we had done in the earlier analysis. Each team member read and analyzed all non-HMO interviews on a specific cluster of questions to see if there were differences on dimensions or utilization between the insured and non-insured non-HMO members and between non-HMO members and the HMOs. When we met on 5 June 1985 we could find no differences between the insured and non-insured within the non-HMO sample. (The question of how to characterize both types of non-HMO respondents with a single typology continued to occupy us into early 1986 and will be discussed in detail shortly.)

At the same time we were still working on comparing the HMOs and non-HMOs. In June we tentatively started to confirm some themes that seemed to differentiate the non-HMO from the HMO members:

> ND: There is a sense that I did not get with the HMOs   .... This use of alternatives. There is acupuncture, a hypnotherapist, a strong use of alternatives. I don't get a sense of the linearity of self-care that leads in some cases to professional care.

vo: The linearity thing sounds real interesting ... the non-HMOs have all systems going at once: acupuncture, Gold Seal (a kind of herbal therapy), mental therapy.

DH: Their self-care is not as systematic. It is fragmented.

While we struggled with these differentiations, we were also deeply involved in data analysis for two conceptual papers for presentation and publication to research audiences in social science and nursing: one on the social psychology of managing ordinary ailments (Olesen, Schatzman, Droes, Hatton, Chico and Chesla 1985) and another on the surgical construction of reality (Hatton and Droes 1987). These papers did not focus on comparison of the HMO and non-HMO samples, but, rather, looked at specific conceptual issues in all data collected to date, for instance, the social psychology of body and self in the mundane ailment and in the more dramatic case of the ostomy. These exercises forced us to clarify these elements in our data in order to make them comprehensible to other audiences and to lift our concepts to the more theoretical levels expected of social science research reports. We returned to the work of comparing the samples for our HMO study sponsor in late winter and early spring of 1986.

By early summer of 1986 this analysis began to produce detailed differences between the samples, namely that the HMO members had a calculating approach to care and services, whereas the non-HMOs' use appeared haphazard at best. A team analytic memo of 2 June shows that our characteriza-tion of the sporadic and disjointed non-HMO approaches had become more abstract:

the non-HMO search for health care is episodic, arising when need does and involves brokering alternatives (acupuncture, etc.) for care. Their framework of relating to care givers is disjunctive rather than adjunctive.

More fully defined, these dimensions were: (1) adjunctive versus disjunctive use, referring to seeking out and co-operating with a health care professional versus not discussing ailments with providers and failing to follow orders; (2) episodic versus periodic, referring to incidental or sporadic use of services versus regular use for examinations, ailments, etc. These distinc-tions emerged again in the team meeting of 5 June 1986:

While the HMO members assess efficacy of self-care efforts and the capacity of medical science to determine whether they will use professional services, they seek attention when self-care no longer handles the situa-tion or the situation is unfamiliar ... the HMO structure which provides access to low cost services supports such calculation. With the non-HMOs one does *not* get the calculation or assessment that HMOs report .... In the non-HMOs' episodic approach to seeking services, there is no support for this type of calculation. Could it be that the HMO ideology actually teaches or supports self-care? Let's check this.

This last question would become a probe for further analysis. We also at this time, as the notes show, detected further differences, responsibility in caring for self, a change from the interpretation of a year before noted above, and abruptness in seeking formal care. This prompted additional re-analyses of previously formulated dimensions:

> While the HMOs frequently monitored ailments with considerable sophistication, the non-HMOs do not report in detail such behaviors. Rather, one gets a sense of an abrupt decision to seek care .... The non-HMOs lack the considered judgements regarding health that the HMOs demonstrated. There is cruder management of health, and in particular, self-care .... Unlike the HMO members' reports which show responsibility in managing one's illness with self-care prior to seeking professional help, this is not as evident in the non-HMO accounts. We need to re-read their accounts for the dimensions of severity, persistence and consequentiality which we have seen to be related to self-care and seeking help.

Analysis blinded, analysis liberated

Late in the summer of 1986 we were floundering. Self-care and use of services were linked, but within our non-HMO sample we could not make sense of the patterns of those who did and did not have insurance. We could not seem to find a way in which we could compare these subgroups with the HMO members in our first analysis.

Later it became clear that our emphasis on the link between the type of coverage or insurance the non-HMO respondents did or did not have and their use of services blinded our analysis. This blinkering was probably a consequence of our focus on the study question (How are services used by those with and without insurance?). It may also have reflected the tenacity of our earlier analyses which described episodic and disjunctive dimensions of use and implicitly linked these to lack of insurance.

Droes's methodological memo of 15 August 1986 provided a breakthrough. Rather than looking at the adjunctive–disjunctive and episodic–periodic dimensions of the non-HMOs' use *as related to insurance status*, she put aside respondents' insurance status. She then re-categorized all non-HMO respondents using only two criteria: a recent visit to a health provider and health providers' services being used by respondents adjunctively, periodically, etc. She then intersected these dimensions so that the cases, without regard to insurance status, could be deftly and parsimoniously located within the four quadrants created by the dimensions intersecting one another (see Figure 6.1).

This broke our stalemate, for it became clear that there were diverse patterns. In the episodic–disjunctive quadrant (upper right) we found,

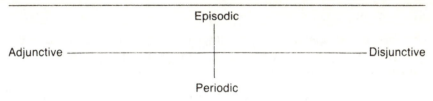

Figure 6.1 Use of health care providers

not surprisingly, a predominance of our non-insured respondents, but we also found those with fee-for-service insurance in this quadrant. Conversely, in the adjunctive–episodic quadrant, the upper left, we saw both non-insured and fee-for-service respondents. Thus, some individuals who were insured acted disjunctively and episodically, while those without insurance and who, for instance, used emergency rooms, behaved in an adjunctive and periodic manner.

To break our analytic stalemate, it was necessary to depart from our solidly entrenched thinking on insurance and literally to reshuffle the analytic process. This breakthrough led to reaffirmation of a higher-order set of categories based on respondent reports, e.g. adjunctive–disjunctive, periodic–episodic. These could be used more productively to characterize respondents rather than the lower-order attribute of the presence or absence or type of insurance. That had not only been unproductive but, as we have shown, blinding.

Analysis of clusters

It still remained to link self-care with the intersecting dimensions of adjunctiveness and periodicity noted above. Here we each took clusters or themes and examined cases in the quadrants to discern differences or similarities. Finding such differences was to prove more elusive than we anticipated, as is suggested in Olesen's memo of 22 August 1986:

> Nellie's memo [Droes, mentioned above] of August 15 led me to resort all the cases into the four quadrants of the use table [Figure 6.1] and read all cases in each quadrant for trust in the body simply to see if there were any discernible differences. No distinctive themes emerged that can be tied to particular groups; rather some of our familiar themes, e.g. relationship of trust in self to trust in body appear in all groups. It is more likely that trust and styles and types of self-care are related in a complex way with the patterns of provider use that we have identified. We will have to examine this carefully when we integrate our analysis for the final report.

We then met again as a team, argued and debated over our findings in this thematic analysis. Where disagreements arose, individuals had to sustain their position or criticisms with both data and logic. Where agreements occurred, sharp questioning forced those agreeing to document their agreement. Each team member then wrote a section for the final report on his or her themes.

Final comparisons

Our final step was to compare the HMO and non-HMO samples along the five questions set out at the beginning of the study. Here is our answer to the key question of differences in self-care practices (Olesen *et al*. 1987):

> We find no striking differences. Both samples have well-tested strategies for managing mundane ailments, using palliative remedies, consulting others (not providers), evaluating the efficacy of their efforts, using tolerance of symptoms, limits to their own expertise and anticipated consequences as guides. The difference between the samples seems to lie in the departure from self-care strategies to use of services, for the HMO members moved smoothly to use HMO services, whereas the non-HMOs used services impetuously and in some instances after considerable delay. On the basis of this very small sample, we conclude that HMO members linked their self-care practices to their HMO membership, albeit very conservatively, for we were impressed with the extent to which they first relied on self-care practices. The non-HMOs, both those with and without insurance, did not seem to tie self-care to provider services.

CONCLUSION

As is true in all qualitative work, our goal was to raise the respondents' comments, whilst respecting the integrity of those comments, to a higher order of abstraction or generality that reflected the patterning seen in the comments. In part we could realize this because of our long mutual immersion in the study of self-care. That immersion honed our analytic skills, and also provided a safeguard against any team member, faculty or not, dominating the analysis or manipulating agreement; others simply knew too much and too well the subtleties of self-care ethnography readily to agree even on non-problematic categories or themes.

What did we learn from our collective experience? The enduring necessity to be unremittingly and relentlessly reflexive was borne in on us time and again, as we stumbled through some parts of our analysis, but anticipated others. Equally important, we thought, was the capacity to be flexible, to look around the corners and beyond some of our dimensions and conceptions and not to shy away from mixing analytic styles and modes, being careful, of course, to heed to exactly what we were doing. In particular, when stalemates loomed we discovered the importance of having the courage to reshuffle the data and to shelve once-important themes in order to break through to more productive categories and analyses. Lastly, we found that we could be systematic without being rigid, we could achieve reliability without forcing the data, we could realize plausibility without torturing ourselves or our data. Some of our styles and strategies could be applied in another study where further innovative analytic tactics, as they inevitably do in qualitative work, would emerge.

NOTE

We acknowledge with appreciation our funding sources: the Division of Nursing Resources, US Public Health Service; the Academic Senate Research Committee of the University of California, San Francisco; the Maxi-Care Foundation; the School of Nursing Research Committee, UCSF. Also participating were David Barrows, Kit Chesla, Katerin Jurich, Marvin Prosono, Joan von Ruden, Barbara Sackoff-Lampert, Robin Saltonstall, Norman Trondsen and Irma Zuckerman.

REFERENCES

Bresnen, M. (1988) 'Insights on site: research into construction project organizations', in A. Bryman (ed.) *Doing Research in Organizations*, London: Routledge.

Burgess, R.G. (1984) *In the Field: an Introduction to Field Research*, London: Allen & Unwin.

Denzin, N. (1978) *The Research Act: a Theoretical Introduction to Social Research*, 2nd edn, New York: McGraw-Hill.

Finch, J. and Mason, J. (1990) 'Decision-taking in the fieldwork process: theoretical sampling and collaborative working', in R.G. Burgess (ed.) *Studies in Qualitative Methodology*, vol. 2, *Reflections on Field Experience*, London: JAI Press.

Glaser, B.G. and Strauss, A.L. (1967) *The Discovery of Grounded Theory: Strategies for Qualitative Research*, Chicago: Aldine.

Hatton, D. (1990) 'Enhancing research through perspective interaction', unpublished paper presented at the Society for Applied Anthropology, York.

Hatton, D. and Droes, N. (1987) 'Surgical reconstruction of reality: trajectories in reconstructing a self following ostomy surgery', unpublished paper presented at the Association for Behavioral Sciences and Medical Education, Fallen Leaf Lake, California.

Latour, B. and Woolgar, S. (1986) *Laboratory Life: the Social Construction of Scientific Facts*, 2nd edn, Princeton, NJ: Princeton University Press.

Lofland, J. and Lofland, L.H. (1984) *Analyzing Social Settings: a Guide to Qualitative Observation and Analysis*, Belmont, Calif.: Wadsworth.

Olesen, V. (1988) 'Plausibility, credibility and adequacy in contemporary ethnography', unpublished paper presented at the Mid-West Sociological Association, Chicago, Illinois.

—— (1992) 'The extraordinary context and the mundane ailment: the contextual dialectics of the embodied self', in C. Ellis and M. Flaherty (eds) *Windows on Lived Experience: Research on Subjectivity*, Newbury Park, Calif.: Sage.

Olesen, V. and Schatzman, L. (1982) 'Trust in the body: notes on the embodied character of mundane ailments', unpublished paper presented at the British Sociological Association meeting, Manchester.

Olesen, V., Schatzman, L., Droes, N., Hatton, D. and Chico, N. (1985) 'HMO membership and self-care practices, part I: Analysis of the HMO members', report to the Maxi-Care Foundation of Hawthorne, California.

—— (1987) 'HMO membership and self-care practices, part II: Analysis of the non-HMO respondents' interviews', report to the Maxi-Care Foundation of Hawthorne, California.

—— (1989) 'The mundane ailment and the physical self: analysis of the social psychology of health and illness', *Social Science and Medicine* 30: 449–55.

Olesen, V., Schatzman, L., Droes, N., Hatton, D., Chico, N. and Chesla, K. (1985) 'Ordinary people, ordinary ailments: conceptual increments from a study of ethnocare', unpublished paper presented at the Social Science and Medicine Conference, Korpalampi, Finland.

Schatzman, L. (1990) 'Dimensional analysis: notes on an alternative approach to the grounding of theory in qualitative research' in D. Maines (ed.) *Social Organization and Social Process: Essays in Honor of Anselm Strauss*, Hawthorne, NY: Aldine de Gruyter.

Spradley, J. (1979) *The Ethnographic Interview*, New York: Holt, Rinehart & Winston.

Stacey, M. (1986) 'From being a native to becoming a researcher: Meg Stacey and the GMC', unpublished paper, Department of Sociology, University of Warwick.

Strauss, A. and Corbin, J. (1990) *Basics of Qualitative Research*, Newbury Park, Calif.: Sage.

Van Maanen, J. (1991) 'Playing back the tape: early days in the field', in W.B. Shaffir and R.A. Stebbins (eds) *Experiencing Fieldwork: an Inside View of Qualitative Research*, Newbury Park, Calif.: Sage.

Wiseman, J. (1987) 'The development of generic concepts in qualitative research through cumulative application', *Qualitative Sociology* 10: 318–38.

Chapter 7

Four studies from one or one study from four?
Multi-site case study research

*Robert G. Burgess, Christopher J. Pole,
Keith Evans and Christine Priestley*

The terms 'fieldwork' and 'field research' have an omnibus quality to them. In common with many aspects of qualitative research they cover various elements of the research process: gaining access, the selection of sites, the collection and analysis of data, and strategies associated with reporting and disseminating data. Yet each of these aspects of the research process is not discrete, for each phase of qualitative research has implications for another. The choice of research questions has implications for the topics and themes of data analysis. The selection of research sites will have implications not only for data collection, but also for the data that are available for analysis and dissemination. Clearly, these are issues which demand exploration in the context of a qualitative project so that the relationship between data analysis and other aspects of the research process can be examined.

At the heart of this chapter is a project on the introduction of a Records of Achievement scheme into Warwickshire secondary schools. While this was a qualitative study, it was far from 'typical', being based on a multi-site investigation, using a team of four researchers. In the account which follows, we go back to the origins of the project, as issues of project sponsorship, project staffing and site selection all had different parts to play in the issues and topics which were pursued in the analysis of data.

THE WARWICKSHIRE RECORDS OF ACHIEVEMENT PROJECT

During the 1980s there was a considerable policy debate in the UK about styles and strategies for recording student achievement in secondary schools. As a consequence of these debates, a considerable literature developed around the topics 'profiling' and 'Records of Achievement' (Broadfoot 1986, Burgess and Adams 1985, Evans 1988, Garforth and Macintosh 1986). Much of this literature was prescriptive in tone, and suggested ways of promoting and implementing Records of Achievement. Empirical studies were few, apart from national evaluations that had been conducted on behalf of the Department of Education and Science (PRAISE 1987, 1988, 1991) and small-scale studies conducted by individual teachers working alone or in small interrelated groups. This area of educational development was therefore ripe for research.

When Warwickshire local education authority (LEA) approached Burgess in 1987 to conduct an authority-wide study of the implementation of Records of Achievement in its secondary schools, no such study existed. While members of the local authority wished to provide financial support for the study, it was only sufficient for one researcher to work across the LEA over two years. Accordingly, Burgess suggested that a more detailed study could be achieved if the local authority was prepared to second a teacher to the project for two years.

Initially, this was to be one teacher over two years, but a subsequent decision by the local authority resulted in two different teachers (Evans and Priestley) being seconded to the project to work with Burgess and Pole (who was the full-time researcher) for one year each.

At one level, it could be argued that this discussion relates more to the politics of research sponsorship than to data analysis, but we would argue that the resources which were made available influenced project design, the selection of research sites, research questions and, in turn, the analysis of data.

With a team of four, Burgess agreed that a study of the introduction of Records of Achievement into Warwickshire schools could take the form of a multi-site case study in which two schools could be studied by Pole and one school each by Evans and Priestley. In addition to the four case study reports, each one of which would be produced by a case study worker (Evans 1989, Pole 1989, 1991, Priestley 1990), there would also be a thematic report for which Burgess would have executive responsibility with other members of the team (Burgess *et al.* 1991). In this respect, a number of issues that were pertinent to data analysis had been resolved at the outset of the project. They were:

1 Four school case studies were to be conducted, two by Pole and one each by Evans and another teacher, Priestley.
2 The topics and themes to be studied would not merely be determined by social science and sociological concerns, but by professional issues that were of interest to teachers (cf. Oja and Smulyan 1989).
3 Issues concerning selection and sampling would be crucial to the project, so as to facilitate cross-site comparisons.

In these ways, the initial aspects of the project held implications not only for data collection, but also for data analysis. The remaining parts of this chapter will therefore deal with issues of selection and the treatment of analytic themes within the case studies. However, it will be noted that Burgess was joined by Pole and by Evans in year one, with the latter being replaced by Priestley in year two. Accordingly, it was Burgess, Pole and Evans who determined the selection of case study schools in year one of the project, and they were also responsible for the selection of case study themes. While Priestley was willing to work within this framework, she also built upon the analytic themes and added to them in year two.

THE SELECTION OF CASE STUDY SITES

The opportunity to work in Warwickshire local education authority provided an arena in which the impact of Records of Achievement could be studied in a range of different secondary schools. Warwickshire is an LEA which includes urban and rural areas, has both selective and non-selective secondary schools in these different areas, and offers a range of schools with differences in social class, gender and race. The complexity of secondary education in Warwickshire therefore provides an interesting problem for fieldworkers whose resources only permit four schools to be studied.

The project required an approach which focused on the processes involved in reporting and recording pupil progress. To this end, it was important to view the use and development of Records of Achievement, not only in the context of LEA support for them, but more important, in the context of the individual schools within which they were being developed. In this respect, to provide the required level of detail and to look at the Records of Achievement holistically within the school, a case-study approach was adopted, which would enable the researchers to spend one term in each school, working with teachers and pupils, observing, and where possible, participating in activities relating to the Record of Achievement process. The case was, therefore, identified as the Records of Achievement within the school in which it was located.

The problem of selection had two related aspects. First, there was the question of how the four sites should be identified; second, on what criteria should they be selected. If it was the intention that the schools selected should be representative of the twenty-two secondary schools in Warwickshire, then it would have involved a large number of schools, given the different types of schooling available within the authority.

However, as is often the case with contract research (cf. Burgess 1989, 1991), the level of funding available from the LEA for the project meant there was a limit to the number of sites in which the work could be conducted. Logistically, the number of staff available also limited the number of schools which could be included as case studies. Ultimately, the funding and logistical considerations, when placed alongside the requirements for a detailed case-study approach which focused on social processes, meant that four schools could be selected for the project.

The schools finally selected were not representative of Warwickshire secondary schools in general, but were nevertheless illustrative of the range of schools which existed within the authority in 1988. The principles of selection involved may in some respects be seen as the kind of compromise which is common in research, allowing research and evaluation to be conducted rigourously, yet within the parameters of a specified budget (cf. Bryman 1988).

The key characteristics of all twenty-two secondary schools eligible for the research were considered by Pole and Evans, who engaged in discussions with LEA personnel about the extent to which Records of Achievement had been developed in individual schools. Initial data collection about the key characteristics of Warwickshire secondary schools had to be examined. In this respect, preliminary data analysis on school characteristics and the implementation process associated with Records of Achievement was central to the selection process. It was these data which Burgess, Pole and Evans used in order to select four schools. The criteria upon which the selection was based were: location (i.e. urban or rural), size of secondary school (i.e. number of pupils on roll), secondary school type (i.e. comprehensive, grammar or secondary modern), social class composition (as described by LEA staff) and the prevalence of ethnic minority pupils (as described by LEA staff).

The four schools incorporated variants of these social characteristics in the following way:

Benton School:	Small, rural, secondary modern, coeducational, predominantly white, working-class pupils.
Four Ways School:	Large, urban, comprehensive, coeducational, multi-ethnic, working-class pupils.
Herbert Marshall School:	Medium size, urban, grammar school, single sex (boys), predominantly white, middle class.
Rowan Hill School:	Large, urban comprehensive, coeducational, predominantly white, middle class.

Underlying the social criteria upon which selection was made was also the question of the degree to which the school had been exposed to, or had developed a Record of Achievement scheme prior to the start of our project. Although Warwickshire had developed a county scheme over the previous five years, use of it had not been mandatory. Consequently, the extent to which it had been adopted varied considerably from school to school. In the four case study schools, the following pattern was evident:

Benton School:	Five years' experience of Records of Achievement, an initial pilot school for the Warwickshire scheme, well-developed programme through the school. Records of Achievement are the main reporting mechanism.
Four Ways School:	Some development, though no clear policy.
Herbert Marshall School:	Limited development with fifth-year pupils during one academic year.
Rowan Hill School:	Scheme in existence for 2–3 years, under review and being developed throughout the school.

An overview of the four sites reveals that collectively they incorporated many of the social and educational characteristics of Warwickshire schools generally, and with relation to the introduction of the Warwickshire Records of Achievement scheme in particular.

The criteria upon which the four schools were selected are summarized in Table 7.1.

Table 7.1 The four case study schools

Benton	Four Ways	Rowan Hill	Herbert Marshall
Small	Large	Large	Medium sized
Rural	Urban	Urban	Urban
Secondary	Comprehensive	Comprehensive	Grammar (boys)
White	Multi-ethnic	White	White
Working class	Working class	Middle class	Middle class
High develop- ment of Records of Achievement (5 years)	Some develop- ment of Records of Achievement	Some develop- ment of Records of Achievement (2-3 years)	Limited develop- ment of Records of Achievement (1 year)

This table highlights the kinds of comparisons that could be made between:

(a) urban and rural schools,
(b) selective and non-selective schools,
(c) schools serving predominantly working-class and middle-class groups,
(d) all white and multi-ethnic schools.

In addition, consideration had been given to the range of experience with the Warwickshire Records of Achievement scheme (with Herbert Marshall having little experience and Benton much experience, with the other two schools coming between). Accordingly, this selection of case study schools influenced the key analytic categories that were to be used in this study.

For example, the inclusion of urban and rural schools had implications for the way in which the schools approached that part of the Record of Achievement which focused on out-of-school activities. Often those pupils from the rural areas did not enjoy the same variety of leisure activities as their peers from urban areas. The size of the school was considered to be important as far as teacher–pupil relations were concerned, and the extent to which teachers and pupils could get to know each other. This had particular consequences for the emphasis which was placed on teacher–pupil dialogue for Records of Achievement. On the basis of this range of schools, issues of race and gender in relation to the identification and recognition of achievement could also be addressed, as could the broader question of social class. Similarly, the inclusion of selective and non-selective schools enabled achievement to be viewed in relation to perceived academic ability according to the

LEA's annual 12 + examination. In this way, the research team considered analytic categories at the time they selected the schools.

In total, the four schools provided sufficient scope for a comprehensive picture of the operation and development of Records of Achievement within Warwickshire to be developed. It was our intention, however, to produce a series of case studies which raised and discussed important issues in relation to Records of Achievement within a variety of different contexts. In this way, heads and teachers could read the case studies and appreciate the specific context in which the data were collected. It was our view that these case studies could be used to facilitate the development of Records of Achievement, not by prescription, but by practitioners reading and using the findings of the studies within the context of their own schools. This was also to be assisted by the production of a thematic report which would generalize about the processes associated with Records of Achievement that had been identified within and across the four schools.

We have already indicated that in our view, a key aspect of a multi-site case study is the selection of individual sites. However, this is only one aspect of the research process contributing to the data analytic procedures. Accordingly, we now turn to the four cases in which we highlight the research topics and themes which were covered, before returning to the whole study. By way of illustration we highlight the comparisons that could be made between the non-selective Benton School and the selective Herbert Marshall School, which were both studied by Pole, before turning to the coeducational comprehensive schools studied by Evans and Priestley.

TAKING FOUR SCHOOLS

Benton School

Of the four schools included in the Warwickshire Records of Achievement project, Benton School was the one with by far the greatest experience of the scheme. The school was well known in the LEA for its association with Records of Achievement, having been an initial pilot institution for Warwickshire for five years. The head enjoyed a reputation as something of an expert on the implications and development of the scheme. In this respect, Benton School offered a standard against which other schools could judge themselves, and be judged, as they developed their own Records of Achievement.

From the outset, we were encouraged to include Benton School in our study by advisers from the LEA, who wanted an independent view of the school and its scheme. In terms of our selection procedures, however, the inclusion of the school could only be justified on the same grounds as any other school, namely, in accordance with the criteria specified earlier, and not because the officers and advisers from the LEA thought it would be a 'good idea' or that the school was an example of 'good practice'. The reasons for including Benton

School therefore related to its size, its location and its experience of Records of Achievement. These factors combined to provide a set of circumstances which were sociologically interesting in relation to the development of Records of Achievement, and from which several other secondary schools in Warwickshire and elsewhere could draw guidance. The inclusion of this school related to the analysis we wanted to develop.

The language of Records of Achievement pervaded many of the school's activities (cf. Pole 1989); pupils and teachers accepted it as part of everyday life. Here was an opportunity to study a school where Records of Achievement were not novel, but a regular part of school business. On the basis of his initial observations, Pole decided that he needed to examine the extent to which the integration of Records of Achievement went beyond the rhetoric of the head and senior staff, and actually affected the experiences of pupils, classroom teachers and parents. Much of the literature developed around Records of Achievement was speculative and policy focused (see Broadfoot 1986, DES 1984, James 1989, Stansbury 1985), as it emphasized the far-reaching effects of Records of Achievement in terms of their potential to bring about wide-scale change in many different areas of education. In Benton School lay the possibility of 'testing out' many of the claims made in the literature, as it was a school where Records of Achievement had existed for a number of years, and where their existence and the demands which they made were in many respects taken for granted by teachers and pupils.

Being a small school with 288 pupils and 17 teachers, it was often asserted (by heads and teachers from larger schools) that Benton School had been able to implement Records of Achievement more easily than larger institutions. Given that the scheme is dependent for its success upon communication between teachers and pupils, a small school in which most staff taught all pupils at some stage during their time in the school would perhaps be deemed particularly conducive to the demands of Records of Achievement. Here, these assertions could be 'tested out' and a context was provided within which questions about communications within small schools more generally could be posed. Allied to this was the rural location, which allowed Pole to examine whether geographical location had a significant effect on the pupils' out-of-school activities, and which of these are thought 'worthy' or 'appropriate' by teachers to include in a Record of Achievement. In these ways Benton School allowed the team to make comparisons with other schools located in urban or suburban districts.

Benton School was a secondary high school (equivalent to a secondary modern), which meant that its pupils were not among the 20 per cent selected for a grammar school education through the 12 + examination in Warwickshire. In this respect, it was a site which allowed Pole to examine definitions of achievement held by teachers so that the team could contrast these with definitions held in the comprehensive and grammar schools in the study. Associated with this was the use to which the summative Document of Record (issued to pupils during their fifth year prior to leaving the school) was put by

Benton School pupils and the status which they accorded it in relation to examination passes, references and other traditional material assembled for use in the job-finding process (see Ashforth 1990). Again this allowed the team to make comparisons between Benton School and the other schools as to the reputation which they enjoyed in the local labour market, the aspirations of the pupils and the expectations of the staff. In Herbert Marshall School for example, the summative Document of Record seemed likely to have little relevance or status with fifth-year pupils, the majority of whom intended to remain in full-time education, at least for a further two years. In Benton School, however, many school leavers expressed intentions to use their Documents of Record, which in the absence of public examination passes could portray them in a positive light to potential employers (see Stronach 1989).

Generally, therefore, Benton School, when viewed beside the other schools, enabled us to pose questions about school size and location, about selective education and the ability and achievements of pupils, and about leaving school and the search for work. All of the questions were addressed in connection with the Record of Achievement but again the comparative case study approach meant that they were a resource which went beyond issues relating to reporting and recording pupil achievement. However, as far as the scheme itself went, the fact that Benton School had a programme in operation that had been accepted in all years enabled us to examine critically many of the claims made for Records of Achievement in the policy-making literature.

Overall, the strength of the study rested in its comparative nature. The research design facilitated the examination of a wide range of substantive educational issues in different contexts. Similarly, the different contexts also gave rise to the examination of issues which were not apparent either in the literature or in the rhetoric of Records of Achievement.

Herbert Marshall School

Herbert Marshall School was selected for inclusion in the study as it provided an example of an all boys grammar school of medium size located in a market town. The school drew on a wide catchment area and the pupils were predominantly white and from middle-class homes. Since the boys were selected by the 12 + examination the staff inevitably perceived them as above average academically.

As far as exposure to Records of Achievement was concerned, Herbert Marshall School provided an opportunity to study the scheme in a context where relatively little development had occurred. During the previous academic year, some small changes in the reporting and recording system had been introduced to the school and then fourth-year pupils began to follow a limited Records of Achievement programme. So the school had begun to adopt Records of Achievement, but had chosen to adapt them to suit the pupils and the organization of the school. Herbert Marshall School was, therefore, an interesting place in which to study the gradual integration of Records of Achievement throughout a school, and to examine the processes and procedures developed which were thought most appropriate for such a school.

The reason for selecting Herbert Marshall School was that it would answer a range of questions about the operation, meaning and suitability for a grammar school of the Records of Achievement scheme. For example, much has been made of the applicability of Records of Achievement for pupils of all abilities (see Burgess and Adams 1985, DES 1984, Hitchcock 1986). In Herbert Marshall School there was an opportunity to examine the impact, perceived relevance and suitability of Records of Achievement for pupils of above average ability who were attending a school placing a high premium on academic success and scholarship.

Prior to the introduction of the Record of Achievement, Herbert Marshall School had relied on traditional methods of school reports (cf. Goacher and Reid 1984) as the principal means of communicating information about pupil progress to parents. Traditional reports, unlike Record of Achievement, were merely documents completed by teachers. They were documents about the pupils rather than documents for the pupils, produced with their co-operation. Studying the scheme within this context allowed the examination not merely of the operation of a new reporting and recording programme, but also of the challenges and changes it presented.

Questions were posed about the role of the teacher and his or her authority. Involving pupils in the reporting process, encouraging them to reflect critically on their own performances and on that of their teachers, had the potential to challenge teachers, particularly those who saw their role as that of an instructor who was beyond such challenges. The traditional grammar school also enabled questions about authority and power to be posed. In so doing, such questions went beyond the introduction to the Record of Achievement, to address issues at the heart of the teaching and learning process. The grammar school context also allowed questions about achievement to be examined. The Record of Achievement attributed importance to all kinds of achievement (see DES 1984, RANSC 1989), not merely academic. In the context of an academically selective school which placed a primacy on success in public examinations, it was possible to examine which kinds of non-academic activities were deemed worthy of inclusion in a Record of Achievement, and which were not. What was deemed appropriate behaviour, and what were seen as worthy achievements, was also raised in analyzing data from this school.

Herbert Marshall School helped us to conduct an investigation related to gender. Being all male in terms of pupils, and predominantly male in terms of staff, the school placed emphasis on what might commonly be described as 'macho' activities and qualities; for example, the game of rugby was seen as important not only for exercise but also for character formation. There was also a general air of 'getting things done' within the school. The emphasis was on 'doing' rather than talking. Again, here was a context in which to study Records of Achievement which place great importance on talking and retrospection. Encouraging pupils to talk about emotions and feelings, for example, was something which was not common. In this respect Records of Achievement would be viewed as a scheme that presented a challenge to school norms, and to aspects of school organization, both being themes which were analyzed in this study.

Herbert Marshall School therefore offered a means by which a range of issues could be studied. The criteria on which the school was selected for inclusion in the project enabled data to be collected on issues which related directly to the Record of Achievement, its development and operation, and in doing so it also provided an opportunity to look at issues of power, status, gender and definitions of achievement within the school. This school provided a context within which these issues could be examined and subsequently compared with other case study schools.

Four Ways School

This school was selected to give a contrast with the rural location of Benton School, the single-sex intake of Herbert Marshall School, and the predominantly white middle-class catchment area surrounding Rowan Hill School. In addition, Four Ways School was the only school among our four case studies to have a multi-ethnic pupil population.

Four Ways School was studied by Evans at the same time Pole was conducting a case-study of Benton School. Here it was important that both case-study workers focused on similar issues concerning the introduction of Records of Achievement, yet it was also important to highlight issues that were particular to this case, and could be subsequently explored through data collection and analysis in the other case studies.

Evans, who was one of the teachers on the project, focused on the data from his case study that had been collected from teachers. He found that the topic of 'time' emerged as a key issue, because teachers saw that Records of Achievement accounted for increased amounts of time in their work-loads and had implications for their roles. Accordingly, by looking at the way in which teachers talked about time, it was possible to examine the Records of Achievement scheme from a different perspective. In particular, Evans found that time had implications for the Records of Achievement process, including the discussions between pupils and teachers, and the negotiation that occurred. Furthermore, time was also important in relation to completing the documentation and obtaining a finished product (the Document of Record).

Allocation of time also had an impact upon school organization as the school closed earlier, and the school day was re-organized in order that discussions between pupils and teachers could take place for the Record of Achievement. Time as an issue took the researcher into the heartland of the project by addressing school organization and the teaching–learning process. It also allowed Evans to pose questions about the extent to which the traditional pattern of school organization facilitated teacher–pupil interaction for the purposes of Records of Achievement. Furthermore, it led him to examine the involvement of the head and the governors of the school in the introduction of Records of Achievement.

From these data, Evans was able to explain aspects of management and policy-making, as well as definitions of achievement. In this way, he was able to complement the work being done by Pole in Benton School, but here he focused on the Records of Achievement co-ordinator and that individual's role within the school system. In particular, Evans utilized the teacher data in his case study to examine substantive issues of concern from a teacher's point of view, as well as data that would lead to further exploration of abstract matters, such as definitions of achievement. This study therefore facilitated the development of issues that Pole had identified, but also other topics such as 'time' that were examined in the other case studies. Altogether data from Evans's study allowed further comparisons to be made, which would contribute to the thematic report where key themes from all the studies could be explored (see Burgess *et al.* 1991).

Rowan Hill School

Rowan Hill School was studied by Priestley. Throughout this case study the emphasis was upon issues that could be examined from a teacher's perspective (in common with Evans) as well as upon those themes that had been identified in the other case studies. The issues were identified by staff and students in the school. The questions posed by the researcher were against the background of two major propositions. First, the level of integration of Records of Achievement practices within the overall teaching and learning process was crucial to determining the continued effectiveness of such schemes. Second, recording schemes were as dependent upon the personal resources (staff and students) as upon material resources. The questions which Priestley posed were designed to highlight the level of commitment to Records of Achievement amongst staff and students.

By the time Priestley came to conduct this case study, she was building upon the earlier studies conducted by Pole and by Evans. In particular, her study drew upon teacher and pupil perceptions of Records of Achievement. Like Evans, she was also interested in all aspects of the management and co-ordination of the Records of Achievement process. Accordingly, she focused her study on these aspects, which in turn led to the analysis of time management in the school generally, and in relation to recording achievement specifically. Similarly, Priestley's analysis allowed an examination of discussions and negotiations between teachers and pupils which in turn fed into the work which Pole and Evans had conducted, and also shed new light on the ways in which achievement was defined, and power was utilized during teacher–pupil discussion.

In this respect, Priestley's study, like those conducted by Pole and Evans, took up issues which were perceived as central to the Record of Achievement process. In addition, Priestley followed up specific areas of interest such as equal opportunities and the practicalities of recording through the use of log books, which were key instruments in the recording process. In this way, Priestley's work facilitated the elaboration of further themes as well as consolidating those that had been examined in the other studies.

Among the key issues which were explored in all studies was time, a topic to which we now turn to explore the way in which a subject was developed within and between case studies.

TIME AND RECORDS OF ACHIEVEMENT

Each of the case studies demonstrated that an important element in the development and implementation of Records of Achievement was the availability of time for reporting and recording procedures. In particular, time for one-to-one teacher–pupil discussion was central to Records of Achievement in each school. From early discussions with both school and LEA staff it became clear that the availability, use and allocation of time was central to the Warwickshire Records of Achievement and would need to be explored in each case study.

The recognition of this crucial element in the Records of Achievement process enabled us to ask a number of different questions in the schools and to analyze time allocation, timetabling and other organizational arrangements. For example, the initial research suggested that the amount of time that headteachers, and other school policy-makers were prepared to commit to Record of Achievement was an indication of the status and importance that was attributed to them, or at least by those making decisions about priorities within the school (Pole 1992). To consider the perceived importance or status of the Record of Achievement it was essential to collect not only those data that related to the amount of time given to the programme in each school, but also to consider how time was allocated and used. We were concerned to consider the place of Records of Achievement activities on the school timetable, any special arrangements made to accommodate them, the time spent on these activities by staff of different status, and the allocation of incentive allowances to develop and manage the process. The topic 'time' led us into a series of questions that had implications for the collection and analysis of data.

By looking at issues relating to the wider implications of time allocation we could begin to construct an analysis of Records of Achievement which went beyond mere description and placed them in the context of, for example, curriculum development, whole school reporting and recording procedures, timetabling, resourcing, the integration of reporting with teaching and learning, and issues of power and control. The way in which each of the four schools approached time allocation for Record of Achievement could be used as a key to analyzing a range of sociological issues which were identified as centrally important to the process of recording achievement in the schools. For example, in Benton School all pupils received a half-hour of one-to-one discussion with their form tutor to consider their Record of Achievement, followed by a twenty-minute follow-up meeting with the same tutor later in the year to discuss progress. The significance of this approach was in the timetabled allocation of time on a regular basis for the Record of Achievement process. For both teacher and pupil the one-to-one discussion sessions became an integral part of reporting and recording procedures and ultimately of the experience of schooling. For staff, particularly those acting as personal tutor for twenty-eight pupils, the discussion sessions came to be an important aspect of their work-load. The timetabling of the sessions for all pupils and all form tutors was an indication of the commitment to Record of Achievement made by the head and other senior staff. Furthermore, time was allocated for discussion purposes throughout the school year and one-to-one sessions became part of staff timetables on a daily basis. In Benton School Record of Achievement were central not only to reporting and recording pupil progress, but also to much of the child-centred teaching and learning philosophies which underpinned the approach to education. They had high status in the school, and were attributed considerable importance; this was demonstrated by the time commitment to them. Focusing on time therefore led into analyses of other aspects of schooling which linked to the processes associated with recording achievement.

Herbert Marshall School took a different approach to Record of Achievement and the allocation of time to them. For example, the programme was introduced to the pupils from the fourth year onwards. At the time of the research, they were not part of the lower school reporting procedures. For fourth- and fifth-year pupils one-to-one discussion sessions were organized as part of a Record of Achievement week in the summer term, when teaching demands on staff were lower owing to the public examination programme. During this week all fourth- and fifth-year pupils underwent a thirty-minute discussion session with their form tutors. The blocking of the Record of Achievement activities into the period of one week enabled the staff to dispense with the process in a short period of time and to ensure that it did not detract from the academic pursuits upon which the school's reputation had been established and in which many of the staff took pride.

To draw the sociological and educational significance from these observations the different approaches to time and Records of Achievement need to be set in the context of the two sites. Benton School was a secondary high school (equivalent to a secondary modern school) whilst Herbert Marshall was a secondary grammar school. In Benton School a very positive view of Records of Achievement was held by the head and many staff. Investment of time in Records of Achievement was seen to pay dividends in pupil–teacher relations, the development of interpersonal and social skills, enhanced pupil motivation and improved pupil behaviour. The Records of Achievement scheme was integral to the activities of the school. In Herbert Marshall School there was support for the scheme as an additional activity which could prove useful for some pupils, rather than as an integral part of the teaching and learning process. Any time spent on Records of Achievement was carefully calculated not to impinge upon time for the academic content of the curriculum, hence the blocking of discussion sessions at a time when the normal timetable had been suspended for public examinations.

Although both schools spent equivalent amounts of time on Records of Achievement procedures in the fourth and fifth years, the way in which the time was organized within the two schools reveals the status of Records of Achievement, their perceived use and value, their contribution to teaching and learning and to pupil development. This example has highlighted the way in which our team was able to take a particular analytic theme and follow it, through the formulation of questions, the collection of data and the subsequent analysis of data on a range of topics. By comparing data across the four research sites we were able to construct a picture of the way in which time could be used to enhance or inhibit the development of Records of Achievement in four different schools, which were illustrative of a range of educational and social characteristics in schools throughout Warwickshire and elsewhere.

FOUR STUDIES FROM ONE OR ONE STUDY FROM FOUR?

In writing about our study, we have focused on the four case studies and the key themes that arose within them. As will be seen, the four case studies were chosen simultaneously to facilitate the collection and analysis of data which would be common to all four sites, and which would also highlight particular issues that related to a site or that the researcher wished to follow.

The organization of our project involved each researcher (Pole, Evans and Priestley) taking responsibility for a particular school. In this respect, the individual case study was of importance in the multi-site design. However, the themes which emerged from a case study not only informed data collection in the parallel case which was being conducted but also the analysis of data across all four sites (an issue that is demonstrated in the thematic report (Burgess *et al.* 1991). However, given the phasing of the project with two sites studied in year one and a further two sites in year two, the themes for cross-case analysis were systematically developed towards the end of the project. Yet this could not have been achieved if similar themes common to all schools had not been used in posing questions and collecting data. So the topics and themes within individual cases led to cross-site comparisons; data from individual sites could subsequently be compared across sites, though the strength and virtue of the traditional case study were retained.

In our view, data analysis is not a discrete element of the research process which can be neatly bracketed off from the other phases of the project. Instead, we would argue that data analysis is integral to the way in which questions are posed, sites selected and data collected. In our project we have attempted to demonstrate how the purpose of conducting four case studies relates to the questions which are posed, but also to the data that can be generated. Indeed, some writers (cf. Burgess 1984, Stenhouse 1984) have suggested that multi-site case study projects are a means of overcoming the problems associated with the traditional single case study. In our project we have had four researchers, of whom three have conducted the four studies. In part, the themes within each study rest upon the sociological and educational literature, the sociological and professional interests of the researchers and the issues which teachers and pupils in the schools considered important to the introduction of Records of Achievement. The key issues and themes across all four studies were brought together in the thematic report (Burgess *et al.* 1991). As we indicated in the introduction to that report, our study was designed to portray an ever-changing situation in four contrasting schools. This allowed us to examine schools in different phases of development and with different experiences of Records of Achievement. The contents of the report highlight the key themes of the project, which were:

1 time,
2 the integration of Records of Achievement with other school activities,
3 the applicability of Records of Achievement for all students,
4 negotiation or discussion in recording achievement,
5 equal opportunities and Records of Achievement,
6 the status of Records of Achievement,
7 organization and management implications in Records of Achievement,
8 student perceptions of Records of Achievement,
9 the Document of Record and its completion.

Here, we have focused on the first theme and the analysis associated with it. Like this theme, many of the key issues could not be neatly isolated as a debate in the literature or a sociological or professional concern. Instead, they required a range of skills present in our team, in order to generate data that would engage academics, practitioners and policy-makers in a constant dialogue about achievement and the introduction of Records of Achievement in schools in Warwickshire and elsewhere. At the heart of such a process is a set of questions and research procedures which combined with creativity and imagination results in the analysis of data: a key element of the research process that cannot be reduced to steps and stages. Indeed, our multi-site case study, like all such investigations, relied on the insights and imagination of the investigators who contributed the data. The data in each case study could be compared with that in other case studies, so as to produce four studies in one, and one study from four.

REFERENCES

Ashforth, D. (1990), *Records of Achievement in the Market Place*, Windsor: NFER-Nelson.

Broadfoot, P. (ed.) (1986), *Profiles and Records of Achievement: a Review of Practice*, London: Holt.

Bryman, A. (1988) *Quantity and Quality in Social Research*, London: Unwin Hyman.

Burgess, R.G. (1984) *In the Field: an Introduction to Field Research*, London: Allen & Unwin.

—— (1989) 'Contractors and customers', paper presented to Educational Research and Evaluation for Policy and Practice Conference, University of Warwick, September.

—— (1991) 'Paying the piper and calling the tune?', paper presented to American Educational Research Association Annual Conference, Chicago, April.

Burgess, T. and Adams, E. (1985) *Records of Achievement at 16*, Slough: NFER-Nelson.

Burgess, R.G., Evans, K., Pole, C.J. and Priestley, C. (1991) *The Warwickshire Record of Achievement Project: Issues and Themes*, Centre for Educational Development, Appraisal and Research (CEDAR), University of Warwick.

DES (1984) *Records of Achievement: a Statement of Policy*, London: Department of Education and Science (DES)/Welsh Office.

Evans, K. (1989) *Records of Achievement in Warwickshire: Four Ways School, a Case Study Report*, CEDAR Report, University of Warwick.

Evans, M. (1988) *Practical Profiling*, London: Routledge.

Garforth, D. and Macintosh, H. (1986) *Profiling: a User's Manual*, Cheltenham: Thornes.

Goacher, B. and Reid, M. (1984) *School Reports to Parents*, Windsor: NFER-Nelson.

Hall, G. (1989) *Records of Achievement: Issues and Practice*: London: Kogan Page.

Hitchcock, G. (1986) *Profiles and Profiling: a Practical Introduction*, London: Longman.

James, M. (1989) 'Evaluation for policy: rationality and political reality: the paradigm case of PRAISE?', paper presented at CEDAR Conference on Educational Research and Evaluation for Policy and Practice, September, University of Warwick.

Munby, S. (1989) *Assessing and Recording Achievement*, Oxford: Blackwell.

Oja, S. and Smulyan, L. (1989) *Collaborative Action Research*, Lewes: Falmer Press.

Pole, C. (1989) *Records of Achievement in Warwickshire: Benton School, a Case Study*, CEDAR Report, University of Warwick.

—— (1991) *Records of Achievement in Warwickshire: Herbert Marshall School, a Case Study*, CEDAR Report, University of Warwick.

—— (1992) 'Time to talk: time for Records of Achievement', in M. Morrison (ed.) *Managing Time for Education*, CEDAR Occasional Paper 3, University of Warwick.

PRAISE (1987) *Interim Reporting: the Pilot Records of Achievement in Schools Evaluation*, London: HMSO/Welsh Office.

—— (1988) *Report of the Pilot Records of Achievement in Schools Evaluation*, London: HMSO/Welsh Office.

—— (1991), *Records of Achievement: Report of the National Evaluation of Extension Work in Pilot Schemes*, London: HMSO/Welsh Office.

Priestley, C. (1990) *Records of Achievement in Warwickshire: Rowan Hill School, a Case Study*, CEDAR Report, University of Warwick.

RANSC (1989) *Records of Achievement National Steering Committee Final Report*, London: Welsh Office.

Stansbury, D. (1985) *Programme to Develop Records of Experience as an Element in the Documentation of School Leavers: Report on the Preliminary Phase*, Totnes: Springline Trust.

Stenhouse, L. (1984) 'Library access, library use and user education in academic sixth forms: an autobiographical account', in R.G. Burgess (ed.) *The Research Process in Educational Settings: Ten Case Studies*, Lewes: Falmer Press.

Stronach, I. (1989) 'A critique of the "New Assessment" from currency to carnival?', in H. Simons and J. Elliott (eds) *Rethinking Appraisal and Assessment*, Milton Keynes: Open University Press.

Chapter 8

From filing cabinet to computer

Lyn Richards and Tom Richards

INTRODUCTION

There are major discomforts in pioneering. Excitement, anticipation and thrill of achievement are balanced against uncertainty, delay and sheer inconvenience. When the frontier in question is methodological development, discomforts include waste of time, even of data, and the competition between demands for testing new methods and demands for full and rigorous analysis of data. This chapter tells part of the story of a project that pioneered changes in the methodology of qualitative analysis.

A longitudinal study of family ideology in an outer suburban housing estate, the Green Views project, was the stimulus for and test-bed of NUDIST, a new approach to computer handling of qualitative data. Publications now report both the family study (Richards 1990) and the computer method (Richards and Richards 1987, 1990, 1991a, 1991b). This chapter is about the interaction of researchers, data and technique. It has five sections. First, we explore the manual methods of data handling used in the Green Views project and the methodological requirements it produced. Second, we outline the processes by which techniques now encapsulated in the software were developed, and the changes they brought to methods of handling data and analysis. Third, we recount the processes of analysis using this early software. The fourth section summarizes the ways in which the shift to computer transformed the analysis. Finally, we reflect on implications for the method and methodological development.

MANAGING DATA BY MANUAL METHODS

One of the discomforts of pioneering is that it takes time. This story begins in 1979, when the Green Views project, funded for five years, had completed one year. It had already amassed a vast quantity of very rich, very unstructured material: informal interviews, field notes and taped discussions. This material obviously exceeded the capacity and flexibility of manual systems for handling qualitative data. To take as an example just one area, the project design had emphasized understanding of neighbour relations. This outer sub-urban area was sold as a 'family community' but bore all the characteristics stereotypical of suburban isolation. In the first year, the data on neighbouring came from very many sources: open-ended questions in surveys, participant observation in groups, unstructured interviews. Simply co-ordinating these records was a formidable task, and understanding them a major challenge. Bulk records defied sensitive interpretation, and multiple data sources defied co-ordinated analysis. The normal response to bulk records from multiple sources is to summarize, and summarized, these data surprised. They reported contradictory results: negative attitudes to neighbouring, but positive ones to community.

As the material built up, the task of controlling it became paramount. The choice appeared to be between reducing most of the data to statistical format and creating innovative methods. The project design was not hostile to statistical reduction, indeed it relied on survey data for many purposes. But it aimed at questions whose answers could not be quantitative. Neighbour behaviour, to use the same example, could easily be tapped in survey data. But two surveys later, we had accrued a substantial body of superficial responses to questions about interaction with and attitudes to neighbours. Everybody knew several people. Everybody affirmed the goals of family community. But by far the most common definition of a good neighbour was two-faced: 'There when you need them but not in your pocket.' We were no nearer to understanding what they did with their neighbours, or what they thought they should do. It was evident that we must turn from simple accounts of behaviour to evidence of the ideological backdrop of the 'community'. Researching ideology involves exploring people's detailed accounts of their ideas and experience of family and community, the ways these ideas are linked, and their social results (Richards 1989).

Attempting these goals, the project met the methodological ceilings that confront much qualitative research. Most obvious of these are restrictions on the bulk of data and their complexity and on the size and complexity of the conceptual framework developed during analysis (Richards and Richards 1987). Mere bulk was the immediate problem. The data records of a year of unstructured interviewing and field notes from participant observation were formidably bulky, and in various paper forms (typescript, field-note diaries, handwritten accounts). To control this increasing volume of records had become a high priority. Filing systems and methods of identifying different types of data seemed at times the major preoccupation of the project staff.

Most researchers respond to this need for control by developing systems for organizing the data (Tesch 1990). But the methodological implications of controlling techniques are seldom considered. Decisions are made about the *system* of data control and the *timing* of control early in a project, and these decisions strongly influence its subsequent development.

Data control: the code-and-retrieve system

The *system* of control adopted for Green Views data appears to be the most common response to the accumulation of very rich data. Typically, researchers identify segments of data records for orderly copying and filing under topics ('neighbouring', 'good neighbours', etc.). The purpose is retrieval: later, you can retrieve everything filed under that topic. This process of lowly clerical work has been reinvented by countless embattled researchers across the world and reported by few. Few monographs describe it, and it has only recently been documented in texts (Lofland and Lofland 1984, Miles and Huberman 1984, Tesch 1990). It is a highly successful method of data control.

It is also a powerful shaping process, determining the ways the researchers can approach data (via the specified categories). The tasks of segmenting and filing became all-demanding. To avoid backlog, systems were developed to process material as it came in. (If it moves, code it!) Records of these stages in the working of a team (between three and five staff) show a high priority was put on 'catching up on coding'. This efficient coding system served to distract and distance the researchers from the tasks of analysis. Coding becomes an end in itself, a tedious job but one you have to get through. Miles and Huberman sum it up well: 'Coding is hard, onerous work. It is not nearly so much fun as getting the good stuff in the field' (1984: 63).

Timing control: postponed analysis

The effect of such a method is to impose one of several possible answers to the timing of control. It appears to postpone analysis (until all the stuff on that topic is processed). This may, ironically, exacerbate the need for data control: if you don't know what it's saying, you have to file all of it under all possible categories. Given the scale and pace of the project, and the reliance on manual code-and-file methods, the Green Views project increasingly appeared to defer analysis. To pursue the example of neighbouring, analysis stalled, as more and more records were accrued, and continuing research was informed by the impression of uniformly positive ideas of local relationships.

In retrospect, this appearance is evidently false. Rather, we would argue, the method obscures and obstructs much analytical work. It obscures the fact that much of the activity of coding for retrieval is a theorizing process. Even the identification of 'purely descriptive' codes (Miles and Huberman 1984) is a theorizing act. (Is gender likely to matter in this data? Should we bother to collect all the stuff on hostility to migrants – just because it is there? What does it have to do with attitudes to local relations or family life?) And yet the method actually obstructs theorizing. To treat these decisions as a pre-analysis is to risk pre-empting the two analytical processes. By the time you get around to looking at all the stuff on definitions of good neighbours, the filing system has determined what you will find there. And if you have not explored the theoretical relationships between the categories created, it may be far too late to do so.

In the dispersed, ill-organized and rarely cumulative literature of qualitative methodology there are few clearly agreed rules. But many writers assert or imply that in qualitative research, data collection and data analysis should not be regarded as sequential stages. Analysis commences with the process of data acquisition, and continues to the end of the project (Burgess 1984, Hammersley and Atkinson 1983). This implies a very different choreography from the organization of most quantitative projects. In survey research, teams of data collectors and coders dominate the early action, moving off-stage when data collection is completed, to clear the way for the dramatic finale of analysis.

This different choreography is required by qualitative research. To talk of data 'collection' as a prior stage is inimical to the theoretical assumptions behind qualitative research. The goals of producing theory from data, rather than merely testing prior theory, require that researchers remain open to ideas, patterns, new categories or concepts, that may emerge during the process of making data. Hence methods of handling qualitative data must contain ways of catching and developing ideas, exploring fleeting hints, and drawing connections between them and the data from which they derived.

So data control methods must be processes of analysis, not merely of data disposal. But these goals are not easily achieved. Most qualitative researchers know the frustration of trying to manage growing data and finding that the more efficient their management methods, the more desiccated the data become. The Green Views project produced this experience at an early stage. The data immediately grew beyond expectations, not merely in bulk but in complexity. Every aspect of life in the housing estate seemed to have something to do with the dreams and realities of family and local relations. Data control methods built up bigger and bigger files on each topic, but defied attempts to explore links between them. To take a simple example, questions about family life were answered with very complex accounts of the meanings of home ownership. (Asked about home, on the other hand, they gave you complex accounts about family privacy.) Clearly it wouldn't do to file all the stuff on home in one place, and stuff on family elsewhere; but it also wouldn't do to give all this stuff two codes, and put off exploring the complexities and the ways these ideas were entangled.

Methods of managing the data were urgently required, but they had to be methods that encouraged the exploration of emerging ideas, rather than postponing them. In retrospect, it seems that this requirement was dictated not so much by commitment to the technique of 'grounded theory' as by the irrepressible data. The idea of 'grounded theory' influenced this particular project rather as, we suspect, it still influences most large-scale qualitative research, as a general indicator of the desirability of making theory from data, rather than a guide to a method for handling data.

What do you do with the text?

Many of the problems came from the approach taken to the linking of theory and data. The project operated from the start with a requirement that in order to support exploration of ideas and verification of claims, theories emerging should retain very detailed links to the data. A requirement in all the methods we developed for recording emerging ideas was that they record exact links with the data that produced those ideas. Those links could be pursued in the process of checking out and testing theories.

This assumption is *not* built into the grounded theory method, though it is our impression that most researchers working under that banner have imported a commitment to retaining access to data records, and often to original full transcribed text. This commitment comes from various sources, including training in variable analysis. By contrast, the classic grounded theory method takes off from the data. In a very clarifying discussion with Turner, one of us commented about concern at the ways the grounded theory method 'jettisons' data; Turner mildly agreed that yes, he too jettisons data. In the process he calls 'concept discovery' the goal is 'moving from data to abstract categories' (Martin and Turner 1986: 147). The subsequent process of theory-construction is at a distance from original data, consisting instead of 'ordering sets of already discovered cognitions and propositions into logically consistent constructions' (Turner 1981: 228).

Few would disagree with these goals, since theory emergence and theory construction are goals of qualitative research. But researchers in fact differ strongly in their methods of seeking these goals and particularly in whether these methods retain text. The Green Views project quickly showed that the code-and-retrieve method is not only a technique of data control but also one of data retention. Researchers' language showed this: the data had become 'stuff', physical stuff that must be put somewhere, not ideas to be explored. The method is backed by two purposes, both foreign to the grounded theory approach. One is data conservation; *nothing* is to be jettisoned if it might later be useful. The other is a particular approach to theory testing, the ability to produce *all* the evidence to validate claims about it.

Stretching the filing cabinet

Manual code-and-retrieve methods of data control were expanded, and improvements explored. In the first year we attacked urgent problems, some about the data *documents* – field notes, transcripts, printed records, and some about the indexing *categories* – the topics designated to receive data. These attempts (and the fact that documents and categories were by now visualized as different parts of the project) strongly influenced the development of NUDIST. But in this part of the story, 'we' refers to Lyn Richards and her colleagues in the Green Views project.

The data documents seemed increasingly distant and dead, killed off by the coding process. This effect had not been so pronounced in smaller projects, where records could be known and reviewed constantly. Now, the filing system segmented documents and ripped segments from context. It became evident that we needed techniques to reinstate context and retain knowledge of the multiple meanings of any segment. Context was retained by various means of copying identifying information, not just an ID number, with every segment of text coded for filing. (One innovation was to record this information on stick-on labels that could be slapped on any page of a document before copying! As the wonders of word-processing were explored, we used copy and paste with search and replace techniques to label all pages or sections of each document.) We attacked the problems of retaining multiple meanings with several attempts to record context and cross-references on text segments before they were filed, arriving at a coding system whereby the code was recorded numerically (much easier to write and read than a mnemonic), and written in the margin of text prior to copying.

Some time in the first year, our approach to categories shifted. They were reorganized by what we now see as two specific strategies. First, we started to produce an index *system*, incorporating in hierarchical structures at least some of the relationships between categories and subcategories. For instance, we rapidly generated several categories to do with neighbour relations, some about values (definitions of a good neighbour, need to 'keep your distance') and some about behaviour ('dropping in', 'helping out'). The two sets were gathered in subcategories of the major categories, 'neighbouring values' and 'neighbouring behaviour'. We labelled separate files for major categories, and put in them separate folders for subcategories. This had the effect of freeing us to explore additional possible subdivisions. Further categories were suggested by logic. (If all the ideas of good neighbours are negative should we be asking where we would find entirely positive definitions?) We started *seeing* the index as structured, using a diagram of hierarchical 'trees' of categories and subcategories to represent where we were at with coding. In various versions this diagram was copied for studying, critiqued and used during coding sessions. We found we could handle more codes in this way, and could code much more efficiently.

Second, we began to use the index system as a container for ideas, not merely bits of text. As reflective notes or memos accrued, we faced the problem of what to do with 'emerging theory'. It became harder to link them to the data from which the ideas emerged. A place was made for memos or comments *at* the category, simply by keeping coloured folders for the memos in the front of the hang-file for that top-level category. And we started thinking about the index categories as places you could put ideas, as well as text that belonged there.

We experimented with ideas for expanding the code-and-retrieve method by add-on non-computer methods. The most successful was the development of card indexes of categories and subcategories in the now rapidly developing filing system. The cards could contain not only notes of cross-references to topic files but also ideas about the material being placed there and memos about emerging patterns. A major technological advance was the use of different coloured cards for the different levels in the index 'trees'! But moving between cards and hang-files to seek the text referred to became a formidable task when several categories were in play as ideas emerging from the data were explored. The system worked adequately so long as the material to be filed was limited in size and was generally in single-topic data segments. Ours wasn't.

By the end of the first year we had generated a series of goals for a dream data handling system that would work. First were requirements for capacity and efficiency. We needed a system imposing no limits on the *number of codes* or the *number of times* that a rich passage could be coded. If it was about twenty different things it had to be filed in twenty different places. In the manual system, as the costs in time and copying bills mounted, we felt pressure to code it in the most obvious place so that it wouldn't get lost, rather than insist it be copied and filed many times. As a result, we had quickly lost confidence that *all* instances of a category were filed in any folder. There was also an urgent need for efficient ways of checking that the *meanings of codes* did not shift, and that different members of the team used them consistently.

Second, we constantly needed a system that would support asking questions about the *relationships of categories*. It is extremely hard to ask further questions of a hang-file. Even simple questions (Is it mainly the men who are coming up with this attitude to lending equipment?) require dealing the copied segments out into new heaps, risking inaccuracy, and taking time. Further questions strain the limits of coding information. (Do young men sound more like young women than like older men? Well, did we identify each extract by age of speaker as well as gender? Damn! Of course that information is available on the interview schedule in the store room!) And even if the coding has been done, it will usually not support further questions. (Do *women's* (but not men's) accounts normally show this link between home and stability?)

Third, we needed a system that linked data with *memos* about emerging theory. By locating a memo only at a particular index category we found we ossified thinking: what of the relation between two categories or more? Theory emergence was not always located on categories, so memos about it could not be filed only there.

Related was a fourth set of goals about *flexibility*. Towards the end of its first year, the Green Views data very clearly indicated patterns that were not only unexpected but also occurred in unexpected ways. These required not only the late incorporation of new topic files, but also constant searching back through earlier data to locate overlooked instances of the now-recognized patterns. The task of *reworking earlier data* became almost impossible as material built up. And we recognized that often these new categories were combinations of old ones, but inaccessible through the hang-files.

Finally, we sought ways of avoiding the problems of *segmentation of data*. Copying and cutting bits of copy paper proved not only inefficient but also distancing. Tagged with their contexting identifiers, segments were still segmented. Whole cases seemed harder to access. We found we almost always cut text into paragraphs, since it was absurd to identify a slightly different set of lines for each of several codes. For many purposes very large segments of a document should have been copied to a category, but cost-conscious researchers settled for small segments. We needed a new way of locating exactly the text that belonged in a category, and of doing so without losing the flow of the document.

We investigated the then available computer methods, including data base management systems and the use of word-processors. These efforts produced clear conclusions: they helped with cost but not with further theorizing or flexibility. Evidently, the manual filing method was a process very easily replicated by and improved on with computers. Computers easily attach labels to text and as easily find anything with a given label. Computerized, the method is faster, cleaner and much more thorough than manual systems, and takes much less space. But computerized, the code-and-retrieve technique remains simply a method of disposing of text in an orderly manner, for later retrieval and analysis. None of the code-and-retrieve techniques available then (or now) offered to answer our goals.

Those goals were sharpened by the decision to design software. Merely providing electronic storage for a now-rejected system was not enough to warrant the major dislocation of a mid-project move to computer analysis. So on top of the sets of methodological goals, we added specific requirements for software that would make changing methods in midstream worthwhile. First, the system should be able to handle a variety of different *types* of data. It should not be restricted to the sort of data that can easily be typed into a computer, indeed it must be able to combine analysis of such 'online' data with data remaining 'offline'. The Green Views budget would be unable to support the retyping of paper records, and was rapidly generating records that were untypable – field research diaries, diagrams of discussion patterns, photographs. Second, the shift to the computer must also completely remove the constraints on *size of records* and *complexity of coding* with which the project had been burdened. And third, and most important, it must *go beyond the data-control techniques of coding for retrieval*. In particular it should encourage the creation of new categories for thinking about the data, rethinking and reordering of old ones, the recording of emerging ideas and exploration of their relationships and their links with the data.

INTO THE COMPUTER: DESIGNING NUDIST

In the following months, we (the present authors) began what is now a constant process of knowledge-engineering during which the boundaries between our disciplines became hazier. The challenges of the sociological techniques were clearly related to the challenges of data base storage and access. In talking through those programming issues we developed new qualitative data handling approaches. Through clarification of the normally unspelt-out assumptions about what was valuable, what was necessary, what was a problem, and what might possibly in future contribute to generating theoretical ideas, we moved towards the design of a system whose most obvious immediate effects were to remove the ceilings on size, complexity and detail of data and its analysis. Less obvious effects included the results of methodological innovation and of removing constraints. One result was a delay of five years before the book from the Green Views Project appeared!

We were not of course alone in tackling the tasks of computer assisted qualitative analysis, but at the time we seemed very alone, unfunded and isolated from other researchers addressing these tasks. The first version of NUDIST appeared for mainframe computers in 1985 and subsequent versions for Macintosh and DOS machines developed from this. The Green Views project was handled in a prototype version on mainframes from 1979. This was before published accounts of other qualitative software (e.g. Drass 1980, Seidel and Clarke 1984, Shelly and Sibert 1986) and it was not until 1989 that a world conference was organized on qualitative computing (Fielding and Lee 1991). By that time, in separate developments in several countries, specialist programs had been produced for coding and retrieval and data organizing tasks. And the Green Views research was completed!

It is beyond the scope of the present chapter to review the different programs. At the time of writing there are at least a dozen commercially available programs for qualitative analysis, and innumerable software packages for handling text that can be applied to some of the qualitative researcher's tasks (for summaries see Miles and Huberman 1993, *Qualitative Sociology* 1991, Richards and Richards forthcoming). Nor is it our task here to detail the architecture and functioning of NUDIST; we have done that elsewhere (Richards and Richards 1990, 1991a and 1991b). Here we describe only those aspects necessary to recounting the research experience of the shift from filing cabinet to NUDIST.

Reshaping records: separating documents from indexing

Many of the goals listed above were addressed by a decision to separate the document data from the thinking about it: there would be two data bases, one of documents and one of the indexing. This decision meant that whilst NUDIST would perform any of the code-and-retrieve tasks, it performed them in a different way from the approach taken (at about the same time) in a set of programs designed for coding and retrieval. Code-and-retrieve programs typically format text and attach codes to it, allowing retrieval by any one code or set of codes linked in the simple relationships usually called Boolean (this code *and* that, *not* that, *or* that). NUDIST formatted text and put references to it in the separate index data base of categories developed by the researcher. Searches of that data base could ask Boolean questions and a large range of other, often more interesting questions (about proximity, context, background data). And the separation of data bases answered several of our other goals.

First, the same program could now handle a range of different sorts of data, including data that would not be typed on to the computer. Documents were provided with headers of information giving the context for any segments subsequently retrieved. Online documents were formatted and lines numbered to enable the researcher to identify exactly the text to be indexed at a category. For offline documents the researcher could specify what units would correspond to the numbered lines of online documents. Field note diaries were indexed by page number, newspaper articles by date, even tapes by tape count when the budget would not allow their transcription. The effect was to 'thicken up' the data available in any line of enquiry, and in several areas of analysis the results were dramatic. One was the intransigent data on neighbouring: with access to all material, from a wide range of different sources, the picture of neighbouring in the estate was now clearly far more complex than the polite, ubiquitous accounts of family community.

Second, despite the dramatic increase in access to data, the research team found an extraordinary lightening of clerical loads. In later NUDIST projects this change shows in different grant application budgets. Projects using the software needed far less low-level clerical labour for cutting, filing, controlling the data. Instead, researcher decisions about indexing were recorded in NUDIST in very rapid processes requiring no typing skills. So the tasks of handling data, hence the staff hours, were reduced, and more time could be given to other tasks. In the word-processor, data documents were given their 'headers' of identifying information, then saved as text-only files, introduced into NUDIST and automatically formatted in seconds. The result is a different experience of data processing, in which putting stuff in places is no longer a problem; so thinking about the relationships of those places is possible.

The third and most immediate effect of the shift to NUDIST was to focus on the index categories rather than the bits of text to which they were attached. Detached from the documents, the indexing data base was from the beginning of the project a centre of methodological development. NUDIST supports (though it has never required) an index system within which categories and sub-categories are logically ordered. As mentioned above, the Green Views project index had already grown a hierarchical structure of categories and subcategories (ideas about neighbouring, definitions of a good neighbour). For convenience of coding in margins of text, we had begun to refer to these by numerical category labels. (Our fourth major category, 'neighbours', had five numbered subcategories, 'good neighbours' being the first: thus its numerical 'address' was 4 1). The computer could now support the development of this structured index into any number of 'trees' of branching categories and subcategories.

As the data were moved to the NUDIST program, the index system was freed from the filing cabinet. The result was extraordinarily exciting. Now if a category should be subdivided into five, it could be. New sets of categories were created for grey areas hitherto simply not coded. If previously the categories had overlapped or contained many meanings, they could now be carefully specified and sorted into independent 'trees'. One of the first results for the Green Views project was the creation of different trees of categories for values and behaviour – not only about neighbouring, but about family life, social environment, and several other areas where the separate coding would permit exploration of the relationship between values and the ways people acted. Figure 8.1 shows how a tree results and how numerical addresses are used. The 'values' tree was the second, values/interaction the fourth subcategory, values/interaction/neighbours the fifth category below, values/interaction/neighbours/'good neighbour' the first below that – so its address was 2 4 5 1!

At this stage we made some terminological decisions. One, argued in later papers, was to avoid 'code' (Richards and Richards 1991b). Both as a noun and as a verb, it carried multiple meanings in qualitative research, and yet

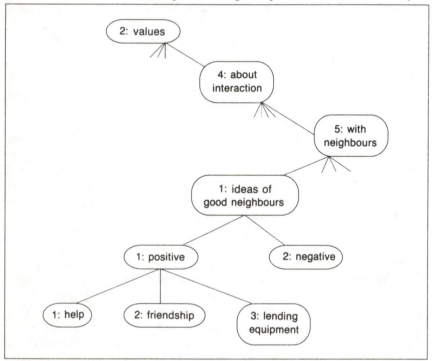

Figure 8.1 Conveying concepts

other meanings in survey terminology. We aimed to provide software support for at least two sorts of qualitative 'coding', coding for retrieval of text segments and 'open coding' for theory generation. So we established a convention of referring to the *categories* in an index system, and to the process of allocating text references to them as *indexing*. So values/interaction/neighbours/'good neighbour' was a category, at which the researcher could put references to the segments of field notes, interviews or other data documents about good neighbours.

But indexing was only one of the processes supported by this system. The researcher could also add *comments* about the category, patterns emerging in data to do with it and so on. The computer too added comments, recording when the category was introduced and ways in which it was subsequently altered. So there was a need for a name for the *place* in the index system where category, comments and indexing information were stored. We chose *node*, in reference to the branching points of the trees. In the figure, 2 4 5 1 is a node, as are 2 4 5 and 2 4 and so on.

Using tree structures to convey information

It is hard to recall how long it took to exploit the potential of index data bases that were independent of document text, and hierarchically tree-structured. It now seems self-evident that many different sorts of information can be carried in this way. (In version 3.0 the trees are shown graphically).

The new system expanded not only the number of categories but also the variety of information they could store. Documents or any part of documents were indexed using a 'background information tree' for data *about*, not *in*, those documents. Categories represented demographic or other variables whose values were represented in subcategories (e.g. background information/ gender/female). This improved on our earliest attempts to contain information about people or events, which had used methods of attaching computerized 'face sheets' to documents (an approach which we later discovered had been taken at the same time in the design of the Ethnograph (Seidel and Clark 1984)). Handled in the same way as other indexing data, the base data categories were unlimited and could refer to whole documents or any parts of documents. The Green Views index system contained such a background information tree of forty-five variables. All respondents in one-to-one interviews could be classified on these by indexing the entire document at that category; participants in group discussions could be classified by index-ing just the lines of a document where that person was speaking.

NUDIST projects since then have used much more strongly the power of this index system to give different modes of access to data. Nodes in an index tree can (1) convey facts (a woman is speaking here, or, this is a document from the re-interview series); or (2) represent relationships with statistical data (this text was coded 2 in the five pre-coded responses to question 26); as well as (3) containing categories for thinking about the data (these lines are about the dangers to privacy when neighbours drop in). See Figure 8.2.

Creating indexes

The immediate result was expansion. Where the project had worked in the filing cabinet with fewer than two hundred folders, it now suddenly had more than a thousand index categories. The difference was not felt as changing size; indeed, the effect was oddly that bulk was immediately removed. The new plethora of categories was no problem to the computer and two four-drawer filing cabinets were freed! The index system was unlimited in size and complexity, but rapidly accessed, easily recalled. What used to be an onerous stage of copying and filing became in NUDIST a very simple process of telling the computer the document to be indexed, the category at which indexing was to go and what text units went there.

The new challenge was not dealing with expansion but guaranteeing quality of the index system. As in several other NUDIST projects since, this was experienced as a human inadequacy: how to impose new organization worthy of a program whose capability for organization of categories appeared unlimited.

It took a year to adapt the Green Views index system to NUDIST; such is the price of pioneering. By comparison, it takes, in the experience of several NUDIST projects since, less than a week from the commencement of a project to establish a strongly tree-structured index system. In retrospect, we see our efforts as a quixotic attempt to produce a perfect index system a priori. Not only can that not be done, it should not be done, since qualitative research requires the incorporation of emerging categories. But anxious researchers see the computer as requiring an index system before analysis can start.

They are right, of course, in expecting that the code-and-retrieve method will reward the researcher prepared to produce and stick with an a priori index. We set out to remove the requirement by supporting flexibility of indexes. In the Green Views project it took some time to recognize that the index system works not merely as a repository for categories but also as an image of the researchers' thinking about the project and as a tool for developing theory. Thus it is necessarily tentative early in the project, and should develop as the data do.

But it didn't. Flexibility of indexes remained a problem throughout the project. The early manual filing techniques had operated with a large number of categories, sorted into subcategories as their folders grew thicker and the complexity of the material they contained became evident. So the project entered its computer stage with what we expected would work as a ready-made index system, and the basic structure remained unchanged. We had learned a lot about the inertia of established filing systems.

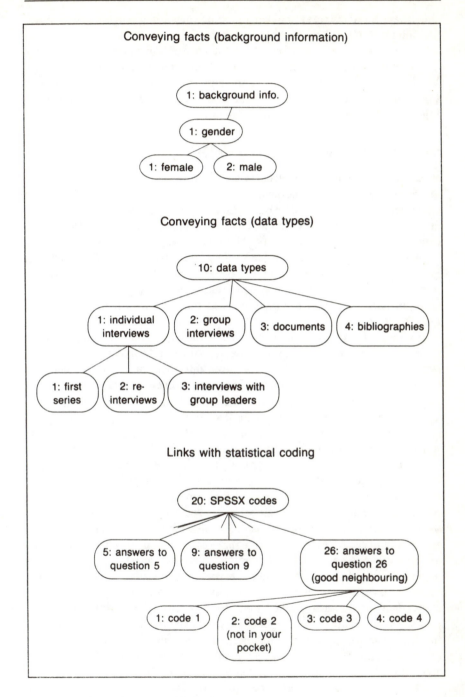

Figure 8.2 Different uses of indexing trees

And access to context remained a problem. Documents in the system could now be browsed and read whole or in part. This made it easier to return to the context of a retrieved segment, but an early disappointment was the discovery that such return trips to the whole document were still rarely taken. We have since heard the same complaint from users of other programs. Computerizing code-and-retrieve techniques did not remove the tendency to segmentation, they merely made it easier.

New categories from old: building theory

What we had produced was certainly a super filing cabinet. Code-and-retrieve techniques were now very easy, very efficient and unlimited in scope. Complicated searches could be quickly carried out. But the goals of flexibility and theory construction remained. How to support the emergence of new categories and the exploration of relations between categories?

New categories were no problem: they could be introduced (or deleted) in seconds. But locating the material that should be indexed at the new category remained a formidable task. We found researchers rarely tackled the task of going back to recode earlier material, and this became a major problem in interpretation.

Exploration of the relation between categories was harder – and far more important. It required seeing the nodes, or points in the tree-structured index system, as entities. Researchers could put into them not only references to text to be indexed at that category, but also comments. Nodes were related to some other nodes through the tree structure.

It took a few months to recognize that in NUDIST a retrieval involving several nodes in the index system could itself create a new node (i.e. one storing the references to the retrieved data). Version 1.0 allowed the building of 'virtual nodes', new categories built from old, whose contents were, as in any other node, title, comments and indexing information.

These could be built by a series of Boolean techniques and, importantly, two non-Boolean ones (the researcher could specify retrieval from files which *somewhere* contained specified indexing, or which did not contain it, for instance all the references to text indexed at 'danger of neighbouring' from documents indexed somewhere at 'financial stress/concern at furnishings'.) The results of the retrieval could be saved, if that was wanted, and further explored, creating more new categories for further exploration and so on until the questions asked of the data, or the data indexed there (or the researchers) were exhausted. Do the responses about the danger of neighbouring from people anxious about furnishings come more from women than from men? Build a new node out of the resulting references. Now, about those responses from women anxious about furnishings and seeing danger in neighbouring: what are the things they want of a neighbour relation? A new process of iterative interrogation of the data was set up, and the Green Views project entered a new stage.

WORKING WITH IT: EXPLORING NEIGHBOURING

The project had set out to explore what rapidly proved to be complex tangles of ideas about family in an outer housing estate, home of the private nuclear family in outer suburbia. This section concentrates on just one tangle: gender and neighbouring. The literature, the survey data and the filing cabinet full of field research records offered incompatible pictures of neighbouring at Green Views. The critical feminist accounts of suburbia interpreted suburban developments as prisons of women, predicting that whilst men would find private havens there, women would find isolation and loneliness. The survey data reported overwhelming, and ungendered, satisfaction. Only tiny proportions said they were lonely, and both women and men reported startlingly high numbers of neighbours 'known' and neighbourly things done for and by them. While the literature said women would be lonely, and the survey data said nobody was lonely, the qualitative data said nobody *wanted* to be close to their neighbours. Few gave entirely positive pictures of good neighbours. Research team meetings recorded recurrences of surprise at the two faces. 'How's this for a contradiction? She felt it was important to get to know people here. "Neighbours are the only people we do know *really*, but then we hate people who live in your yard." Perhaps I should have coded her differently?'

People produced instant definitions of 'good neighbours' that sounded very similar. Partly this was because the same keywords turned up frequently, partly because of a repeated pattern to answers; positive ideas were always balanced by negative:

> Someone who's there if you need them. Not living in each other's home all the time. You can say hello to them when you go to the letter box. You borrow a cup of sugar off. That sort of thing. Someone you don't see too much of.

In the filing cabinet we collected people's accounts of neighbouring, distinguishing positive and negative. The categories filling up were the negative ones. Meanwhile, the categories of 'loneliness' and 'isolation' in fact were collecting remarkably little material, and what was there was usually accounts of the loneliness of *other* women (Richards 1990). Hostility to neighbouring contacts, especially the casual ones of 'dropping in', was linked with a pervasive sense of their danger. Early memos were all about danger and the keywords that hung around were 'not in your pocket' and 'too close for comfort' (title of an early paper). We created a collection of places neighbours should not venture: your pocket, your lap, your hair, your yard, your doorstep or your life. These people clearly had as much neighbouring as they wanted, in many cases more than was desired. And this passion for privacy was equally evident in the accounts of women and men. There were no statistically significant gender patterns in the survey data on ideas of a good neighbour.

There were strong patterns in the data reporting what people actually did with neighbours – but not by gender, as the literature would suggest, but by life-stage.

At this stage, the project was transferred to NUDIST. The clerical steps were simple. All the transcripts already typed online were introduced as NUDIST documents, line-numbered print-outs were obtained, and the member of the research team closest to that data took the transcript away, with a copy of the now growing index system, and recorded in the margin the category at which particular lines should be indexed. A typist entered those indexing references. At this stage, the process *felt* much like that of dropping segments in hang-files, and the analytical results were similar.

The difference was not felt until we overcame the instinct for parsimony in allocating the same text to only a few categories. Slowly, we adapted to the system's tolerance of multiple indexing, and to the speed with which indexing data could be entered. The shift from indexing a passage at the obvious place to indexing it at all the categories to which it is relevant was hardly felt as increased work-load. But it remade our understanding of the complexity of our data and the interrelationships between categories. Most obviously, half-hidden meanings, or less dominating ones, were now recorded in indexing information. If a passage of text was about privacy, the dangers of casual dropping in and if it *also* contained suggestions of sadness, duty to control invasions of the family home, inability to find other women who felt similarly; if it linked workforce participation with the need for company and juxtaposed this with the difficulty of negotiating reciprocity in caring for children, it could be indexed at all of these. Suddenly the categories under 'neighbouring' values and behaviour grew in number and complexity, as did the categories that had something to do with isolation. Suddenly, we were 'finding' material that documented not simple accounts of inability to find company, but the complexity of the social construction of isolation within an ideology of family privacy.

The multiplication of categories was not only a result of ability to 'find' many more meanings in text. Subcategories were also created, now, by logical work on the index system. The computer invited logical sets of subcategories, so the discovery that almost all categories for good neighbours were negative led to a search for positive ones.

Back to the survey data: had it been lying? Following the lead of the complex meanings to neighbouring, we sought not simple gender differences but complex types. The open-ended answers to the 'good neighbour' questions could now be accessed through NUDIST, so we could explore *which* of the negative 'not in your pocket' answers had themes about protecting the privacy of the home, and whether these were women's. (They were.) Seeking varieties of neighbouring, we had asked people to look through a series of statements about relationships ('We prefer to keep our distance', 'We have a lot in common', etc.), and circle those that applied to each of the four people they knew best in the estate. A cluster analysis of these binary data produced a very strong typology. Both women and men were dealt into each of the types. In NUDIST we used categories indicated as central to each type to explore the different attitudes to community they linked with.

The first strong theme to emerge from this exercise was not gender but life-stage. Each cluster analysis type collected people in the same life-stage. Case studies, explored by 'line by line analysis', produced new categories linked by NUDIST indexing to categories about the needs and dangers of neighbours. For instance, the *in vivo* category 'getting set up' turned out to occur constantly with codes about positive ideas of neighbours, and further node-building established that the accounts producing this overlap came from young childless couples. Get all the stories about 'neighbourly things' divided by life-stage and it becomes clear that those 'getting set up' accept help more readily, and see the threat of neighbours 'in your pocket' as less salient; they are, after all, unlikely to be at home and if at home will be less hassled. The new category also intriguingly links with other tangles of ideas: text indexed at 'getting set up' very often is also indexed at nodes under both family and home ownership. At the other end of the life cycle, women (not men) whose children were older tended to produce accounts in which *not knowing what's going on* was strongly linked to avoidance of neighbouring:

> *A woman*:   I've just never gone out of my way. Like, I sort of just know my neighbours' names and that's all. I don't even know the neighbour next door's name. I don't know a thing that's going on around the place.

Theory construction here was often by a sort of quasi-variable analysis. After early time-consuming efforts, ability to run sorting algorithms in background mode was added to NUDIST. Now, combinations of base data indexing could be used for very rapid sorting of all of the text indexed at a category by life-stage and gender, for instance. This showed immediately why the statistical data had produced muddled pictures of life-stage differences: several life-stage categories contained very different experiences of family. Following sociological custom we had used very broad life-stage coding categories (lumping together all those with pre-school-age children, for instance, without regard to the age of their other children). These had served to mask in the statistical data strong differences between the experiences of women.

Both need and danger now proved to be strongly gendered *for some life-stages*. None of these gender patterns was simple enough to have found their way into the statistical categories or the hang-files. But they could be firmly established by building new categories from the original indexing of the qualitative data. These were then pursued in further category-building explorations in NUDIST.

What of the apparent flurry of neighbourly activity? People's reports could be examined now to find the associated ideas, using simple Boolean retrievals (e.g. all the text on neighbourly acts that is indexed at 'time in estate/first weeks'). Such enquiries established that those neighbouring acts were normally defined as 'little things', and normally occurred either during moving in or in an emergency. In both contexts they were seen as once-off, context-specific events: 'hot water, and just those neighbourly things'. Such emergency aid was regarded as available almost by right, and the phrase 'without being asked' turned up often, as did 'what anyone would do', but these often substantial favours were regarded as obviously consistent with a distancing definition of a good neighbour. The accounts showed no apparent problems with this bundle of contrasting requirements for a good neighbour.

> *A woman*: One who doesn't want to live in your pocket, but someone who's there. I mean, we've had examples the last couple of weeks. She was ready to drop everything if you need help, which we did.

Privacy is not a uni-dimensional concept. And for women it has much more clearly several dimensions. As they appeared, the different dimensions were incorporated in new subnodes under 'privacy', then their relation to other aspects of social interaction could be explored. First is about privacy of information, having someone 'knowing your business'. Second are references to the physical invasion of constant visits. A third, loss of control over your life, turns out to be linked in all accounts with the threat of being 'used' in situations where reciprocity doesn't work. The program can explore the interrelationship of these. Retrieval of the text indexed at either category when they overlap will show which people produce complex accounts of the need for privacy. That new node constructed by this retrieval can be divided according to gender, justifying the impression that the men's accounts are more complex.

> *A man*: A good neighbour I would like to be friendly with, be able to have a talk to. Oh, perhaps socialize with them occasionally, in a family get-together. I wouldn't like to think I had a neighbour that was continually on my doorstep (I don't think we've got any like that) but someone you can rely on, if you needed help at any time, in case of an emergency or something. Someone that you can trust. People that are good people, I think, that's what you're after. Not sticky-beaks or anything like that.

WHAT'S NEW? THE IMPACT OF NUDIST

Many of these questions could have been tackled through the quantitative data, and some very usefully were. But the survey data obscured crucial differences. Some of these differences might well have been thrown up by filing-cabinet code-and-retrieve analysis, but they would have been reported as impressions, and could not have been pursued in the same way. Clearly major sectors of analysis were newly possible, and most of these were the most important sectors. It was no exaggeration to say the experience was of a method transformed.

The transformations can be summarized under three heads. First, the *handling* of data was quite different. It took surprisingly little time to become used to relating to data on the screen rather than on paper, and to adjust to the speed and facility of browsing text on screen. It took longer to find new routines of indexing and inputting indexing data, but as those became smooth the process of indexing was remade, from a cut-and-file clerical drudgery that was felt as data-damaging to an index-building exercise that was flexible and constructive.

Second, the *routines of analysis* were changed. Code-and-retrieve is an in–out technique: get out the hang-file, study its contents, shove it back (if it will still fit!). NUDIST analysis, even in this early version, was experienced as a category-exploration and category-building technique. For much of the analysis in the Green Views project, there was a new sense of being able to strain the exploration of ideas as far as the data allowed. The end of an interrogation came when the data ran out – or our indexing of it let us down – never when the data-handling method would not support the enquiry required. Increasingly, the analysis moved between the impressions of case study exploration, the productive routines of open coding, and the computer-supported interrogations that allow exact location and exploration of suggested patterns and discovery of new ones.

Third, analysis became far surer, with provision for *constant interrogation of themes*. The processes of building and interrogating themes gave an impression of constant working at theory built up and peeled back in onion-skin layers. In this process, we found a strong defence against one of the dangers of qualitative research, the fascination of a theme that appears to dominate the data. Once you see it, it's always there. Most researchers know the frustration of trying to verify a hunch that is colouring everything they hear, or an impression that everyone is really saying the same thing. Working within a grounded theory tradition, the researcher is strongly assisted in confirmation and thickening-up of emerging theory, but not so strongly pushed to seeking disconfirming evidence or hidden patterns. Such a theme was the apparently ubiquitous hostility to neighbours, 'too close for comfort'. In the early manual stages of the project, this hostility coloured every aspect of the data on neighbouring; and could not be seen, as it later was, as ideological, masking the need of at least some women for neighbour friendships.

And finally, the program transformed the processes of concluding, claiming and validating claims. Some of these changes were to do with *confidence and thoroughness*. Rigorous coding allowed thorough cross-classification. Flexible size and development of indexes allowed teasing out of the emerging meanings of neighbour danger and their incorporation in new index categories that could in turn be explored. Very thorough indexing of all relevant material gave a new certainty to the exploration – was it really *all* men? If not, *which* men? New links could be drawn to quantitative material, through statistics offered by NUDIST or indexing linking to survey data. Deviant cases could be identified and explored. In short, techniques permitting complex structured indexing and manipulating of that *structure*, plus text search that adds its results to the indexing system, plus a large palette of retrieval operations that also add their results to the indexing system, together provide an elegant tool-kit for construction of theory and testing of that theory through the relevant data.

WHAT'S NEEDED NEXT? DEVELOPING NEW DEMANDS

While the Green Views project shifted methodologically a long way from the original data-control techniques, it took some time for this shift to be reviewed. In retrospect, the extent of the shift is clearly shown in the shopping list of developments it demanded of NUDIST. Most of these, now in later versions of the software, were aimed at combining the two forms of coding in stronger ways.

Improving on the code-and-retrieve technique

Some immediate developments improved on handling of documents for segmenting and indexing. *Subheaders* were added to provide speaker identifiers or context comments (and exploited to allow the user to nominate sections of documents, between subheaders, as the arena for certain enquiries). The rigidity of line-numbering had proved unnecessary for much of the data; later versions allow as text units in online documents *any unit that can end with a hard carriage return: lines or paragraphs, speeches, verses, even single words*.

Later developments addressed the apparent need to create a 'perfect' index up front. This meant flexibility not only to delete indexing categories but, more importantly, to *recombine, re-examine or rethink them,* or to recode their contents and to introduce new nodes. We had used the ability to delete a node very little, since deletion meant loss of indexing time. The Green Views project ended with large numbers of poorly used indexing nodes (just as manual systems accrue half-empty forgotten folders).

The problem of the new category created late in a project had remained one of the great frustrations of the Green Views project. It's no use if you can't afford the time to go back to the start and re-index material. The harried researcher had to be able to locate all, or at least most material likely to be relevant for a new category. This problem provided one of several reasons for a demand for *string searching capability*. It is much easier to search for 'getting set up' than to search through all categories that might be related to it! If words occurring in the text may indicate that material, a series of string searches could be conducted. In the prototype NUDIST in the Green Views project, string searching had been done using the UNIX editor; the clearly required next step was to allow the results of a string search to be automatically indexed. String searching was implemented in version 2.0, with wild cards to allow more flexible searches, and the *ability to save the results to a new or existing index node*, with any required amount of surrounding text. We also rapidly added the ability to specify that only documents indexed (or not indexed) at particular nodes were to be searched (avoiding the searching of all the bibliographic references, for instance, or selecting out people in a particular category).

But what if they had said not 'getting set up' but 'in the first weeks'? Other ways of locating the material for a new category were required. In the Green Views project we had often resorted to going through all the nodes likely to be related to the new one. In version 2.0 we exploited tree-structuring by allowing the researcher to *collect* all categories below one specified, so material could be recoded without a return to original documents. This ruse provided a surprise answer to another source of irritation, the need to trudge through *all* the meanings of good neighbour, for instance, if you wanted to find the overlap of ideas of good neighbour with ideas of family privacy. Now all those good neighbour subnodes could be temporarily collected whilst questions were asked about them.

Similarly, if you could explore the interrelationship of two or more sets of subnodes, pairwise, you clearly had to. Definitions of good neighbours by gender and life-stage gave an $8 \times 2 \times 5$ three-dimensional matrix. Storage of node-building instructions to create these eighty new categories in background mode did not remove the problem of creating the instructions. And such qualitative matrices were becoming increasingly popular as a method of display of qualitative data (Miles and Huberman 1984). They were controversial, risking distortion of rich data, since the 'cells' of manually drawn matrices must contain only illustrative quotes. Yet the technique clearly assisted in the recognition of patterns and their demonstration. Discussions with Matthew Miles and Jane Ritchie persuaded us that the need was for access to the entire contents of any given cell.

We implemented in version 2.0 of NUDIST automatic building of matrices of any number of dimensions, using the subnodes of any specified nodes. Each 'cell' is represented as a node, containing all the text, as well as comments, and also statistics about the proportion of documents, and of their text units.

The coding game: rethinking data processing

The Green Views project attempted to combine two sorts of qualitative coding, and the NUDIST project attempted to support this effort by computer. It was some time before the difference between the two sorts of coding became clear. The literature rarely distinguished between code-and-retrieve methods and coding for grounded theory: texts described one technique only. The difference is indicated in the tone of account. In Strauss's writing, coding is an adventure, almost a game. Miles and Huberman, by contrast, warn that coding is 'hard, obsessive work'.

In papers since, analyzing the experience with NUDIST, we have argued that the method requires clarification of these two meanings of 'code' (Richards 1991a and 1991b). In the specification of techniques in NUDIST, we have avoided the term and its duality, referring instead to indexing, and to index categories, at nodes. Our goal was to master the techniques of code-and-retrieve in order to support linking of theory with data and testing through it, then to develop techniques of emergence and interrogation of theory from data. In retrospect, we recall no concern that the two approaches would not easily combine, given the technology.

One of the strongest lessons from the Green Views analysis is that the two techniques do not easily combine. Code-and-retrieve is not a problem. On the contrary, the facility with which the computer performs this technique is problematic. Compared with the grounded theory method of open coding it is very easy, and very easily dominates time. Managing the proliferating categories was a constant challenge. By solving the problem of managing categories, NUDIST made more coding for retrieval possible. The technique is exhausting and lonely, easily routinized and continues its demands on time as long as data are coming in. The more vulnerable and tentative ideas emerging from the data are harder to incorporate in ordered categories than are codes describing characteristics of the data or allocating material to major known topics. So the code-and-retrieve method is to open coding as the root stock is to a grafted exotic plant. It takes over.

Open coding produces categories whose relationships have to be discovered: most coding for retrieval is done in categories whose relationships are logically set or logically discoverable. The codes produced by the grounded theory approach thus require constant care and attention. Relationships between categories are explored, while data are interrogated for comparative examples and for distilled meanings. The categories are rarely known in advance of data exploration, and the relationships between categories must always be discovered during data analysis. So prior shaping of index structures is impossible. Introduction of new categories is no mere extra requirement; all categories, in this method, are new, with the attendant problems of locating the data that fit them.

Supporting theory-building

New demands were generated by the experience of domination by the code-and-retrieve method. First, it was necessary to support the creation and linking of memos. They could of course be introduced into NUDIST as further document data, and then indexed at the nodes to whose categories they referred. But this tended not to happen, largely, we concluded, because as Strauss puts it, 'memos are cumulative'. In version 1.0 it was possible to locate memos about a single category in its comment field, but the challenge of providing multiple links to other categories remained for version 3.0.

Second, it was essential *to widen the range of retrievals*. Version 1.0 contained a complete set of Boolean search patterns: six ways of combining one category *and*, *or* or *not* another (all the material indexed at 'ideas about good neighbours' and also at 'privacy'). But these were often unable to specify what was wanted in detailed analysis processes. The first version also contained the ability to conduct the much more interesting request for 'all the ideas about good neighbours from women who mentioned (somewhere) their dislike of neighbours dropping in unannounced'. Building on this, we produced two groups of further requests. We needed to be able to explore *proximity or sequence of occurrence* of codes, to find, for instance, all the material on dangers of dropping in that was near (you specify how near) to, or that came before or after discussions on the privacy of the home. We needed ability to locate text coded at one category if it was *inside text coded at another* or *outside* it. (A search for the linked ideas of ideology would be assisted by being able to select all the material on home ownership that occurred within discussions of family life.) Once these were implemented, it was possible to explore the proximity or sequence or nested location of *occurrences of strings*, since the results of string searches could be made into nodes. With 'collect' and 'matrix', these made a set of fourteen retrieval and node-building commands.

The next move was to explore ways that the new nodes created in analysis could become part of the index system, rather than merely being separately stored as 'virtual nodes'. In version 2.0 the program was given the ability to place built nodes into the index trees, where they could be handled just like any other node. (Very shortly thereafter, it was given the further ability to encourage deletion of new nodes no longer wanted before the hard disk became cluttered!) Thus the explorations described above could be conducted with a set of temporary built nodes, thoroughly explored and then deleted, whilst ones now central to analysis (like 'neighbour-danger') could be retained.

As the project began to exploit the structure and capacity of the index system, it produced new demands for further flexibility. The program was changed to allow the user to shift, copy or delete nodes, so the index system could be pruned, reorganized and strengthened, new nodes incorporated in the logically required locations, duplication cleaned up, fuzzy boundaries between categories clarified.

The freedom of node-building was a heady and sometimes alarming experience. It proved amazingly easy to scale enticing beanstalks of guesswork and conjecture, as ideas emerging from the data were pursued – and very hard to figure out how you had got up there when you located an interesting body of material. A trail-marker was clearly needed. In version 2.0 nodes were given *comment fields*, which served multiple purposes. The system automatically logged anything it had done to that node: when it was created, whether it was built from other nodes, if so, what comments were at those, and so on. And the researcher could use them as a jotter pad, to note the patterns of the moment, ideas still to be pursued, etc. In version 3.0 memos can be edited for nodes or documents.

CONCLUSION: NEW COMBINATIONS OF METHOD?

Experience in the Green Views project suggested the program could act as catalyst for new combinations of techniques: quantitative and qualitative; case study and pattern-seeking; theory construction and theory testing. Each is achieved through the combination of coding for retrieval and open coding. The two techniques are not incompatible. They can be (and arguably should be) regarded as different loops of enquiry and theory-production, appropriate to different stages of research, types of data and, perhaps most importantly, different theoretical purposes and styles of enquiry. They contain comparable processes for widening and narrowing interpretative sweeps.

But the combination is far from easy, and the routine techniques of code-and-retrieve dominate. The segmentation of data is no mere clerical convenience: it imposes the choreography of delayed analysis and the view of the data as segments. New chronologies of research processes as well as new skills are required to exploit these possibilities. In NUDIST projects since, it has become far less important to produce up front an elegantly structured and comprehensive index system, since the program now offers very considerable support for revising and reviewing indexing data and reshaping the index system. At the same time, projects have begun to exploit the potential of a system that allows constant inspection and review not only of the categories currently being used, but of what is in them and the relationship between them.

The main task of qualitative research is always theory construction. Theories are actively constructed, not found, as Miles and Huberman nicely put it, like 'little lizards' under rocks. They will continue to be constructed by human researchers. They are 'mental maps, abstracted webs of meaning, that the analyst lays over bits of data to give them shape without doing violence to them' (1984: 83). The researcher must weave these webs. The computer can assist, by holding a myriad threads, exploring the sticky links to other categories, by allowing the exploration of many patterns and the building of one web on another, and by testing the strength of the resultant fabric. But the task of theory discovery remains for the human researchers; the questions are theirs, the combinations of categories specified by them. They see the links and draw the threads together, often by creative leaps or imaginative analogies or sheer field research luck, factors that have little to do with the carefully constructed index. But the resultant web of meaning will be certainly more complex and more confident than the manual method would have supported, the knowledge of the data far deeper, and the researcher equipped for interrogating results in ways that were not possible in the filing cabinet.

NOTE

The NUDIST project (Non-Numerical Unstructured Data Indexing, Searching and Theorizing), has been supported by the Victorian Department of Industry, Technology and Resources, and by La Trobe University. The software for mainframes, Macintosh computers and DOS machines are copyright to Replee Pty Ltd. For information and addresses of local agents, write to Qualitative Solutions and Research, 2 Research Drive, La Trobe University, Melbourne, Vic. 3083, Australia. 'NUDIST' is a trademark of Replee Pty Ltd.

REFERENCES

Burgess, R. (1984) *In the Field: an Introduction to Field Research*, London: Allen & Unwin.

Drass, K. (1980) 'The analysis of qualitative data', *Urban Life* 9: 332–53.

Fielding, N. and Lee, R. (1991) *Using Computers in Qualitative Research*, London: Sage.

Glaser, B.G. and Strauss, A.L. (1967) *The Discovery of Grounded Theory: Strategies for Qualitative Research*, Chicago: Aldine.

Hammersley, M. and Atkinson, P. (1983) *Ethnography: Principles in Practice*, London: Tavistock.

Lofland, J. and Lofland, L.H. (1984) *Analyzing Social Settings: a Guide to Qualitative Observation and Analysis*, Belmont, Calif.: Wadsworth.

Martin, P.Y. and Turner, B.A. (1986) 'Grounded theory and organizational research', *Journal of Applied Behavioural Science* 22(2): 141–57.

Miles, M.B. and Huberman, M. (1984) *Qualitative Data Analysis: a Sourcebook of New Methods*, Beverley Hills, Calif.: Sage.

Qualitative Sociology (1991) 14. Special issue on computing.

Richards, L. (1989) 'Family and home ownership in Australia: the nexus of ideologies', *Marriage and Family Review* 40: 173–94.

—— (1990) *Nobody's Home: Dreams and Realities in a New Suburb*, Melbourne: Oxford University Press.

Richards, L. and Richards, T. (1987) 'Qualitative data analysis: can computers do it?', *Australian and New Zealand Journal of Sociology* 23: 23–36.

—— (1991a) 'The transformation of qualitative method: computational paradigms and research processes', in N. Fielding and R. Lee (eds) *Using Computers in Qualitative Research*, London: Sage.

—— (1991b) 'Qualitative computing: a healthy development?', *Qualitative Health Research* 1: 234–62.

—— (1993) 'Using computers in qualitative analysis', in N. Denzin and Y. Lincoln (eds) *Handbook of Qualitative Research*, Newbury Park, Calif.: Sage.

Richards, T. and Richards, L. (1990) *NUDIST 2.1: Manual*, Melbourne: Replee.

Seidel, J.V. and Clark, J.A. (1984) 'The Ethnograph: a computer program for the analysis of qualitative data', *Qualitative Sociology* 7: 110–25.

Shelly, A. and Sibert, E. (1986) 'Using logic programming to facilitate qualitative data analysis', *Qualitative Sociology* 9: 145–61.

Strauss, A. (1987) *Qualitative Analysis for Social Scientists*, Cambridge and New York: Cambridge University Press.

Strauss, A.L. and Corbin, J. (1990) *Basics of Qualitative Research, Grounded Theory Procedures and Techniques*, Newbury Park, Calif.: Sage.

Tesch, R. (1990) *Qualitative Research: Analysis Types and Software Tools*, Basingstoke: Falmer Press.

Turner, B. (1981) 'Some practical aspects of qualitative data analysis: one way of organizing the cognitive processes associated with the generation of grounded theory', *Quality and Quantity* 15: 225–47.

Chapter 9

Qualitative data analysis for applied policy research

Jane Ritchie and Liz Spencer

The last two decades have seen a notable growth in the use of qualitative methods for applied social policy research. Qualitative research is now used to explore and understand a diversity of social and public policy issues, either as an independent research strategy or in combination with some form of statistical inquiry. The wider use of qualitative methods has come about for a number of reasons but is underpinned by the persistent requirement in social policy fields to understand complex behaviours, needs, systems and cultures.

'Framework', the analytic approach described in this chapter, was developed in the context of conducting applied qualitative research. It was initiated in a specialist qualitative research unit based within an independent social research institute (Social and Community Planning Research (SCPR)). The work of the institute spans all areas of social and public policy and is undertaken on behalf of central or local government, voluntary organizations, universities, or other public bodies, or it is grant funded by research councils and foundations. All the institute's work can be broadly classified as applied policy research, some of which is initiated by institute members but most of which is generated by the sponsoring bodies.

'Framework' has been refined and developed over the years but the general principles of the approach have proved to be versatile across a wide range of studies. Our aim here is to describe the method in detail; we use examples to show how the approach can be used to move through the various stages of the analytic process. Because the method has been developed for applied policy research, we begin with a brief overview of the kinds of objectives and requirements this sets.

THE NATURE OF APPLIED POLICY RESEARCH

Applied research can be broadly distinguished from 'basic' or 'theoretical' research through its requirements to meet specific information needs and its potential for actionable outcomes. The social policy field makes use of both applied and basic research, but a great deal is of the former kind. However, a very high proportion of applied policy research is quantitative in form, a heritage from the early years of empirical social inquiry and the result of the dominant requirement of policy-makers for facts (Bulmer 1982: 40–9). Fortunately, this is changing, as is the role played by qualitative methods. At one time, the use of qualitative methods was seen as acceptable if it was confined to a developmental role for statistical investigation. Now it has become recognized that the contributions of qualitative research are much more wide-ranging and that it has an important place in its own right. Most significantly it has a key role to play in providing insights, explanations and theories of social behaviour.

> What qualitative research can offer the policy maker is a theory of social action grounded on the experiences – the world view – of those likely to be affected by a policy decision or thought to be part of the problem.
>
> (Walker, 1985: 19)

In applied policy research, qualitative methods are used to meet a variety of different objectives. The questions that need to be addressed will vary from study to study but broadly they can be divided into four categories: contextual, diagnostic, evaluative and strategic:

Contextual: identifying the form and nature of what exists

e.g. What are the dimensions of attitudes or perceptions that are held?
What is the nature of people's experiences?
What needs does the population of the study have?
What elements operate within a system?

Diagnostic: examining the reasons for, or causes of, what exists
e.g. What factors underlie particular attitudes or perceptions?
Why are decisions or actions taken, or not taken?
Why do particular needs arise?
Why are services or programmes not being used?

Evaluative: appraising the effectiveness of what exists
e.g. How are objectives achieved?
What affects the successful delivery of programmes or services?
How do experiences affect subsequent behaviours?
What barriers exist to systems operating?

Strategic: identifying new theories, policies, plans or actions
e.g. What types of services are required to meet needs?
What actions are needed to make programmes or services more effective?
How can systems be improved?
What strategies are required to overcome newly defined problems?

Most research attempts to address more than one of these groups of questions. But in applied policy research, the objectives are usually clearly set and shaped by specific information requirements. Hence any output from the research needs to be appropriately targeted towards providing 'answers', in the form of greater illumination or understanding of the issues being addressed. This in turn has important implications for the form and functions of the analysis undertaken.

In addition to the research objectives, there are other features of applied policy research which may shape the way analysis is undertaken. First, time-scales tend to be shorter rather than longer – usually months rather than years. If government departments and other public agencies are to maximize their use of research, then they need 'answers' in time to influence their policy or planning decisions. Although all public bodies do commission longer-term research, a high proportion has a specified deadline, related to some key activity in the policy process.

Partly as a consequence of limited time-scales, applied research is often carried out by teams of researchers. These may comprise researchers from different disciplines, or be organized to allow individuals to take responsibility for different parts of the research process. Either way, this requires an explicit research methodology which can be viewed, discussed and operated by individuals within the team.

Another common feature is the need for generated data. Although desk research or document analysis usually forms part of a social policy research project (and occasionally is confined to these approaches alone), it is more usual to find that new data is collected. This may be in the form of individual interviews, group discussions or observational work. Certainly, within SCPR, most of the studies have newly generated interview data (either individual or group) and sometimes an observational component.

Qualitative research meets quite different objectives from quantitative research, and provides a distinctive kind of information. For applied policy purposes it may therefore be carried out with some kind of linkage to statistical inquiry (i.e. to help develop, illuminate, explain or qualify statistical research), or it may be entirely independent. Either way, it is important that the particular contributions that qualitative research can make are fully exploited.

Finally, there is an important issue to address in relationship to the visibility of qualitative methods. One of the factors that has almost certainly inhibited the greater use of qualitative methods in social policy fields is the lack of access that commissioners and funders have to the research process. This is particularly so in the conduct of qualitative data analysis. If decisions or actions are to be based on qualitative research, then policy-makers and practitioners need to know how the findings of the research have been obtained. The research community needs to respond to this by making its methods more explicit. This will bring not only greater confidence in the methodology, but also a deeper understanding of what qualitative research can do, and the way in which it can do it.

AIMS OF QUALITATIVE DATA ANALYSIS

Material collected through qualitative methods is invariably unstructured and unwieldy. A high proportion of it is text based, consisting of verbatim transcriptions of interviews or discussions, field notes or other written documents. Moreover, the internal content of the material is usually in detailed and micro form (e.g. accounts of experiences, descriptions of interchanges, observations of interactions, etc.). The qualitative researcher has to provide some coherence and structure to this cumbersome data set while retaining a hold of the original accounts and observations from which it is derived. All of this has implications for the methods of analysis which are developed.

Qualitative data analysis is essentially about detection, and the tasks of defining, categorizing, theorizing, explaining, exploring and mapping are fundamental to the analyst's role. The methods used for qualitative analysis therefore need to facilitate such detection, and to be of a form which allows certain functions to be performed. These functions will vary depending on the research questions being addressed, but, certainly in applied policy research, the following are frequently included:

Defining concepts: understanding internal structures;
Mapping the range, nature and dynamics of phenomena;
Creating typologies: categorizing different types of attitudes, behaviours, motivations, etc.;
Finding associations: between experiences and attitudes, between attitudes and behaviours, between circumstances and motivations, etc.;
Seeking explanations: explicit or implicit;
Developing new ideas, theories or strategies.

'Framework' has been developed to help these aims and outputs to be achieved. It is also designed to facilitate systematic analysis within the demands and constraints of applied policy research previously cited. To both these ends, the method has certain key features, which were central to its development. These are summarized in Figure 9.1.

Grounded or generative: it is heavily based in, and driven by, the original accounts and observations of the people it is about.
Dynamic: it is open to change, addition and amendment throughout the analytic process.
Systematic: it allows methodical treatment of all similar units of analysis.
Comprehensive: it allows a full, and not partial or selective, review of the material collected.
Enables easy retrieval: it allows access to, and retrieval of, the original textual material.
Allows between- and within-case analysis: it enables comparisons between, and associations within, cases to be made.
Accessible to others: the analytic process, and the interpretations derived from it, can be viewed and judged by people other than the primary analyst.

Figure 9.1 Key features of 'Framework'

'FRAMEWORK' AS A METHOD OF QUALITATIVE DATA ANALYSIS

'Framework' is an analytical process which involves a number of distinct though highly interconnected stages. Although the process is presented as following a particular order – indeed some stages do logically precede others – there is no implication that 'Framework' is a purely mechanical process, a foolproof recipe with a guaranteed outcome. On the contrary, although systematic and disciplined, it relies on the creative and conceptual ability of the analyst to determine meaning, salience and connections. Real leaps in analytical thinking often involve both jumping ahead and returning to rework earlier ideas. The strength of an approach like 'Framework' is that by following a well-defined procedure, it is possible to reconsider and rework ideas precisely because the analytical process has been documented and is therefore accessible.

The approach involves a systematic process of sifting, charting and sorting material according to key issues and themes. In order to illustrate the method, and to reflect the context and diversity of its applications in applied social policy research, five studies are referenced, one or two for each stage of the analytical process. Table 9.1 outlines the aims, sample, type of data and time-scale for each study.

Table 9.1 Summary of research studies used for illustrative purposes

The study	Type	Aims or objectives	Sample	Type of data	Time-scale
Talking about Sex *	Contextual	To explore sexual attitudes and behaviours. To study perceived links between sexual practices and health. To develop issues and clarify language for survey.	40 individuals	Depth interviews	10 months
Thirty Families *	Contextual	To explore the processes that lead to changes in living standards and the impact of these changes on families.	30 families	Depth interviews, 2 interviews per family	2 phases (9 months) with interval of 5 years)
Barriers to the Receipt of Dental Care *	Diagnostic and strategic	To identify the range of factors which inhibit people from seeking dental treatment. To generate ideas on ways of overcoming barriers.	108 dental attenders and non-attenders	Depth interviews (40) Group discussions (8)	12 months

The study	Type	Aims or objectives	Sample	Type of data	Time-scale
On Volun teering *	Diagnostic and strategic	To identify and explore motivations to volunteer. To examine ways in which volunteers might be attracted and maintained.	70 volunteers and non-volunteers	Group discussions (8)	5 months
Going on YTS: the Recruitment of Young People with Disabilities*	Evaluative	To evaluate the processes of recruitment in terms of: identification of young people with disabilities; their endorsement for special funding; their referral to suitable schemes. To identify good practice.	97 careers officers; government agency staff; managing agents; trainees	Depth interviews (67) Group discussions (4) Observational notes on training schemes provided	12 months

*These publications, based on particular studies, are listed with full details in the References.

The five key stages to qualitative data analysis involved in 'Framework' are:

> familiarization,
> identifying a thematic framework,
> indexing,
> charting,
> mapping and interpretation (this being the stage at which the key objectives of qualitative analysis are addressed).

Each of these analytical stages is described and illustrated below.

Familiarization

Before beginning the process of sifting and sorting data, the researcher must become familiar with their range and diversity, must gain an overview of the body of material gathered. Although she or he will have been involved in some, if not all, of the data collection, and will have formed hunches about key issues and emergent themes, it is important at this stage to set these firmly in context by taking stock and gaining a feel for the material as a whole. Where more than one person has been involved in data collection, the analyst can have only a partial or 'second-hand' grasp of colleagues' material. Even where the analyst has been the sole interviewer, it is likely that recollections will be selective and partial.

Essentially, familiarization involves immersion in the data: listening to tapes, reading transcripts, studying observational notes. In some cases it is possible to review all the material at the familiarization stage, for example where only a few interviews have been carried out, or where there is a generous timetable for the research. However, more often than not in applied policy research, the timetable is too pressing or the volume of material too extensive, and a selection must be made for this initial stage.

How the material is selected will depend on a number of features of the data collection process, such as:

the range of methods used,
the number of researchers involved,
the diversity of people and circumstances studied,
the time period over which the material was collected,
the extent to which the research agenda evolved or was modified during that time.

When making a selection, it is important to ensure that a range of different cases, sources, and time periods are reviewed. For example, in the study of barriers to dental care, material was collected by three researchers, through individual and group interviews amongst regular, intermittent and non-attenders. The analyst chose to review both individual and group data for different types of attenders and to include data collected by different researchers. For the study of sexual attitudes and behaviours, five researchers were involved in interviewing, partly to ease the interviewing burden, but also to evaluate the impact of interviewer characteristics, such as age and gender. Consequently, interviews were selected for review to include different interviewers at different stages of the fieldwork period as well as a mix of gender and age of respondents.

During the familiarization stage, the analyst listens to and reads through the material, listing key ideas and recurrent themes. Where a study aims to explore aspects of the research process as well as substantive issues, for example in the study of sexual attitudes and behaviour, notes are also made on the general atmosphere of the interview and the ease or difficulty of exploring particular subjects.

Identifying a thematic framework

During the familiarization stage, the analyst is not only gaining an overview of the richness, depth, and diversity of the data, but also beginning the process of abstraction and conceptualization. While reviewing the material, the analyst will be making notes, recording the range of responses to questions posed by the researchers themselves, jotting down recurrent themes and issues which emerge as important to respondents themselves.

Once the selected material has been reviewed, the analyst returns to these research notes, and attempts to identify the key issues, concepts and themes according to which the data can be examined and referenced. That is, she or he sets up a thematic framework within which the material can be sifted and sorted. When identifying and constructing this framework or index, the researcher will be drawing upon a priori issues (those informed by the original research aims and introduced into the interviews via the topic guide), emergent issues raised by the respondents themselves, and analytical themes arising from the recurrence or patterning of particular views or experiences.

The first version of an index is often largely descriptive and heavily rooted in a priori issues. It is then applied to a few transcripts when categories will be refined and become more responsive to emergent and analytical themes. For these refinements, the researcher looks for conceptualizations which encapsulate and represent diversity of experience, attitude, circumstance, etc.

Devising and refining a thematic framework is not an automatic or mechanical process, but involves both logical and intuitive thinking. It involves making judgements about meaning, about the relevance and importance of issues, and about implicit connections between ideas. In applied social policy research, it also involves making sure that the original research questions are being fully addressed.

The development of a thematic framework can be illustrated from the study of the living standards in unemployment, where one set of issues to be explored concerned patterns of expenditure in unemployment compared with those when last in work. This area of questioning (as outlined in the extract from the topic guide) and the emergent issues noted at the familiarization stage led to index categories as in Figure 9.2.

It will be seen that some of the index categories were virtually identical to specified areas of questioning (e.g. 1.3 Items and activities reduced), others were newly defined from the emergent themes (e.g. 1.5 Changing patterns over time). It should also be noted that the full index contained a total of 59 categories (i.e. 1.1, 2.1, 2.2, etc.), within 8 major subject headings.

Indexes provide a mechanism for labelling data in manageable 'bites' for subsequent retrieval and exploration. They should therefore not be over-elaborate in detail at this stage as the analyst needs to retain an overview of all the categories. The more interpretative stages of analysis, which take place later, will produce the refinement of what is contained in each category.

If there is more than one population being studied (as, for example, in the case of the YTS study), then it may be necessary to develop separate indexes for each group. Alternatively, it may be possible to keep a common index but deal with additional elements in the material through extra subcategories. Generally it is preferable to keep a common index for the different groups being studied as this helps immediately to identify both common and divergent themes.

Indexing

'Indexing' refers to the process whereby the thematic framework or index is systematically applied to the data in its textual form. Although any textual material can be indexed in this way, the method has mainly been applied to

TOPIC GUIDE (extract)

Income and expenditure

Current income:
Sources level (in detail)

Income when last employed:
Level, extent of change

Main effects on expenditure:
What has changed; how has
it changed?

Identify items or activities
which have been

Withdrawn:
Why; how important before,
what does the loss mean
to them; what is the effect?

Reduced:
Why; how important before,
what does the reduction
mean to them; what is the
effect?

Maintained:
Why; what is their
importance, why not
reduced or cut out?

Increased:
Why; what is importance?

Change in patterns of expenditure:
Did changes all happen
immediately or over time?
What caused change in
patterns?

INDEX (extract)

Patterns of expenditure

1.1 Expenditure management
1.2 Items and activities maintained,
    increased and newly adopted
1.3 Items and activities reduced
1.4 Items and activities withdrawn
1.5 Changing patterns over time
1.6 Two weekly patterns

Patterns of management

2.1 Methods of money management
2.2 Methods of control
2.3 Changes in lifestyle, financial
    demands
2.4 Critical times, abnormal
    demands
2.5 Previous financial commitments
2.6 Other

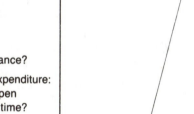

RESEARCH NOTES AND JOTTINGS
Managing style variable
Critical times when money management,
expenditure hard to control
Control mechanisms
Changing patterns in early and later stages of unemployment.

Figure 9.2 Development of a thematic framework

transcriptions of individual and group interviews. All the data, not just those selected for review, are read and annotated according to the thematic framework. Indexing references are recorded on the margins of each transcript by a numerical system which links back to the index, or by a descriptive textual system based directly on the index headings.

Again, applying an index is not a routine exercise as it involves making numerous judgements as to the meaning and significance of the data. For each passage, the analyst must infer and decide on its meaning, both as it stands and in the context of the interview as a whole, and must record the appropriate indexing reference. Single passages often contain a number of different themes each of which needs to be referenced; multiple indexing of this kind can often begin to highlight patterns of association within the data. Of course, this process of making judgements is subjective, and open to differing interpretations. By adopting a system of annotating the textual data, however, the process is made visible and accessible to others; others can see for themselves how the data are being sifted and organized, research colleagues can 'try out' the framework and pool their experiences; the analyst can 'check out' the basis of his or her assumptions.

Figure 9.3 shows a page of an indexed transcript from the living standards study. The first column on the right hand side replicates the index numbers assigned and any research notes that were made. The far column shows the content of the index categories to which these relate. These would not normally appear on the transcript but have been shown here for the purpose of clarification.

In Figure 9.3, it is possible to see that several different index prefixes appear on one page, even within one speech passage (e.g. 4.1, 1.3, 1.6, 1.4). It is quite common to find that different major topics are connected and interwoven in this way and this is one of the values of indexing. Once labelled, the analyst is able to access each reference and, more crucially, to see patterns and the contexts in which they arise. As already suggested, these juxtapositions are often one of the early clues to associations for subsequent stages of analysis.

Charting

Having applied the thematic framework to individual transcripts, the analyst needs to build up a picture of the data as a whole, by considering the range of attitudes and experience for each issue or theme. Data are 'lifted' from their original context and rearranged according to the appropriate thematic reference. This process, referred to as charting, is described below.

Charts are devised with headings and subheadings which may be drawn from the thematic framework, from a priori research questions, or according to considerations about how best to present and write up the study. How the charts are laid out will depend on whether analysis is to be thematic (for each

Transcript	Code	Theme
F: We just live from day to day. Sometimes I make the kids pancakes if they're hungry and things like that where I never used to before. They could always go and help themselves to an extra bowl of cereal but the cereal	4.1	Impact on children
has to be rationed, it's got to do. What I get at the weekend has to do for so many days.	1.3	Items reduced
	1.6	Two weekly patterns
You know, things like that. And so, I say, fresh vegetable and fruit, I cut right down. Right down. And they all used to take an apple going to school, the older ones or a banana or an orange or something, they don't do that any more. Or I'd give them the		
money to get something extra at school. Can't do that any more. Just can't, it's just impossible. It's either that or we lose our home. Because they've already taken us before.	1.4	Items withdrawn
M: County court.		
F: The county court and, as I say, it's £400 we're behind isn't it?	3.7	Loans/debts/arrears
M: What's that on?	1.3	Items reduced
F: Our mortgage, £400 isn't it?		
M: It was but over the last 2 months - er - we've got it, we've kept the last 10 months up to date, £72 per month. Next month and the following month we'll try and get off the arrears £30 per month, which is –	1.1	Expenditure management
F: Extra.		
M: (baby shouting) It's all more – I'm trying to say you're getting the tourniquet tightening on you all the while. That's why I'm hoping	2.3	Changes in lifestyle/ financial demands
I can get a – with the weather, can get some work.	7.1	Employment prospects
F: Yes, 2 months we've got.		

Figure 9.3 Example of an indexed transcript

theme across all respondents) or by case (for each respondent across all themes). Where a thematic approach is adopted, charts are drawn up for each key subject area, and entries made for several respondents on each chart. The ordering and grouping of the individual cases may be linked to characteristics or dimensions that are known or believed to have a significant effect on patterns of experience or behaviour etc. The essential point, however, is that *cases* are always kept in the same order for each subject chart, so that the whole data set for each case can easily be reviewed. Where a case approach is used, one or two charts may be drawn up for each case, with *subjects* recorded in the same order.

In the case of the living standards study, a thematic approach was followed, and six major subject charts were constructed. These covered:

patterns of management,
patterns of expenditure,
personal and social effects,
effects on family life,
standards of living (definition and changes),
employment: activity, attitudes to and job search.

Figure 9.4 shows some of the headings for the chart 'Patterns of expenditure'. Several families were entered on each chart, grouped according to the ratio of their income in unemployment to that when last employed, known as the replacement ratio. By keeping a consistent order for the families on each chart, comparisons could be made between or within cases. It can also be seen that some of the chart headings were identical to index categories (e.g. Items reduced, Two weekly patterns), others reflected newly emergent themes identified while indexing the data (e.g. Periods of new control). For example, this latter heading was introduced to chart data about a period often described in the interviews when families had to introduce new levels of expenditure control.

Whereas some methods of qualitative analysis rely on a 'cut and paste' approach, whereby 'chunks' of verbatim texts are regrouped according to their index reference, charting involves abstraction and synthesis. Each passage of text, which has been annotated with a particular reference, is studied and a distilled summary of the respondent's views or experiences is entered on the chart. The level of detail recorded varies between projects and between researchers, from lengthy descriptions to cryptic abbreviations for each entry. However, the original text is referenced so that the source can be traced and

CHART 3. PATTERNS OF EXPENDITURE FAMILIES WITH REPLACEMENT RATIO 75-90%				
Family	Items maintained	Items reduced	Two weekly patterns	Periods of new control
1				
2				
3 etc.				

Figure 9.4 Example of subject chart headings

the process of abstraction can be examined and replicated. Illustrative passages for possible quotation are also referenced by transcript page numbers at this stage.

In the study of recruitment of young people with disabilities to YTS, one of the key subjects to be charted was the way in which different parties defined and interpreted the term 'disability'. Under the overall heading 'definitions of disability', further subheadings were elaborated to include: the 'official definition' (as endorsed by the government agency), the respondents' 'own definition', and 'grey areas' or ambiguities of interpretation or application. Charts were then constructed separately for each group of respondents: careers officers, agency staff and scheme providers. Transcripts were studied according to the appropriate index references, and a summary of each respondent's views entered on the chart. Figure 9.5 shows an example of the chart constructed for careers officers, and illustrates the kind of entries recorded together with the page referencing system.

Respondent	The recruitment of young people with disabilities to YTS CHART 3: DEFINITIONS OF DISABILITY (Careers Officers)		
	3.1 Official definition	3.2 Own definition	3.3 Grey areas
CO1	Includes physical/ sensory handicaps and learning difficulties. (p. 10) Area officers more flexible than the official guide-lines. (p. 18)	Also add moderate learning difficulties and behavioural problems. (p. 12) 'The naughty boys'. (p. 13)	What about people who are socially disadvantaged? (p. 22) Is inequality a disability? (p. 27) Official view would not accept this. (p. 29)
CO2	Physical/sensory/ mental handicap + behavioural. (p. 15)	Go along with official view. Find it very helpful. (p. 19)	Problem is managing agents take a very narrow view - physical/ sensory only - and the official statistics are based on their returns. (p. 27)
CO3			

Figure 9.5 Example of subject chart entries

Mapping and interpretation

When all the data have been sifted and charted according to core themes, the analyst begins to pull together key characteristics of the data, and to map and interpret the data set as a whole. Although emergent categories, associations and patterns will have been noted and recorded during the indexing and charting phases, the serious and systematic process of detection now begins. It is here that the analyst returns to the key objectives and features of qualitative analysis outlined at the beginning of this chapter, namely:

> defining concepts,
> mapping range and nature of phenomena,
> creating typologies,
> finding associations,
> providing explanations,
> developing strategies, etc.

Which of these the analyst chooses to attempt will be guided by the original research questions to be addressed, and by the themes and associations which have emerged from the data themselves.

Whichever route is followed, the basic processes are the same: the analyst reviews the charts and research notes; compares and contrasts the perceptions, accounts, or experiences; searches for patterns and connections and seeks explanations for these internally within the data. Piecing together the overall picture is not simply a question of aggregating patterns, but of weighing up the salience and dynamics of issues, and searching for a structure rather than a multiplicity of evidence.

This part of the analytical process is the most difficult to describe. Any representation appears to suggest that the analyst works in a mechanical way, making obvious conceptualizations and connections, whereas in reality each step requires leaps of intuition and imagination. The whole process of immersion in the data triggers associations, the origins of which the analyst can scarcely recognize. Because this crucial part of the process is so difficult to encapsulate, a number of different examples are given below, and an attempt made to crystallize and convey the logical and creative pathways followed.

Defining concepts

In the course of charting references to a particular phenomenon, the analyst may well have begun to identify a number of associated features or descriptions. At this stage, however, she or he systematically examines the charted material, searching for key dimensions and themes.

So, for example, in the living standards study, an analysis was undertaken of how the terms 'living standards' and 'standards of living' were defined by study participants. The case study families, between them, identified nine factors that had a bearing on their judgements of living standards. These were:

the amount of disposable *income* they had,
the items of *expenditure* they could or could not afford,
the level of *choice* or constraint that surrounded their pattern of expenditure,
the level of *financial security* that was felt,
the degree of *struggle* involved in making ends meet,
the material *possessions* they had, or could attain,
the degree to which *expectations* were fulfilled,
the extent to which *self-esteem* could be upheld,
the feelings of *contentment* that surrounded life.

These elements emerged during the course of people describing their present standards of living, or what it had been like before, or how they defined a good or poor standard of living or simply their understanding of the term.

A further example of clarifying definitions is taken from the study of the recruitment to YTS of young people with disabilities, where identifying the range and diversity of concepts of disability was important in order to understand how guide-lines were implemented, and to gain an understanding of the recruitment process. By first listing the characteristics associated with

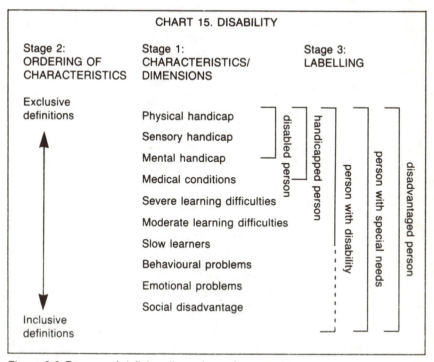

Figure 9.6 Process of defining dimensions of a concept

disability, and then ordering them on the dimension of inclusivity–exclusivity, it was possible to devise a scale of definitions, and to identify how different labels were applied. Figure 9.6 illustrates this three-stage process.

Mapping the range and nature of phenomena

A core function of qualitative research is to identify the form and nature of a phenomenon, and where appropriate, to map the polarities. In the study of volunteering, a central objective of the research was to identify key reasons why people might become volunteers. By reviewing the charts for references to attitudes, experiences, images and deterrents, it was possible to draw out key dimensions of motivations to volunteer (see Figure 9.7).

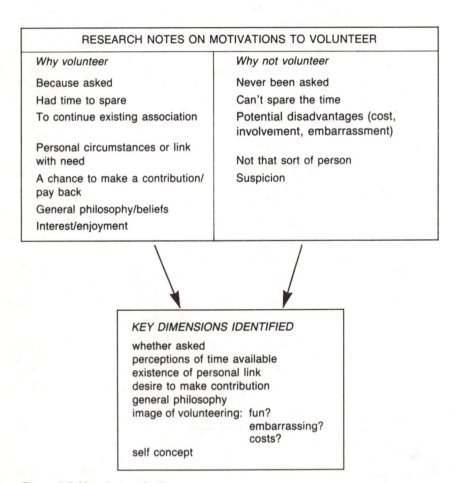

Figure 9.7 Mapping motivations

Creating typologies

Having identified key dimensions or characteristics of particular social phenomena, the researcher may decide to move on to multidimensional analysis, as in the creation of typologies, where two or more dimensions are linked at different points, giving a range of *types* of cases. In the study of sexual attitudes and behaviours, it was important to establish the nature of people's sexual histories and life-styles in order to understand the context of their views and actions. Key dimensions of sexual life-style were identified as the number of sexual partners over time, and the basis of the relationship(s) or encounter(s). By plotting people's histories and current sexual activity along these two dimensions, the following typology of sexual life-styles could be constructed (see Figure 9.8).

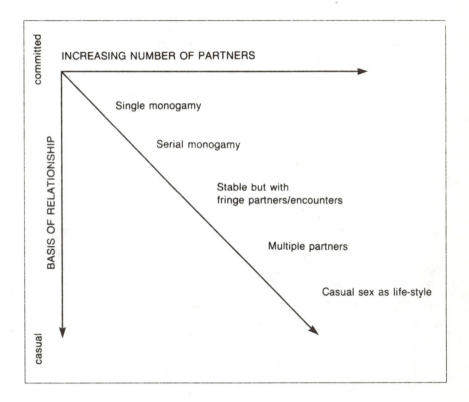

Figure 9.8 Typologies of sexual life-styles

Finding associations

In the course of indexing and charting interview material the analyst may become aware of a patterning of responses; for example it may appear that people with certain characteristics or experiences also hold particular views or behave in particular ways. At this stage the analyst will systematically check for associations between attitudes, behaviours, motivations, etc, either those made explicit by respondents themselves or those derived from implicit connections.

In the study of the recruitment of young people with disabilities to YTS, a systematic search among references to disability revealed that particular groups of respondents interpreted 'disability' and applied labels in quite different ways. This association was identified through the process of constructing a central 'labels' chart across all respondent groups. The five different labels associated with disability were chosen to form subheadings, and respondents were plotted according to their use of particular terms, as shown in Table 9.2. For the sample as a whole, the central chart revealed a clustering of types of respondent under each of the different terms. Whereas careers officers tended to hold the most inclusive definitions and to use labels with the least stigma attached, managing agents of basic schemes held the narrowest definitions, frequently referring to 'the handicapped' and 'the disabled'. This pattern of association is represented diagramatically in Figure 9.9.

Table 9.2 Plotting associations

		USE OF LABELS		
Disabled person	Handicapped person	Person with a disability	Person with special needs	Disadvantaged person
MA 1 (B)	MA 2 (B)	AS 1	CO 1	CO 3
MA 5 (B)	MA 3 (B)	AS 2	CO 5	CO 4
MA 8 (B)	MA 6 (B)	AS 3	CO 8	CO 6
	AS 6	AS 4	MA 4 (S)	CO 7
		CO 2	MA 7 (S)	
			AS 5	

Key: MA (B) = Managing agent for basic scheme
      MA (S) = Managing agent for special scheme
      CO = Career officer
      AS = Agency staff

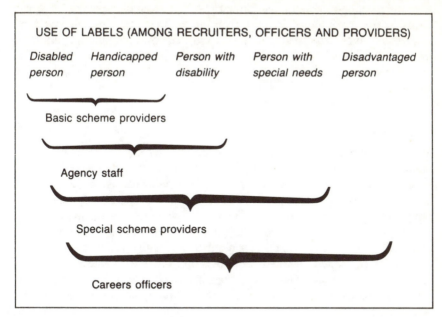

USE OF LABELS (AMONG RECRUITERS, OFFICERS AND PROVIDERS)

| Disabled person | Handicapped person | Person with disability | Person with special needs | Disadvantaged person |

Basic scheme providers

Agency staff

Special scheme providers

Careers officers

Figure 9.9 Mapping patterns

Providing explanations

A common objective in applied qualitative research is to explain, as well as to illuminate, people's attitudes, experiences and behaviour. Explanations may be sought in order to address the questions that triggered the research in the first place, or to account for issues and patterns of behaviour which arise from the research itself.

In the study of sexual attitudes and behaviour, it emerged from the analysis that young heterosexual men and women, whose sexual life-styles suggested they would be wise to practise safe sex, were taking no preventative measures at all. They did not consider themselves to be in a high risk group such as people who 'do drugs', or are 'promiscuous'. By unpacking how people defined the term promiscuous, it was possible to explain why people did not apply the label to themselves. Key characteristics associated with promiscuity were identified as:

the basis of the relationship (casual),
feelings about sexual partners (absence of),
number of partners over time (compared with own experience),
number of partners co-terminously (more than one).

It became clear that whereas others were described as promiscuous on any one of these counts, people did not label their own behaviour in this way unless all the conditions applied. So, for example, people who had casual sexual encounters or more than one partner at a time did not consider themselves promiscuous if they liked their partners and judged them to be 'nice people'; people who changed partners every few months felt they were exempt because the relationship was 'serious' while it lasted, and so on.

Developing strategies

Much of the research carried out in the policy field has a strategic component; policy-makers commission research into attitudes, behaviours and experiences because they wish to inform their policy decisions. As a result of the process of analyzing qualitative data, and identifying underlying motivations, patterns and explanations, it may be possible to develop strategies for change which arise directly from the qualitative material itself. For example, the volunteering study identified a number of positive and negative conditions which accounted for whether or not people became volunteers. By drawing out the implications of these conditions, it was possible to develop a strategy for attracting and retaining volunteers which directly addressed those issues (see Figure 9.10).

ATTRACTING AND RETAINING VOLUNTEERS

change perceptions
need for positive, interesting, caring image, to overcome unprofessional, 'busybody', amateur connotations

practical incentives and help
training
reimbursement for travel expenses

higher profile
provide more information
give a focus for information e.g. identifiable agency

modes of recruitment
personal invitation/overcoming resistance to compulsory schemes

---

Figure 9.10 Developing strategies

A second example is provided by the dental health study, where a number of barriers to dental care were identified. These in turn led to the formulation of a number of specific strategies that would help people become more regular attenders. Some of these arose out of explicit suggestions made by the respondents themselves, others were derived indirectly from the nature of the problems. So, for example, one key area concerned the cost of dental treatment; specific suggestions made in relation to this were:

reduce or abolish dental charges,
introduce a clear charging system,
inform patients of the cost of treatment before commitment to carrying it out,
ensure privacy when determining eligibility for free treatment,
(for long-term attenders) provide an incentive of first course of treatment free.

CONCLUSIONS

Because of the nature of SCPR's work, we (and other researchers with us) have had the opportunity to apply 'Framework' on numerous studies. The method, of course, needs to be adapted to suit the aims and coverage of a specific piece of research, but it has proved flexible for a range of different types of studies. It has been applied to in-depth and group interviewing, longitudinal studies, case studies, and projects involving different groups or subpopulations of participants. 'Framework' has also been successfully used jointly by two or more researchers working on a single project, in some cases cross-institutionally.

It will perhaps be apparent that some parts of the process have been relatively easy to display, while others have been much more difficult to capture. Nevertheless, we believe these more elusive stages, particularly those which involve inductive and interpretative thinking, can be made explicit in some form. As already emphasized, we believe this accessibility is important for those who commission and use qualitative research for public policy purposes.

We wish to stress that the analysis method described above is just one approach for synthesizing and interpreting qualitative data. Although it does accommodate all the features we believe to be important, there are certainly other approaches that would equally satisfy these requirements. But, until recently, this has been difficult to know since qualitative researchers have not made their analytic tools accessible. It is important that individual researchers provide documentation of their methods and techniques of analysis, not just in volumes of this kind, but also in research publications and proposals. Only by so doing will the research community widen its pool of analytic knowledge and extend its methodological base.

REFERENCES

Bulmer, M. (1982) *The Uses of Social Research*, London: Allen & Unwin.

Finch, H. (1988) *Barriers to the Receipt of Dental Care*, London: Social and Community Planning Research.

Ritchie, J. (1990) *Thirty Families*, London: HMSO.

Spencer, L. and Whelan, E. (1988) *Going on YTS: the Recruitment of Young People with Disabilities*, Sheffield: Training Agency.

Spencer, L., Faulkner, A., Keegan, J. (1988) *Talking about Sex*, London: Social and Community Planning Research.

Thomas, A. and Finch, H. (1990) *On Volunteering*, Berkhampsted: The Volunteer Centre, UK.

Walker, R. (1985) *Applied Qualitative Research*, Aldershot: Gower.

Chapter 10

Patterns of crisis behaviour: a qualitative inquiry

Barry A. Turner

INTRODUCTION

Qualitative research comes in a variety of forms. We produce 'qualitative data' in the course of our attempts to understand a range of different events, processes, behaviours or people, and such data are inherently diverse, non-standardized, heterogeneous and difficult to classify. This is not to suggest, though, that such data are peculiar. Even though it often appears as if we live and work in a world where most of the important information is quantitative and standardized, a world in which any qualitative material has to be segregated and treated with suspicion, a deeper understanding of the processes of inquiry and comprehension shows that the reverse is the case. We can regard all of the information which we acquire about the world as qualitative, and then see that under some circumstances we can use this information to create a particular kind of data, quantitative data, to which the properties of number can be applied.

The power offered by numerical systems of analysis can only be developed and used if we can find a sufficiently close correspondence, a sufficient degree of isomorphism, between the properties of the portion of the world under investigation and the properties of the mathematical or number system which we might use. A moment's reflection will reveal to us that, even where the use of numerical analysis seems most self-evident, to use it we need to make certain working assumptions. We may regularly count apples or sheep or pounds sterling. But every apple, every animal, is unique.[1] When we count, we merely agree, tacitly, that for this everyday purpose, we are willing to apply rules which disregard the differences between individual apples or individual sheep, and which stress their similarities for numbering purposes. If we are buying a flock of sheep, we are likely to want to know whether there are twenty or fifty of them, and how much we are paying per head. But we might regard the flock differently if it includes the two baby lambs which our children have hand-reared and given pet names to. Such an individual relationship would then make us much more aware of the uniqueness of the separate entities, and thus of the differences between them.

And, even though a monetary system embodies an assumed equivalence of monetary units (Weber 1978: 166–80) which leads us to think it irrational that we should prefer one coin to another of the same denomination, it is still the case that any individual coin or currency note is unique. I would have this uniqueness drawn to my attention with some force if a coin which turned up in my change was identified as a valuable rarity, eagerly sought after by collectors. Ironically, I would then lay myself open to charges of irrationality if I proposed to disregard its uniqueness in order simply to spend it for its face value at the supermarket.

We are obliged, though, to categorize to some degree the events and phenomena which we encounter in the world if we are to bring any order to our experiences. To make it possible to learn from them and to avoid the madness of total unpredictability we have to typify or construct general classifications. We cannot function in our everyday life unless we are able to escape from the presumption that the future will be a stream of unique and unprecedented events, unrelated and unrelatable to anything which we have already experienced.

We work, then, with typifications, but for more of our activities and for most of our investigations, the kinds of typifications which we use do not closely match readily available mathematical models. When we find numbers useful, we are willing to adopt 'strong' rules for categorizing our data, rules which assume that the inherent differences between objects or events can be disregarded. When 'weak' rules for categorizing data are more appropriate, we cluster phenomena together more loosely and more of the diversity of the world which we are confronting remains apparent (Gherardi and Turner 1987). Handling qualitative data makes us particularly sensitive to the need to deal with variety and diversity.

One method for analyzing diverse, non-standardized texts, transcripts or other kinds of qualitative social scientific data is the approach initially described as 'grounded theory', which was pioneered by Glaser and Strauss (1967) and which has been further developed by Strauss and others (Martin and Turner 1986, Richards and Richards 1987, 1991, Strauss 1987, Strauss and Corbin 1990, Turner 1981, 1988). In essence, this approach involves: first, the 'chunking and coding' of data, dividing facets of the available data into segments which are given labels, names or codes; second, the accumulation of those central codes which recur, and the development of abstract definitions to specify the properties associated with these core codes; and third, identifying links between the codes, links which may merely be associational, but which in some cases will be causal. Exploration and elaboration of these links make it possible to develop 'local' or 'grounded' theoretical patterns to account for aspects of the data under scrutiny. Such procedures are not exclusive to social science for they embody very general processes of cognition and comprehension, processes which may be used in fields as diverse as real estate finance (Glaser and Crabtree 1969), structural engineering

(Pidgeon *et al*. 1986) or the elicitation of knowledge for use in expert systems (Pidgeon *et al*. 1991).

In spite of its widespread scope, though, grounded theory does not cover every kind of qualitative inquiry, and to see something of the diversity of qualitative investigations, it may be instructive to look at some kinds of analysis which fall on its fringes. The example which I would like to consider more closely here is an analysis carried out by Brian Toft and myself of the patterns of crisis-behaviour discernible during a tragic and disastrous fire which occurred in 1973 at the Summerland Leisure Centre, Douglas, Isle of Man.

APPROACHING THE CASE STUDY

I had already carried out one analysis of the inquiry into this fire, paying particular attention to its social and organizational *preconditions* (Turner 1978, Turner and Pidgeon forthcoming) as one step in building up a more general theory of the social preconditions of disaster. In this first analysis, I had begun with the documentary account provided by the public inquiry into the fire (*Summerland 1974*) and used the 'grounded theory' method already referred to, labelling file cards with the titles of categories which I teased out of the documentary data, and then juggling the categories on these cards to produce an appropriate theoretical account. In the second analysis, though, we had access to additional data and we wanted to look not at preconditions, but at the behaviour which occurred when the emergency actually *started*, so that we could express our analysis in a narrative form for use as a case study of crisis decision-making for teaching purposes. This required us to pay attention to a different section of the public inquiry data, as well as our additional material. We could not readily add further to this stock of information by collecting new data, since the incident was already some fifteen years old when we embarked on the second analysis.

In the first analysis, I had used the 'grounded theory' approach to the Summerland documents, along with other reports on major accidents, in order to develop a theory about the events which caused them. In the second, more recent analysis, my colleague Brian Toft and I set about building upon the first by preparing a narrative account of one particular stage of the development of the catastrophe, the onset of the crisis. The completed narrative could then be used as training material from which students could attempt to draw their own lessons about the handling of crisis.

First analysis: developing the initial 'grounded theory'

At this point, it might be helpful to look back briefly at the way in which the original grounded theory was developed before going on to consider the problems of constructing a case study narrative. The original analysis of Summerland was based upon data drawn entirely from the official public inquiry into the incident (*Summerland 1974*). I worked paragraph by paragraph through this report, as I did for all of the accident reports published between 1965 and 1975. I asked, for each paragraph, what names or 'labels for ideas' I needed in order to identify those elements, events or notions which were of interest to me in my broad and initially very unfocused concern to develop a theory of disaster preconditions. I then recorded each name or concept label on the top of a 5 inch by 8 inch file card, together with a note of the source paragraph, and added further paragraph references to the card as I encountered additional instances of the concept identified.

Eventually, for my whole study, I ended up with 182 of these cards, which had to be sifted, sorted and juggled into a coherent theoretical model. I produced general definitions for each of the categories which recurred, looked for causal and other links and moved gradually towards a theoretical pattern which helped to explain the range of data which I had about accidents. This sorting stage is the one which is more difficult to write about, or to formulate useful general propositions about. Referring elsewhere (Turner 1988) to the coding process as a set of procedures to lead the researcher into the centre of a maze, I proposed that, once in the centre, the researcher has to fashion a theory out of any resources available in order to make it possible to find a way out again.

The Summerland accident report was the third one I analyzed, after I had tackled those on the major tip slide at Aberfan and the crash at the Hixon level crossing. These three major incidents were sufficient to provide the core of the emerging theory, as the analysis in my early publications shows (Turner 1976a, 1976b). Looking back, I find that I entered references to Summerland on 96 of my 182 cards. Of these, 58 record ideas which *originated* from my reading of the Summerland report (for example, *Reliance on informal networks to communicate about ill-structured problems*, *Waiving of regulations*, *Safety procedures ineffective* and *Unanticipated dual control exacerbating ill-structured problem*) and 38 record my spotting factors in the Summerland report which had already been noted on cards in connection with Aberfan or Hixon. The subsequent generation of cards from other accident reports prompted me to remember and add a note of a similar factor at Summerland (for example, *Use of ambivalent statements which apparently resolve differing views of complex problem*, *Idealistic and unrealistic normative view of problem area by top management*, and *Limited range of action and responsibility for individual whose organisational position and organizational behaviour are influenced by institutional bias*). I can now see that I eventually ended up with 94 cards which included references to Summerland because I decided that the codes or labels on two new cards prompted by reading the Summerland report were essentially the same as those on two existing cards, so that they could be merged.

First analysis: some detailed instances

Let me offer one or two more detailed instances of the coding process.[2] Some categories I think of as very basic 'bread-and-butter' kinds of categories: early on in an inquiry I find it necessary to record those basic terms and ideas which recur in any description of the kinds of phenomena that I am interested in. They constitute a basic vocabulary for any even mildly theoretical discussion of the events. As an example of one of these essential if intellectually unexciting elements in the analysis I can point to card 119: *Problems of restricted access causing hazard.* This code was triggered by paragraphs 27 ff. (*Summerland 1974*) which noted the difficulties of access at Summerland for visitors, for staff and regular services as well as for emergency and firefighting services. I then recorded on this card seven or eight further references to restricted access and its implications which were made at other points in the Summerland report. The question of access recurs in many major accidents, although, as the lack of references on this card indicate, it was not a contributory factor to the Aberfan or Hixon accidents.

A much more general factor, the *Existence of many groups handling a complex problem*, I noted many times in connection with Aberfan and Hixon, as well as for virtually all other major disasters. The Summerland report enabled me to add to this card references to the multiplicity of architects, designers, governmental bodies and commercial companies involved with the planning, construction and operation of the leisure centre.

A key concept in the theory as it finally emerged was that of the decoy phenomenon. This term began life as *Acceptance of partial view of problem obscuring wider view*, which I noted in connection with a range of confused responses to the potential dangers of tip slips at Aberfan, and to overhead electric cables at Hixon level crossing. From the Summerland report, I added notes that in the planning stage, the Fire Staff Officer knew that the plastic material Oroglas, used in constructing part of the centre, was flammable, but that on other grounds – that there were no buildings nearby – he did not object to a waiver permitting its use (Summerland 1974: para. 62); that Summerland, a novel kind of entertainment complex protected from the elements by a new form of canopy, was not *seen* as a large building, or as a theatre, so that possibly appropriate regulations and precautions were not seen as relevant or were not applied (paras 131–6 and *passim*); and a reference (para. 147) to vague and erroneous theories about the possible behaviour in a fire of the materials used, such as that plastic domes in the roof might 'fall out' to permit the venting of lethal smoke. I eventually described or defined the idea involved here as a contributory factor to disaster which arises from 'the attention paid to some well-defined problem or source of danger in the situation which was dealt with, but which distracted attention from a still dangerous but ill-structured problem in the background' (Turner 1978: 60):

the very appropriate term 'decoy' was eventually provided by an anonymous referee of an article (Turner 1976a) submitted to *Administrative Science Quarterly*.

In a discussion in the accident report of the lack of fire protection for the service stairs at Summerland, I was struck by a comment (Summerland 1974: para. 185) which noted that one of the designers 'made the rather startling observation that this staircase was "a notional fire escape at the time . . . an earnest of intentions"'. I labelled card 148: *Talisman: Symbolic safety precautions only: good intentions not enough*. I made a note which linked this with some reading which I had been doing about propitiatory precautions undertaken by Londoners during the Blitz: spending so many nights in the air-raid shelter, but rewarding themselves for good behaviour by spending a night in their own beds, even though the bombing continued. I still find this idea and this kind of behaviour fascinating, but the category never recurred in the reports I was looking at and I did not make any use of it in the finished theory. It remains in my records as a kind of unfulfilled theoretical promise, yet to be taken up.

It is probably worth commenting here on the extent to which personal preferences and idiosyncrasies enter into the process of code generation. I know from discussions with other qualitative researchers that my codes are more extensive and in some senses more messy than the labels which they would regularly use. At the level of 'conceptual focus' at which I seem to prefer to operate, I perhaps take for granted a more basic, sociologically influenced grid of understanding of the world in terms of roles, interaction and so on. What makes this kind of analysis stimulating for me is the search to identify and map complex interlocking clusters of phenomena which relate to the problems I want to understand and explain in my theory. Conversations with Lyn Richards suggest that she is concerned to identify much more 'crisp' facets or dimensions of social phenomena which can be located and compared by multiple researchers using an extensive, shared set of data. By contrast, Strauss's writings suggest that he would like to move towards the identification of key social activities (for example, monitoring) whose dimensions can then be explored and identified (Strauss and Corbin 1990: 61–74). There is no need to search for an orthodoxy here: the format chosen is likely to be one which fits both the investigator and the kind of problem under scrutiny.

SECOND ANALYSIS: THE CASE STUDY

The second qualitative inquiry using the Summerland material, and the one on which we can now concentrate, was the development of a crisis case study in collaboration with Brian Toft. This was quite a specific problem, involving an analysis which was in some senses historical, looking back at an incident which took place in 1973, and trying to make sense of a portion of it fifteen years later. The format in which we anticipated we would present our data was, in a very broad sense, predetermined. Also the set of data available to deal with the problem was given, so that the analysis had a self-contained quality which is not found in many social science investigations. More typically, social science inquiries are 'open-world' inquiries, where boundaries are difficult to specify and where issues ramify in all directions. Knowing that we had only *this* set of evidence, and that we had to use our ingenuity to extract some resolution from it gave to the process a puzzle-like quality which I must say that I quite liked.

In addition, since 'technology . . . is inseparable from catastrophe' (Ronell 1989: 341), the analysis would have to extend beyond the social to take note of technical matters. Accident and disaster studies cannot avoid covering the conditions associated with technological failure since they deal with physical injury and damage. In socio-technical systems, even taking into account all of the caveats necessary to refer to the socially mediated nature of our understanding of the technical world, material factors do sometimes act power-fully to constrain patterns of social behaviour. In the Summerland case, both Brian Toft and I became acutely aware of the way in which the catastrophically changing physical environment of the burning leisure centre, and the time-constraints associated with the rapid spread of the fire placed limits of great severity upon the actions of those caught up in that setting and in those circumstances.

STYLE OF SELF REPORT

Looking back to how we analyzed the Summerland data, I am trying to recall and to write a simple, clear account of our activities. But I also feel that I have to try to take some account of the contemporary professional sophistication – or perhaps the professional suspicion – which we have all developed these days about the sources of different views of events, about coherence and who claims coherence, and about accounts and accounting. I have to add, of course, that the extent of this suspicion ensures that I cannot claim any final authority for my own interpretation of our work.

None the less, in thinking now about the representational style which I am using to construct a persuasive account of our work and of how we dealt with our circumscribed task of qualitative data analysis, I can see that the rhetoric which offers itself as most appropriate for this account is that of a minor epic narrative, the tale of a journey during which difficulties are surmounted (Jeffcutt: 1991). My tale, then, tells how we posed our problem, how we defined our quest. It tells of our ordeals of time-pressure, of our needs to 'make' sense and to create coherence; and in a minor way, it celebrates the success represented first by the creation of a written analy-sis, and second by the acceptance of it for publication (Turner and Toft 1989).

Our own account, though, is manufactured from a multiplicity of other, infinitely more tragic accounts. The polyphonic voices of those who survived the fire at Summerland, and of those who fought it, are heard distantly in our writings, refracted through our reading of their officially presented accounts. And there are also tragic absences: the voices of those who did not survive to give evidence to the inquiry, but perished in the smoke and flames. We were trying in our story to acknowledge the multiple accounts of survivors of the Summerland fire, and to set these multiple voices in the context of the officially sanctioned account represented by the public inquiry, contested though that was and still is (*Summerland 1974*, *The Times* 1974, *Shockwaves* 1991), and then to use our production for training others who might have to deal with similar incidents.

THE CASE STUDY

In my original discussion of the incident, I represented the Summerland fire as follows:

> a holiday leisure complex at Douglas, Isle of Man, with approximately 3,000 people inside, caught fire on 2 August 1973. The building, an open structure clad partly in sheet steel and partly in acrylic sheeting, burned rapidly and 50 men, women and children in the building died.
>
> (Turner 1978: 53)

As we have seen, this first account drew heavily upon the published report of the Commission of Inquiry (*Summerland 1974*), building on this and other incidents from the same period to develop a wider framework for understanding the preconditions of such accidents. My new task, with Brian Toft, was to move beyond these accounts of the tragedy and to concentrate upon the manner in which the crisis created by the fire was handled. In this context, we considered a crisis to be a period which begins when a possible threat is first discerned and when the people involved have to start to make choices about how to deal with the situation. A crisis ends either when no further threat exists or when no further choices are possible. At Summerland, we could say that this period of crisis lasted from about 19.40 on 2 August, when a small fire adjacent to the outer wall of the leisure centre was first spotted and reported to leisure centre staff, to 21.10 when the emergency services indicated that the fire was under control and that the incident was effectively over, a period of only ninety minutes. Our task, therefore, was to try to discern and to reflect upon what happened in those ninety minutes, to see if we could determine what choices individuals had about their response and what conclusions we could draw from our analysis.

We already knew that Summerland was a rather complex entertainment centre, of a novel form. It was organized on several levels: the higher levels were terraced under a transparent roof to create a sunny holiday atmosphere. Galleries with bars, restaurants and sunbathing platforms looked down on to a central entertainment space with a small stage, a bar, a restaurant and an amusement arcade nearby. At lower levels there were other facilities, including a children's cinema. A control room with a public address facility and also a direct emergency line to the local fire station was located in a control tower which overlooked the main open area, although, because of inadequacies in staff training and emergency provision, the control centre and its central fire alarm were not used in the fire. The centre was located at the foot of a cliff, between the cliffs and the sea, and adjacent to a swimming pool building, a location to which access for both the public and the emergency services was restricted.

When the fire started and began to spread through the centre, there was considerable confusion among both staff and customers, in the absence of any authoritative announcements or general guidance about appropriate behaviour. This confusion was exacerbated by the reaction of numbers of parents separated from their children, who were at entertainments in other parts of the centre. Parents struggled against the main flow of the crowd to look for their children. A number of the doors leading out of the building were locked and it took quite a time for the one-way turnstiles to be bypassed at the main entrance to allow people to get out freely, and for an upward moving escalator to be switched off to allow people to come down it to the exits. The turmoil was increased when, at 20.11, the House Manager switched off the electricity supply and, because of flat batteries, the emergency generators failed to come into operation. The emergency stairs were then plunged into darkness. Several people died in this locality since the protection of the stairs from smoke had not been maintained, for an additional doorway which did not meet fire regulations had been built on to the stairwell.

People struggled to escape from the terraces down open stairs adjacent to the burning plastic outer wall, and others were trapped in various rooms in the centre in which they had taken refuge. Some broke large windows to get out on to the terrace, but since this was not a place of safety, they then had to scale a 1.3 m fence to get away from the burning building. Because of the malfunctioning of a two-stage mechanism which had been built into the fire alarm, those who broke fire alarm glasses in the centre did not succeed in sending out warnings about the fire, and the emergency services were not notified until a taxi-driver called in on his radio twenty-one minutes after the fire had been discovered. When it was informed, the fire brigade reacted promptly and efficiently, mobilizing all of the island's fire services and bringing the fire under control in just over one hour.

In carrying out our analysis, our first problem was to decide what might constitute crisis-related behaviour. We were clear that we wanted to set aside the point of view of the emergency services in this instance and so we started by reading through all of the accounts written by staff and customers who survived the fire. Some members of the public reacted promptly and removed themselves and their families rapidly from the centre, even though there had been no official warnings. Others were left without guidance because of the inability of the majority of the untrained staff to respond to an emergency. None of the staff had received emergency training at the centre and, with one or two notable exceptions, their uncertainty about how to behave did not assist members of the public in responding to the fire. A significant number of the customers were restrained initially in their departure by the public announcements made by the compère on the entertainments stage in the open area, for he thought that the best approach was to encourage the audience to remain calm. As noted above, the multiple levels within the centre, the restricted access and locked exits meant that many members of the public who did try to escape found themselves caught up in panicking crowds pressing away from the fire, jamming on to stairways and searching for possible exits.

Having screened and taken notes on all of these individual stories, a process which was greatly facilitated by Brian Toft's exhaustive knowledge of the incident, built up from his interviews on the Isle of Man (Toft 1990) as well as from a detailed reading of the documentary evidence, we puzzled further about the kind of crisis behaviour we needed to note particularly. We came to the conclusion that our central concern in drawing up a case study of behaviour was less with the nature of the public response than with how those holding some formal responsibility for the centre reacted to the emergency. It is not uncommon in a long-running crisis for a communications centre to be set up to handle the emergency. By contrast, the senior staff at Summerland were scattered around the centre at the start of the fire and both the unusual physical layout of the centre and the speed with which the fire spread prevented them from coming together to plan a coherent response. In trying to think about how we might prevent a similar incident recurring, we rapidly came to the conclusion that most of the preventive work in relation to this crisis would have to have been started much earlier, during the design, planning and regulatory stages, as the building was being conceived, constructed and fitted out. Or alternatively, it could have been in the development of emergency plans and training procedures when staff were recruited for the new centre at the start of the summer season. The inquiry, of course, had said all of these things, and, in a different context, we were to reiterate them in our article.

This still left, though, the question of what options and choices *were* available to the staff caught up in the situation at Summerland during the period from 19.40 to 21.10 on 2 August 1973. At this time, approximately 200 staff were working in the building, in bars, cinemas, cafeterias and other facilities. Our initial resolution to look at the behaviour of all of the staff was undermined not only by the number of them, but also by their dispersion and by the fragmented variety of their responses to the situation.

Most staff members had no specific ideas of their duties in case of fire, or about how to set up and direct an evacuation. Nor had they received any fire training. Mostly they were caught unprepared and at a loss. Many of them, in some cases directed by their superiors, made the securing of their tills and cash receipts a priority rather than directing patrons to safety, while others simply panicked. Some staff members did, of course, display great bravery, placing themselves in extreme danger as they assisted people – some losing their own lives in the process – and some members of the public responded in a similarly selfless manner. The public inquiry documented fully the professional behaviour of one staff member, the manageress of one of the bars who had received fire brigade training in her previous employment. She was aware of fire precautions and exits and she directed patrons to an emergency staircase, not leaving until she was convinced that everyone else had left her area. At that time the building was in darkness and she herself was in danger of being overcome by smoke. She was the only member of staff who recalled any fire instructions, which she had become aware of from reading the notices posted in the bar.

In the face of this scattered and variable response, we needed to rephrase our core question about crisis behaviour yet again, focusing attention this time upon those staff who had the greatest degree of responsibility for the whole leisure complex, rather than simply for individual sections of it. And then, to try to get some purchase upon their behaviour, we found that we had to try to build up our own mental picture of their pattern of responses during the crucial ninety minutes of the crisis. It proved not to be possible to do this without more substantive aids: we had already found it necessary to return to the public inquiry report in order to sketch out for ourselves a set of outline drawings of the layout of the leisure centre and its complexities on several levels, and we now tried to map on to our drawings the movements of each of the senior staff at the centre, attaching times to them so that we could look at the possibilities for contact and co-ordinated action. On our sketch plans we showed in coloured ink the paths taken by key staff, although we found it difficult to represent their movements adequately on a two-dimensional sketch when they moved from one level of the centre to another.

Six members of staff had personal radios with them, and these were used for a very limited amount of communication during the early stages of the fire. The General Manager, working in his office, had his radio switched off during the first few minutes of the crisis, and the control tower operator could only be contacted by internal telephone. So, in spite of the existence of some other means of communication, the physical disposition of the senior staff seemed to be a crucial thing to establish. After our preliminary plots of movement and timing, we came to the conclusion that we could narrow the focus of the analysis still further by concentrating upon the three most senior staff at the centre: the General Manager, the House Manager and the Technical Services Manager, together with a fourth, potentially crucial member of staff, the Control Tower Operator.

The amount of contact between these four staff turned out to be very low during the period in question. When we tracked each of them, we found, in summary, the following pattern:

The *Control Tower Operator* was a 19-year-old woman who had worked in the control room for a month, with the duties of playing a programme of music through the day, making public announcements as instructed and controlling stage lighting. She had had no instructions about what to do in case of fire, or about how to operate the fire alarm panel. She saw no reason for great concern in the early stages of the fire, but as the fire began to take hold, and she saw people starting to escape themselves, she judged, sensibly, that she should leave as rapidly as she could, going downstairs and finding her way through broken glass doors into the adjacent swimming pool building.

The *Technical Services Manager* initially became aware of the small external fire which set off the blaze and played some part in directing staff trying to deal with it. When the fire spread inside the centre, he checked that someone had called the fire brigade, and also broke a fire alarm glass himself. He then moved through the centre assisting with fire-fighting, advising people to leave, switching off the escalator which was causing difficulty, opening some locked doors and assisting in breaking open others. Finally he organized the evacuation of people from the outside terrace to the road below.

The *House Manager* used his two-way radio at around 20.00 to tell staff that he was investigating a small fire which had been reported to him, saw the Technical Services Manager and other staff trying to cope with the growing fire on the outside wall and called the fire brigade from a public telephone at the main entrance. He collected cash from the pay boxes at the entrance, and went down service stairs to pick up a number of spare keys to assist with evacuation, only to find that the fire had grown so much in his absence that his original plan had to be abandoned. He then switched off the electricity to avoid electrical fires and left the building through a back entrance, meeting the General Manager who instructed him to make arrangements for a staff roll call the next day.

The *General Manager* heard about the initial fire at about 20.00 and went rapidly to the terrace where he saw the staff tackling the fire and checked that the fire brigade had been called. Moving into the centre and trying to shepherd people off the terrace, away from the external fire, he entered the centre just as a flashover took place in one internal area of the centre and the fire entered a newer and fiercer phase. He ran through the building, telling the entertainers to instruct people to leave, and started to break down locked doors to the swimming pool building. He ran out through the swimming pool entrance and tried to enter the centre again, but was repulsed by the smoke and by the flow of people coming out.

We then documented these four individual stories more fully, set them out in narratives which would form part of the case study, and started to think about their implications for potential actions which *could* have been taken during the crisis period. We also started to turn some of the other material we had analyzed into the format of a case study, summarizing the background, the incident, and the characteristics of those we had now identified as key actors. In looking at the material in a case study context, we also had to consider how the account we had prepared related to relevant theoretical understandings of such events. We were clear that we wanted to discuss the preconditions of the crisis by reference to my own developmental model (Turner 1978) and to relate this to subsequent work which extended or criticized the original model (e.g. Gephart 1984, Rosenthal 1986). I was also guided very much in my own understanding or interpretation of the idea of 'crisis' by the influential definitions which Hermann and his colleagues had developed in their work on administrative crises. Although for some reason we did not cite Hermann's work in the published case study,[3] his definition gave us an orienting perspective which allowed us to proceed with the interpretation of the case (Hermann 1963; see also Smart and Vertinsky 1977). Given the general familiarity of both Brian Toft and myself with the Summerland case, and our previous work on accidents and failures, the theoretical materials mentioned seemed to us to be enough to provide an adequate analysis of the events associated with the crisis.

We had now reached the point where we were able to prepare a reasonably coherent draft analysis of the crisis in a format which could be fitted to the editors' case study guide-lines. This carried us forward to the meeting of contributors. Uriel Rosenthal and Michael Charles, the senior editors of the volume for which our analysis was destined, had been able to arrange for a joint discussion to take place, to allow for a degree of co-ordination between contributions. Compared with the normal minimal degree of contact which is possible between authors whose work comes together in an edited book this experience was a great luxury. The two days of discussion amongst the editors and their twenty authors made for a very creative conference workshop. There was space for a full discussion of the kinds of uncertainties which we ourselves had been experiencing about both the case format and the way in which the idea of crisis might be defined and handled. Representing Brian and myself at this meeting, I realized that, in spite of the sometimes rather desperate urgency which had gripped us while we were working through the analysis outlined above, we were in fact much further advanced than many other contributors.

Moreover, many of the other case studies which were being analyzed involved very lengthy crisis periods, dealing with terrorism, riot, hostage-taking or famine. Because of the truncated crisis period in our incident, a number of the considerations affecting other incidents did not transfer very readily across to our case. This meant that, apart from minor alterations, when our draft chapter was presented to the group, it was allowed to stand more or less unchanged. The one major change, though, which both the editors and the other contributors insisted upon was in the theoretical realm.

Apart from my own model, the other major contribution to the social scientific study of disaster preconditions is that of Perrow, in his review of what he designates 'normal accidents' (Perrow 1984). After the workshop discussion we were pressed not to leave the chapter without reference to Perrow's model of high complexity and tight coupling as factors underlying the production of 'normal accidents'. Brian and I had already discussed this point and we had not initially found Perrow's model useful in assisting our understanding of what had happened at Summerland. Moreover, we had some analytic doubts about the model. At its core is a two-by-two table, and the dimensions of this table, *degree of complexity* and *tightness of coupling*, are both difficult to operationalize and hard to distinguish from each other. In fact, we were uncertain about whether they represented independent dimensions. So far as we could tell, the Summerland Centre might be judged to have been tightly coupled in a technical sense, but it was very loosely coupled socially, and Perrow did not make this distinction. In terms of complexity, the centre was physically fairly straightforward if compared with constructions such as a major hospital or a nuclear power plant, but it did have sufficient complexity to allow events to spread rapidly in a way which those involved could not understand and could not have readily predicted.

In the end we reluctantly acknowledged to ourselves that the suggestions being made for change were probably right, and that it was not reasonable to omit all discussion of Perrow's work. Accordingly, hoping that the editors would accept our solution, we prepared synopses of the two models, and summarized their main features in tables which could be set into the text. We then demonstrated in the final discussion the extent to which each model could be used to understand different features of the Summerland case. The editors accepted this response to their suggestions for change and the paper proceeded to publication.

REFLECTIONS

The process of setting out the above account raises a number of issues for me. First, I need to caution that many of the stages I have mentioned were iterative. The journey which we took did not follow a straight line: we took diversions and doubled back on ourselves. Now, as always in retrospect, the ill-structured problem of what to do looks clear-cut: events look more ordered with the benefit of hindsight. If what we did now seems obvious, and if our problems of analysis now seem trivial, this is in part because a fairly well-structured problem has been retrospectively defined.

It now seems a self-evident strategy to concentrate upon the crucial ninety minutes of the fire, to disregard the accounts of members of the public involved in the fire and to concentrate upon the senior management and the Control Tower Operator, but this is only so in the frame which we have now imposed upon the problem. My initial feelings, as I recall them, were very much of being under pressure, given the time we had available and our other commitments; of feeling bewildered at how we might cope with the large, undifferentiated pile of statements which we had to hand, many discussing matters of potential importance for our analysis not elaborated in the public inquiry report; and of feeling a great deal of uncertainty about how we could best interpret the idea of 'coping with crisis' in the context of Summerland.

I suspect that this kind of anxiety, bewilderment and uncertainty is not untypical of the reactions of many qualitative analysts faced with a new task. Perhaps we need to be particularly tolerant of doubt and ambiguity. Because the kinds of 'weak' methods used do not impose a standardization upon the data, the qualitative analyst is much more likely to vary the methods of analysis according to variations in the data being examined, and so is in much less of a position to impose an orthodox approach which can disregard local variations. This has the consequence, not only that many qualitative tasks have their own distinctive characteristics, but also that these features are not fully evident until after the event. The qualitative analyst assumes that the situation will have a story to tell, but that this will not be told spontaneously. In the interrogation, *what* to ask becomes completely clear only after the story is revealed. Moreover, since the analyst makes an active contribution to the process of qualitative analysis (Turner 1988), sometimes we may find ourselves constructing a story out of responses made by a respondent who did not have a story to tell anyway (Johnston 1981, quoted by Neville 1989: 222–3).

More formally, the process is one of interrogating the data for relevant material according to criteria of relevance which are themselves only developed during the process of analysis (Pidgeon et al 1991). There are reminders in this of Wolff's technique or philosophy of 'surrender and catch': Wolff advocates a complete 'surrender' to the experience of those he is studying, to a non-directed openness and awareness in interaction with them, followed by a scrutiny of what has been 'caught' as a result of this yielding (Wolff 1976). The sensations involved may also evoke rather distant echoes of Walter Benjamin's private pleasure at being able to wander in an unfamiliar city until he was completely lost, in order, then, to be able gradually to find himself again (Sontag 1979).

I began by suggesting that all qualitative analysis was not the same, but our discussion makes it clearer, also, that such analysis does not readily lend itself to being divided into homogeneous, classifiable types. What Brian Toft and I did in writing our case study does not have a distinctive label unless it is 'writing case studies' or the more generic Civil Service term of 'drafting'.[4] We tackled a mixture of sub-tasks which were dictated by our search for an understanding of the larger task to be undertaken and found ourselves involved in a heterogeneous array of activities linked only by the logic that they were all associated in some way with the task we had in hand. We already had a grounded theoretical framework available from my first analysis, but in the second analysis, in writing our narrative case study, we were not looking to extend the theory. Instead, we consulted material from archives. We iterated and redefined our problem, deciding whose accounts to look at and how to shape the questions which we posed of their accounts. We spent a lot of time worrying away, using maps, diagrams and chronologies, at a bounded puzzle which we felt sure that we ought to be able to solve: how to make coherent and instructive sense of crisis-coping behaviour at Summerland. And also, in the final stages we were pushed by what we could loosely call peer pressure to widen our theoretical purview.

Large tasks can best be handled if they are subdivided or limited, so that we mark out what we need to attend to. We can impose boundaries ourselves or they can be suggested by outside factors. In the analysis of the Summerland crisis, boundaries were pressed upon us by the ninety-minute time period, by the constrained physical setting and by the fact that events had occurred a long time ago. I can propose a relevant 'loose classification' of types of problems here, for I have encountered a similar kind of bounded analysis on previous occasions in the study of acute system failures. Such unexpected events, such surprises (Turner 1979), always force us afterwards to revise our understanding of the world: they generate a need to reframe. As a result the issues are always there to be raised of how the two frames of understanding, before and after, are related to one another; of how one needs to be modified in order to be transformed into the other; and of how far it might have been possible to prevent the accident by predicting the new, transformed state on the basis of an examination of the initial, untransformed state. When the situation before the accident can readily be represented by a limited array of information, it is a natural response to interrogate this array for clues which, correctly interpreted, could have anticipated the transformation wrought by the accident.

In the 1973 London smallpox outbreak, for example, this puzzle-like quality was very clearly visible (Turner 1978: 109–17). The outbreak occurred because someone with a misdiagnosed case of smallpox was placed in a public hospital ward, fatally infecting two visitors to the ward. The information needed to *deduce* that she had smallpox was spread around two groups of people, one group knowing that she was ill but not that she had been exposed in a laboratory to a smallpox virus harvesting process, the other group knowing of her presence at this process, but not knowing about or having any responsibility for her health. Disclosure before the event would have required these two groups to exchange information about a situation which they did not know at that time was a potential matter for concern. In this case, to order these quite clearly defined patterns of social relations and the related distribution of information before and after the event, it was very helpful to resort to maps and diagrams, setting out the topography of the puzzle as an aid to coping with it adequately.

Another instance of the bounded pattern of information associated with system failure was the distribution and 'ownership' of an array of clues available before a failed building development project. In this case, before building work began, the clues might have revealed that the old industrial site being converted for building purposes was contaminated with many tons of hazardous industrial waste. The clues and their information were available, but before the event they were ignored or misunderstood, or were in the hands of people who had no use for them (Pidgeon *et al.* 1988).

A series of accounts of epidemiological incidents written up *as if* they were detective stories (Rouché 1967) points up for us that such patterns of clues and transformations link the study of accidents and system failures with the form of the detective novel. The detective novel format itself reflects a particular, characteristically nineteenth-century epistemology in which true knowledge can be revealed by careful enquiry. We understand the world in a much messier and less certain way now, so it is both curious and intriguing to find that in the study of acute system failures, the nature of the phenomena with which we are dealing suggests to us such positivistic parallels.[5]

Our case study account also prompts reflection on the curious role played here by theory, a role which is much less clear than textbook accounts might have us believe. Theoretical issues were not 'up front' for Brian and myself in our interpretation of our task. Looking back we might say that we were working within the 'paradigm' of an existing model, which gave us a way of looking at the portion of the world under scrutiny that we were not concerned to question. But, since close scrutiny reveals that this model had nothing at all to say about crisis, we were really in uncharted territory when we tried to get to grips with crisis behaviour. Ironically, too, Perrow's model is also silent on this topic, and we failed to acknowledge the work of Hermann, our most useful source of conceptual clarification. We did use one of the other major contributions in the area, Rosenthal's discussion of crisis (1986), but his examination of administrative and managerial responses to crisis assumed a much lengthier period of crisis than we were dealing with. We could have been helped by a much more coherent theory of social and organizational responses to acute crisis, but, apart from the ground-breaking work of Smelser (1962) little was available to us. In fact, though, as the full book was assembled, a comparison of the series of crisis case studies in it did make it possible for Alex Kouzmin and Alan Jarman to formulate, together with the editors, a typology of crises and a path model of crisis development in which the Summerland crisis was typified as moving instantly from routine to crisis (Rosenthal *et al.* 1989).

Lowe (1977) proposed, on the basis of a number of self reports of research written by leading sociologists in the 1960s (Hammond 1964), that most social research projects exhibit 'breakdown' at some point, when the original plan or the original theory turns out to be inadequate for coping with the task in hand. While researchers saw themselves as responding to this condition by resorting to what they thought were rather unsatisfactory and *ad hoc* coping mechanisms, Lowe pointed out that the resultant 'patchworking' activities typically constituted the most creative part of the research project. Her quilting image, in which, under conditions of necessity, existing fragments are patched together with whatever theoretical materials come to hand, seems to me to fit well with the kinds of strategies needed and adopted by qualitative researchers. In the absence of 'strong' grounds for ruling out data as erroneous or irrelevant, the qualitative researcher is typically faced with a heterogeneous array of units of analysis – individuals, groups, organizations, events, maps and chronologies – rather than the uniformity more familiar to the survey researcher, so that there is a need to adopt suitably eclectic practices of classification and theorizing.

The outcomes, closer to Feyerabend than to Popper, may not have the sweep and grandeur of the work of major theoreticians. But they often represent a creative and a serviceable response to the variations which have to be handled by those who choose to live with diversity, those who are reluctant to impose strong Procrustean rules upon their data. In our Summerland case study, where our concerns initially were fairly practical ones, I do not think that we can claim to have reached even this modest theoretical conclusion, but my retrospective analysis of our activities shows up more clearly how others (Rosenthal *et al.* 1989) were able to patch up the hole in the quilt which we had found.

CONCLUSIONS

But apart from helping me to identify a hole in the theoretical understanding of crisis behaviour and to see how it has been filled, do any other benefits result from discussions of the present kind? It should follow from my initial contention about the diversity of qualitative research that there will be few benefits in terms of the presentation of a clear model of practice to be followed, copied or modified. If one were planning a whole series of parallel investigations of very much the same type, then, of course familiarization and routine would bring some kinds of benefits. But the conditions of routinization are not often likely to bring out the best in the qualitative researcher who often has most to offer from pressing forward to gain new ideas and insights.

At a more general level, though, I do think that there are gains to be derived from more open reflection upon the broad range of intellectual skills involved in analysis and theory creation. There was a time when pieces like Polya's *How to Solve It* (1944) and the methodological Appendix to C. Wright Mills's *The Sociological Imagination* (1959) were among the few exemplars of the fragmented and scarcely respectable discussion of how to think, or how to develop what Mills's more precise phrase calls 'intellectual craftsmanship'. Then, perhaps, such skills were assumed to be more innate, and thus not worth discussion. Those who could do these kinds of things just got on with it. Today, though, we realize much more clearly that research, analysis and theorizing embody significant elements of skill, and, more importantly, that the level of skill can be raised by externalizing processes and problems so that they can be discussed, and possibly improved upon. Just as the exteriorization of thought which the advent of writing brought about had positive consequences for intellectual reflection and discussion (Goody 1986) so the minor explosion of writing on qualitative analysis since the early 1970s has ushered in much sustained and fruitful reflection on the skills and the possibilities of the qualitative approach. This externalization process is now being accelerated as the development of software to handle different phases of qualitative analysis by computer encourages us to scrutinize such processes even more carefully (Pidgeon *et al.* 1991, Richards and Richards 1987, 1991, Tesch 1990).

I began by referring to some of the constraints on the utility of numbers in social science, in the form of the limits to the isomorphic properties of numbers in relation to social behaviour (cf. also Lawlor 1982). But this now hardly seems to be contentious. A more important concluding point to emphasize is the need to recognize and develop strategies for dealing with diversity in the exploration and analysis of many contemporary problems. For some purposes we may want to overrule and subdue the diversity which surrounds us, but to understand many issues, especially those of what used to be called the 'middle range', we will want to continue to cluster phenomena loosely together and to try to reflect upon and make sense of those important portions of the world where the evident social diversity is precisely what we are interested in.

NOTES

1 Even agreeing how many teeth or nipples a sheep has is not as simple as might at first appear. See Ronell 1989: 337–9.
2 See Martin and Turner 1986 for further detailed examples of grounded theory notes, concepts, definitions and analyses.
3 Hermann's work *is* discussed in the editors' introduction to the published book (Rosenthal *et al.* 1989: 3–33).
4 My understanding of the role played by case studies, however, has been much enhanced by reading Alvarez and Merchán's insightful discussion of narrative, imagination and action (Alvarez and Merchán, forthcoming). Case studies used for training managers and administrators offer *narratives* which serve to bridge the gap between the general propositions and instructions offered in theoretical training and the messy concrete situations encountered when those being trained try to apply their theoretical knowledge. Our case study involved the building of just such a bridging narrative.
5 Note that with chronic injurious conditions with a much more gradual onset, such as much environmental pollution, this particular configuration does not appear, or appears much less strongly (Couch and Kroll-Smith 1985, Gephart 1984).

REFERENCES

Alvarez, J.L. and Merchán, C. (forthcoming) 'The role of narrative fiction in the development of imagination for action', *International Studies of Management and Organization*.

Couch, S.R. and Kroll-Smith, J.S. (1985) 'The chronic-technical disaster: towards a social scientific perspective', *Social Science Quarterly* 66: 564–75.

Gephart, R.P. Jr. (1984) 'Making sense of organizationally based environmental disasters', *Journal of Management* 10: 205–55.

Gherardi, S. and Turner, B.A. (1987) *Real Men Don't Collect Soft Data*, Quaderno 13, Dipartmento di Politica Sociale, Trento, Italy: University of Trento.

Glaser, B.G. and Strauss, A.L. (1967) *The Discovery of Grounded Theory*, Chicago, Aldine.

Glaser, B. and Crabtree, D. (1969) *Second Deeds of Trust*, Mill Valley, Calif.: Balboa Press.

Goody, J. (1986) *The Logic of Writing and the Organization of Society*, Cambridge: Cambridge University Press.

Hermann, C.F. (1963) 'Some consequences of crisis which limit the viability of organizations', *Administrative Science Quarterly* 8: 61–82.

Hammond, P. (ed.) (1964) *Sociologists at Work*, New York: Basic Books.

Jeffcutt, P. (1991) 'Styles of representation in organizational analysis: heroism, happy endings and the carnivalesque in the organisational symbolism literature', paper presented to the Standing Conference for Organizational Symbolism (SCOS) Valhalla Conference, 'Reconstructing Organizational Culture', Copenhagen Business School, June.

Johnston, K. (1981) *Impro*, London: Methuen.

Lawlor, R. (1982) *Sacred Geometry: Philosophy and Practice*, London: Thames & Hudson.

Lowe, J. (1977) 'Facts and frameworks: aspects of the research process', unpublished MA thesis, University of Birmingham.

Martin, P.Y. and Turner, B.A. (1986) 'Grounded theory and organizational research', *Journal of Applied Behavioral Science* 22: 141–57.

Mills, C. Wright (1959) *The Sociological Imagination*, New York: Oxford University Press.

Neville, B. (1989) *Educating Psyche: Emotion, Imagination and the Unconscious in Learning*, Melbourne: Collins Dove.

Perrow, C. (1984) *Normal Accidents: Living with High Risk Technology*, New York: Basic Books.

Pidgeon, N.F., Blockley, D.I. and Turner, B.A. (1986) 'Design practice and snow loading: lessons from a roof collapse', *Structural Engineer* 64A: 67–71.

—— (1988) 'Site investigations: lessons from a late discovery of hazardous waste', *Structural Engineer*, 66: 311–15.

Pidgeon, N.F., Turner, B.A. and Blockley, D.I. (1991) 'The use of grounded theory for conceptual analysis in knowledge elicitation', *International Journal of Man-Machine Studies* 35: 151–73.

Polya, G. (1944) *How to Solve It*, Princeton, NJ: Princeton University Press.

Richards, L. and Richards, T. (1987) 'Qualitative data analysis: can computers do it?' *Australian and New Zealand Journal of Sociology* 23: 23–35.

—— (1991) 'Computing in qualitative analysis: a healthy development?', *Qualitative Health Research* 1: 2.

Ronnell, A. (1989) *The Telephone Book: Technology, Schizophrenia and Electric Speech*, Lincoln, Nebr.: University of Nebraska Press.

Rosenthal, U. (1986) 'Crisis decision-making in the Netherlands', *Netherlands Journal of Sociology* 22: 103–29.

Rosenthal, U., Charles, M.T. and 't. Hart, P. (eds) (1989) *Coping with Crises*, Springfield, Ill.: Charles C. Thomas.

Rosenthal, U., Charles, M.T., 't. Hart, P., Kouzmin, A. and Jarman, A. (1989) 'From case studies to theory and recommendations: a concluding analysis' in U. Rosenthal, M.T. Charles and P. 't. Hart (eds) *Coping with Crises*, Springfield, Ill.: Charles C. Thomas.

Rouché, B. (1967) *Annals of Epidemiology*, Boston, Mass.: Little, Brown.

Shockwaves, BBC Radio 4 documentary, 1991.

Smart, C. and Vertinsky, I. (1977) 'Designs for crisis decision units', *Administrative Science Quarterly* 22: 640–57.

Smelser, N.J. (1962) *Theory of Collective Behavior*, London: Routledge & Kegan Paul.

Sontag, S. (1979) 'Introduction' to Walter Benjamin, *One Way Street and Other Writings*, trans. Edmund Jephcott and Kingsley Shorter, London: Verso.

Strauss, A. (1987) *Qualitative Analysis for Social Scientists*, Cambridge and New York: Cambridge University Press.

Strauss, A. and Corbin, J. (1990) *Basics of Qualitative Research: Grounded Theory Procedures and Techniques*, Newbury Park, Calif.: Sage.

Summerland 1974, Report of the Summerland Fire Commission, Douglas, Isle of Man: Government Office.

Tesch, R. (1990) *Qualitative Research: Analysis Types and Software Tools*, London: Falmer Press.

The Times, 28 August 1974, 'No criminal neglect in Summerland fire, jury decides', p. 2.

Toft, B. (1990) 'The Failure of Hindsight', unpublished Ph.D. thesis, University of Exeter.

Turner, B.A. (1976a) 'The organizational and interorganizational development of disasters', *Administrative Science Quarterly* 12(3): 378–97.

—— (1976b) 'The development of disasters', *Sociological Review* 24(4): 753–74.

—— (1978) *Manmade Disasters*, London: Wykeham Press.

—— (1979) 'Surprise: social aspects of time', unpublished conference paper presented to the 4th European Group for Organisational Studies Colloquium, Netherlands, June.

—— (1981) 'Some practical aspects of qualitative data analysis: one way of organising the cognitive processes associated with the generation of grounded theory', *Quality and Quantity* 15: 225–47.

—— (1988) 'Connoisseurship in the study of organizational cultures', in A. Bryman (ed.) *Doing Research in Organizations*, London: Routledge.

Turner, B.A. and Pidgeon, N. (forthcoming) *Manmade Disasters*, revd edn, Berlin: de Gruyter.

Turner, B.A. and Toft, B. (1989) 'Fire at Summerland Leisure Centre', in U. Rosenthal, M.T. Charles and P. 't. Hart (eds) *Coping with Crises*, Springfield, Ill.: Charles C. Thomas.

Weber, M. (1978) *Economy and Society: an Outline of Interpretive Sociology*, vol. 1, ed. Guenther Roth and Claus Wittich, Berkeley, Calif.: University of California Press.

Wolff, K.H. (1976) *Surrender and Catch: Experience and Inquiry Today*. Boston, Mass.: D. Reidel Co.

Chapter 11

Reflections on qualitative data analysis

Alan Bryman and Robert G. Burgess

In many discussions of qualitative research there is a reluctance of many (if not most) authors to lay bare the procedures associated with the analysis of data. In this respect the chapters that have been included in this book represent a major advance in that contributors do reflect explicitly on the process of analysis. They provide many ideas about qualitative data analysis that can rarely be discerned through other publications. We feel that much will also have been achieved if this collection stimulates a greater self-consciousness about analysis among qualitative researchers when designing and reporting studies.

This chapter brings together a number of themes that have been of particular interest or concern to our contributors. The purpose is not to summarize what they say, but to identify issues that are particularly revealing about qualitative data analysis.

BULK AND COMPLEXITY

It is clear that our contributors regard analysis as a 'problem' because of the nature of qualitative data, which are invariably described as voluminous, unstructured and unwieldy. The difficulty of handling such data is well illustrated by Miles's (1979) description of qualitative data as 'an attractive nuisance'. In fact, remarks about the volume and complexity of qualitative data, and the implications for analysis, have been made by many commentators (for example, Bresnen 1988: 48). Of course, quantitative data deriving from large-scale surveys could equally be described as voluminous and unwieldy, but the availability of standard statistical procedures and computer programs for handling them is generally perceived as rendering such data non-problematic. This comparison could be taken to imply that qualitative researchers might seek to codify or routinize their analytic procedures in a similar manner to that found in quantitative research. A volume such as ours would be a necessary phase in building up the kind of data base that could form the basis for codification. This was essentially Merton's goal when he appealed for researchers to include in their publications a detailed account of the ways in which qualitative analyses *actually* developed. Only when a considerable body of such reports are available will it be possible to *codify* methods of qualitative analysis with something of the clarity with which quantitative methods have been articulated. . . . This codification is devoutly to be desired both for the *collection* and the *analysis* of qualitative sociological data.

(1968: 444, n. 5, emphases in original, quoted in Conrad and Reinhartz
1984: 5–6)

Conrad and Reinharz (1984) agree that this is a desirable goal and see computers as playing an important role in its accomplishment. However, it is clear that our contributors feel such codification in qualitative analysis is not feasible and that even if it were, it would not necessarily be desirable. Turner, for example, argues that researchers are forced to vary their analytic approaches since these will vary according to the nature of the data with which they are confronted. Potter and Wetherell's depiction of discourse analysis as a craft skill reflects a similar scepticism about the possibility of routinizing analysis. In so far as any codification is feasible or desirable, it is likely to be at a general level, as implied by Okely's remark that 'there can be no set formulae, only broad guide-lines', a phrase that suggests data analysis is not confined to one aspect of the research process.

ANALYSIS IS NOT A DISTINCT PHASE

Qualitative researchers have frequently suggested that research design, data collection and analysis are simultaneous and continuous processes (Burgess 1984a, 1984b; Habenstein 1970). Certainly this is a recurring theme in this volume, in that analysis is not perceived as a separate phase as in quantitative research (see Richards and Richards, and Burgess *et al.*). However, the extent to which data analysis is a separate phase in quantitative research is often exaggerated by qualitative researchers. For example, when designing a questionnaire, survey researchers have to be mindful of the kind of data analysis they will be able to carry out. If the respondent's age is one of the questions, it has to be borne in mind that if an open question is asked the resulting data can be treated as an interval variable, but if respondents are asked to assign themselves to age categories the resulting variable will be ordinal. The latter will restrict the range of statistical options available to the researcher, though this will not be of concern if most of the other variables will also be at the ordinal or nominal level of measurement (Bryman and Cramer 1990).

None the less, data analysis emerges from our contributors as a much less discrete process in qualitative research. This echoes the view of Wiseman when she writes that the 'constant interplay of data gathering and analysis is at the heart of qualitative research' (1974: 317). Potter and Wetherell go one step further when they suggest that it is questionable whether the term 'analysis' is appropriate in qualitative research in general and discourse analysis in particular, because it relates to a distinctive set of procedures that belong to the discourse of quantitative research. None the less, all our contributors subscribe to the view that analysis in qualitative research is continuous in that it interweaves with other aspects of the research process. However, it is apparent that researchers vary in terms of how soon they engage in explicit data analysis (in so far as this can be depicted as a distinct activity). Sometimes, analysis seems to begin more or less immediately on entering the field (see, for example, Geer 1964), whereas other researchers appear to delay analysis pending the accumulation of a substantial body of data. The extent to which conceptualization involves either the application of a priori categories or the derivation of emergent concepts may condition the juncture at which analysis takes place. Nevertheless, in either case, careful coding is required.

CODING

The nature of coding in qualitative data analysis was raised in Chapter 1 and has been a prominent topic in several chapters. Mason, and Ritchie and Spencer write about indexing, which seems to refer to a similar process to coding, but which possibly carries the connotation of the process of developing and applying a whole coding scheme, rather than the derivation of individual codes. Coding (or indexing) is seen as a key process since it serves to organize the copious notes, transcripts or documents that have been collected and it also represents the first step in the conceptualization of the data. As Mason recognizes, it is easy to view coding as an end in its own right, but there is always a good deal of intellectual work to be done once coding has been completed (however provisionally). Richards and Richards dislike the term 'code' because it carries different meanings in both qualitative and quantitative research, although they write about codes and coding at a number of junctures in their contribution. They discuss two kinds of coding: 'coding for retrieval of text segments and "open coding" for theory generation'. Not only do there seem to be different types of code, there appear to be different approaches to coding. Turner contrasts his approach with that of other researchers (such as Anselm Strauss and Lyn Richards), noting that he tends to develop a larger number of codes, which are often 'more messy' than those employed by other researchers. Clearly, there is the potential for considerable confusion regarding what coding actually is, so that it is doubtful whether writers who employ the term are referring to the same procedure.

As Ritchie and Spencer note, coding is invariably associated with the cutting and pasting of transcripts or notes, whereby chunks of text are cut out and pasted with other items that fit under a certain heading. Some contributors find this aspect of analysis a little disconcerting because the text that is cut out is then taken out of its natural context. In Mason's case, chunks of interview transcripts were at risk of having lost their moorings in the family groups to which interviewees' replies pertained. She notes the importance of not losing sight of the contextual nature of the transplanted chunks. Meanwhile, Richards and Richards argue that, although the computer software they developed made it easier to retain the sense of context, they and other users rarely used the facility. Retaining a sense of context would seem to be linked to a researcher's theoretical assumptions and not just something associated with certain data handling devices.

CONCEPTUALIZATION

One of the major goals of qualitative research is the generation of concepts that can form the building blocks of theory (Glaser and Strauss 1967). Initially, concepts are likely to be little more than extensions of codes; at a later stage more abstract conceptualization is likely to be possible. Richards and Richards's discussion of their computer software demonstrates that tree-structures can be employed to facilitate the progressive elaboration of concepts into higher levels of abstraction.

As can be seen in the Olesen *et al.* chapter, the elaboration of concepts is a more difficult stage than is sometimes appreciated. A particular difficulty that they refer to is the problem of attaining a higher order of abstraction without compromising the authenticity of the data (that is, the views of those being studied). The naturalistic ethos that pervades much qualitative research can easily engender a phenomenalism that Olesen *et al.* were keen to guard against (Bryman 1988: 85–6, Rock 1973). Mason makes a distinction between descriptive and conceptual categories. The former are essentially the elements in the indexing system that she and her co-worker employed. Conceptual categories were grounded in both the theoretical perspectives that were applied to the research design and the data that had been collected.

A further salient issue about conceptualization is the question of how far concepts in qualitative data analysis are a priori or emerge out of the research context. Most of the contributors emphasize the creation of concepts rather than the imposition of existing ones. Okely is adamant that 'classification is made after, not before fieldwork', though how this view fits with the notion that analysis and data collection are inextricably linked is not absolutely clear. Similarly, Hughes mentions that in her research on stepfamilies, the central issues emerged near the end of the fieldwork.

When research has an applied emphasis, and perhaps especially when it is externally funded, the need to focus on certain concepts which are decided at the outset of the research is more pronounced. In both the Burgess *et al.* and the Ritchie and Spencer chapters there can be discerned a greater recognition of a need to ensure that certain topics are addressed. This tendency is likely to mean that some concepts are 'given' at the outset of the research. However, it does not mean that emergent concepts are unlikely to be found in such investigations; the Burgess *et al.* chapter provides an illustration from within a project with an applied focus of the emergence of 'time' as an important ingredient of their understanding of the four schools studied. None the less, the kinds of preoccupation that are typically discerned in an applied investigation are likely to entail a significant amount of conceptualization in advance of fieldwork, often in relation to issues concerned with policy and practice (Burgess 1993).

While our contributors have provided many insights into conceptualization in their analyses, they are more guarded about the emergence of *theory*. Concepts are, of course, the building blocks of theories, but they do not constitute theories in their own right. Linkages between concepts are mentioned by Richards and Richards, Turner, and others, but the degree to which it is theory that is being created is left somewhat understated. As a result, the question of whether the analyses create substantive or formal theory (Glaser and Strauss 1967) is even less apparent in the discussions. In spite of the frequent mention of grounded theory, there seems to be a lack of certainty about the degree to which, in the process of conceptualization, theory is being generated.

GROUNDED THEORY

Grounded theory is widely cited as a prominent framework for the analysis of qualitative data and is frequently referred to as the approach employed when writers report the results of their research (see the example of Sutton 1987). Our contributors are no exception and a number of them cite the work of Glaser and Strauss (1967) and Strauss (1987) approvingly. The influence of grounded theory extends to its impact on the development of computer software in that Richards and Richards mention that NUDIST was developed with the approach very much in mind (see also Richards and Richards 1987: 26). 'Ethnograph', which is an alternative and probably more widely used package for qualitative analysis, was also influenced by grounded theory (Seidel and Clark 1984: 112).

In spite of the frequent citation of grounded theory among our contributors and others, it is questionable whether it is employed by researchers in its entirety. Richards and Richards write in their chapter that generally it influences qualitative research 'as a general indicator of the desirability of making theory from data, rather than a guide to a method for handling data'. An almost identical view has been expressed by Bryman (1988: 85). We suspect that the influence of grounded theory has been twofold. First, it has, as Richards and Richards say, alerted qualitative researchers to the desirability of extracting concepts and theory out of data. Second, grounded theory has informed, in general terms, aspects of the analysis of qualitative data, including coding, and the use of different types of codes and their role in concept creation. These influences can be seen in the way in which grounded theory is typically cited by our contributors, in that it refers to a general disposition or to a particular phase or aspect of the approach. Turner's contribution does provide a detailed exposition of grounded theory in the manner of Glaser and Strauss, but largely in the context of an analysis which he describes as falling on the fringes of grounded theory. Quite rarely do we find evidence in the contributions of the iterative interplay of data collection and analysis that lies at the heart of grounded theory and, as presaged in the last section, rarely do we find clear indications that theory is being developed.

COMPUTING

The use of computer software has been of concern to a number of contributors in addition to Richards and Richards. Most recognize that the chief benefit of programs like NUDIST and Ethnograph is that they are able to alleviate the arduous cutting, pasting and subsequent retrieval of field notes or interview transcripts. As Richards and Richards make clear, this was precisely the context within which NUDIST was developed. The coding of materials still needs to be done and its laboriousness is not really diminished, but the computer software opens up the possibility of those operations that follow on from coding being greatly eased.

While those contributors who mention the possible role of the computer recognize its potential, they are all realistic about its limits. As Okely says, it cannot substitute for the imagination that is a necessary ingredient of analysis. Indeed, Seidel and Clark (1984) have written that one of their chief aims was to free researchers from cutting and pasting in order to allow them to concentrate on the interpretation of their data. A good number of researchers would seem to be attracted to this possibility in that, between March 1988 and January 1990, 1,600 copies of Ethnograph had been sold (Lee and Fielding 1991: 11). However, an interesting issue for reflection, particularly in light of the fact that there are at least eleven different software packages available, is how far the different programs condition the analysis that is undertaken and hence influence its findings. Certainly, this is an area on which we feel further research is required if we are to get beyond the 'mechanics' of using computer programs in the analysis of qualitative data.

TEAM RESEARCH

It is striking that the majority of our contributors report their experiences in connection with research in teams, but this may be a consequence of age, career phase, the development of qualitative research, or the politics of funding. A number of them have chosen to comment on the implications of doing qualitative research and data analysis in such a context (cf. Wakeford 1985). Ritchie and Spencer observe that applied research often entails limited time-scales, so that teams are required to ensure that all of the work gets done in time. They suggest that when a number of interviewers are used it may be necessary to evaluate the impact of such factors as age and gender on data collection and analysis. Porter reports that in her ethnographic study of communities in Newfoundland the fieldwork was primarily done by research assistants, hence her phrase 'second-hand ethnography'. She writes about the difficulty of having others doing ethnography on her behalf in that she was forced to trust someone else's eyes. In this respect, the skills demanded of the project director are similar to those of researchers who engage in secondary data analysis (Burgess 1992, Reinhartz 1993). In addition, she discusses the problems of maintaining a team structure that was consistent with the principles of feminism since all her research assistants were women, an issue that had considerable significance for the conduct of the project.

An extension of the virtue of team-based investigation is discussed by Olesen *et al.* who show how they developed team analyses of their qualitative interview data. It is rare to find such a detailed exposition of how teams deal with the analysis of such data, and the contribution is revealing for its insights into the role of different team members and what steps can be taken to ensure that no one dominates the analysis. An interesting question to ask in this context is how computer software might be employed within a team environment. Might separate analyses be undertaken by each team member and discrepancies resolved, or would meetings be employed to generate a single, definitive coded set of materials? The speed and flexibility of the computer would allow either approach to be taken with much greater ease than by a manual approach. But as team research becomes more common in qualitative investigations, the special implications of doing analyses in teams will require greater attention.

LINKING QUALITATIVE AND QUANTITATIVE DATA ANALYSIS

Some of our contributors have collected quantitative data in tandem with qualitative research. This raises the question of how far the two types of research can be combined and how far one analysis influences the other. Mason's research on family obligations involved a clear division of labour between quantitative and qualitative research. The purpose was not to 'triangulate' the two sets of data (that is, to check the different findings against each other) but to allow the quantitative component to map out general patterns and the qualitative phase to reveal processes and the perspective of those actually involved in situations in which questions of family obligation have materialized. Thus, a certain topic or issue could be approached from different angles. Mason's general recommendations about linking the two types of research are consistent with the views of those writers who have been enthusiastic about the prospects of their integration (e.g. Bryman 1988,1992; Sieber 1982).

In contrast, Porter is much less sanguine about the role of a quantitative research element in the context of a predominantly qualitative study. This scepticism is at least in part conditioned by her support of the feminist critique of quantitative methods like the social survey. The quantitative research component was introduced primarily in order to triangulate the ethnographic evidence. However, the two types of data were not treated equally: if there was a clash of evidence, the qualitative findings were treated as more valid. In a sense, it is difficult to see why the survey evidence was collected because the qualitative data were highly privileged by such a stance. Richards and Richards also report finding a clash between survey and qualitative evidence, but they did not plump for one finding rather than the other. Instead, they probed their qualitative data in greater detail to reveal that their statistical analysis had employed a classification of life-stages that was too crude. Porter also notes that the research assistants found that their roles as ethnographers were compromised by the surveys that they carried out because they were time-consuming and adversely affected relationships with the people they were studying.

The chapters by Mason, Porter, and Richards and Richards reveal strikingly contrasting views about the problems and prospects of combining quantitative and qualitative research. They also represent very different approaches to the integration of quantitative and qualitative data analysis in terms of what might be achieved and how much conviction they had in the outcomes of the exercises. Richards and Richards go further in their chapter (and in Richards and Richards 1991) in suggesting that the growing use of software programs like NUDIST may break down many of the conventional dichotomies, like the quantitative/qualitative one. However, they may also assist researchers to collect more data and to cover more sites.

MUTLI-SITE STUDIES

Investigations like those of Porter, and Burgess *et al.*, are multi-site studies in which the aim is to draw comparisons between cases. There are signs that this is becoming an increasingly popular research design in policy and organizational research (Eisenhardt 1989, Louis 1982, Yin 1984), although not all are agreed that it represents a fruitful departure (Dyer and Wilkins 1991). Eisenhardt (1989) shows how some recent, predominantly qualitative studies of a number of organizations have adopted a common strategy. An issue that she addresses in the context of data analysis is the question of how comparisons across cases can be made. But where the data for each case in multi-site case studies are collected by different people, as in the Burgess *et al.* and Porter studies, how can the research director be sure that he or she will end up with data that can be meaningfully compared? This point is especially significant in light of the largely unstructured nature of qualitative investigations unless common units of study, common interview agenda and so on are specified at the start of the project (cf. Burgess *et al.* 1989).

Porter's strategy in the context of her study of three communities was to adopt a 'linked ethnographies' approach. This entailed simultaneous data collection in the three communities and regular sharing of field notes and experiences. The four schools in the Burgess *et al.* research were studied sequentially. Here the strategy was for each later case to build on the findings from the earlier case or cases, but to be sensitive to nuances and distinctive features as each new school was studied. This approach, which has affinities with Yin's notion of replication logic, raises the question of how far findings from the initial case constrain the later ones. The criteria for selecting cases will also play an important role in the kinds of cross-case inference that can be made and this is a major focus for Burgess. It is probable that further exploration and developments will take place in this area of data collection and analysis as qualitative researchers move away from the classic 'one-shot' case study (Lacey 1970).

CONCLUSION

In addition to what our contributors have discussed, we have been mindful of what they have *not* addressed. For example, it is still not absolutely clear how issues or ideas emerge in order to end up in the finished written product. The determining factor often seems to be the frequency with which something is observed or is said in interviews and the fieldworker's conceptual elaboration of the phenomenon. If frequency is the critical factor, it is surprising that there are so few counts and percentages in reports of qualitative research, since these could substantially enhance the reader's appreciation of the salience or significance of the perspectives or actions that provide the substance of the report. However, many qualitative researchers would be concerned that this would change the emphasis of their studies and in turn their analyses. Software packages may enhance researchers' preparedness to engage in such primitive counting exercises. But the real problem is that we simply do not know why certain themes emerge as core elements in the report, whether it is persistence of symptoms for Olesen *et al.*, time for Burgess *et al.*, or life-stages for Richards and Richards. If frequency is never or not always the determining feature, it would be helpful to know what is. In this respect, just as qualitative researchers have in the last two decades developed methods of data collection, so the challenge for qualitative researchers in the next decade is to articulate as fully as possible the processess associated with data analysis.

This book is only a beginning. There have been accounts of qualitative data analysis in the past, but they have been isolated and rarely brought together. We hope that this book will stimulate systematic reflection on the subject in the future.

REFERENCES

Bresnen, M. (1988) 'Insights on site: research into construction project organizations', in A. Bryman (ed.) *Doing Research in Organizations*, London: Routledge.

Bryman, A. (1988) *Quantity and Quality in Social Research*, London: Unwin Hyman.

—— (1992) 'Quantitative and qualitative research: further reflections on their integration', in J. Brannen (ed.) *Mixing Methods: Qualitative and Quantitative Research*, Aldershot: Avebury.

Bryman, A. and Cramer, D. (1990) *Quantitative Data Analysis for Social Scientists*, London: Routledge.

Burgess, R.G. (1984a) *In the Field: an Introduction to Field Research*, London: Allen & Unwin.

—— (ed.) (1984b) *The Research Process in Educational Settings*, Lewes: Falmer Press.

—— (1992) 'Linking design and analysis in ethnographic studies', paper presented at British Educational Research Association Annual Conference, University of Stirling, August.

—— (ed.) (1993) *Educational Research and Evaluation for Policy and Practice*, Lewes: Falmer Press.

Burgess, R.G., Candappa, M., Galloway, S. and Sanday, A. (1989) *Energy Education and the Curriculum*, CEDAR, University of Warwick.

Conrad, P. and Reinhartz, S. (1984) 'Computers and qualitative data: editors' introductory essay', *Qualitative Sociology* 7: 3–15.

Dyer, W.G. and Wilkins, A. (1991) 'Better stories, not better constructs, to generate better theory: a rejoinder to Eisenhardt', *Academy of Management Review* 16: 613–19.

Eisenhardt, K.M. (1989) 'Building theories from case study research', *Academy of Management Review* 14: 532–50.

Geer, B. (1964) 'First days in the field', in P. Hammond (ed.) *Sociologists at Work*, New York: Basic Books.

Glaser, B.G. and Strauss, A.L. (1967) *The Discovery of Grounded Theory: Strategies for Qualitative Research*, Chicago: Aldine.

Habenstein, R.W. (ed.) (1970) *Pathways to Data*, Chicago: Aldine.

Lacey, C. (1970) *Hightown Grammar*, Manchester: Manchester University Press.

Lee, R.M. and Fielding, N.G. (1991) 'Computing for qualitative research: options, problems and potential', in N.G. Fielding and R.M. Lee (eds) *Using Computers in Qualitative Research*, London: Sage.

Louis, K.S. (1982) 'Multisite/multimethod studies: an introduction', *American Behavioral Scientist* 26: 101–20.

Merton, R.K. (1968) *Social Theory and Social Structure*, New York: Free Press.

Miles, M.B. (1979) 'Qualitative data as an attractive nuisance', *Administrative Science Quarterly* 24: 590–601.

Reinhartz, S. (1993) 'Empty explanations for empty wombs: an illustration of secondary analysis of qualitative data', in M. Schratz (ed.) *Qualitative Voices in Educational Research*, Lewes: Falmer Press.

Richards, L. and Richards, T. (1987) 'Qualitative data analysis: can computers do it?' *Australian and New Zealand Journal of Sociology* 23: 23–35.

—— (1991) 'Computing and qualitative analysis: computational paradigms and research processes', in N.G. Fielding and R.M. Lee (eds) *Using Computers in Qualitative Research*, London: Sage.

Rock, P. (1973) 'Phenomenalism and essentialism in the sociology of deviance', *Sociology* 7: 17–29.

Seidel, J.V. and Clark, J.A. (1984) 'THE ETHNOGRAPH: a computer program for the analysis of qualitative data', *Qualitative Sociology* 7: 110–25.

Sieber, S.D. (1982) 'The integration of fieldwork and survey methods', in R.G. Burgess (ed.) *Field Research: a Sourcebook and Field Manual*, London: Allen & Unwin (originally published 1973 in *American Journal of Sociology* 78: 1335–59).

Strauss, A.L. (1987) *Qualitative Analysis for Social Scientists*, Cambridge and New York: Cambridge University Press.

Sutton, R.I. (1987) 'The process of organizational death: disbanding and reconnecting', *Administrative Science Quarterly* 32: 542–69.

Wakeford, J. (1985) 'A director's dilemmas', in R.G. Burgess (ed.) *Field Methods in the Study of Education*, Lewes: Falmer Press.

Wiseman, J.P. (1974) 'The research web', *Urban Life and Culture* 3: 317–28.

Yin, R.K. (1984) *Case Study Research: Design and Methods*, Beverley Hills, Calif.: Sage.

Name index

Subject index